D1167659

"This is a remarkable book that describes what happens when a mother's heart is 'pierced by a sword,' a woman's experience of child death. Dr. Mathes introduces powerful archetypal images that serve as containers for bereaved mothers. Speaking from her personal experience, she explores deep emotions and reveals the wisdom of the heart that can come after great loss."

KATHRIN ASPER,
psychoanalyst and author of *The Abandoned Child Within*

"Because I have had a child die, I can testify that Charlotte Mathes has captured the essence of Mother's grief from the profound title of her book and also through the poignant stories bereaved mothers shared with her."

JUDY BONURA,
Chapter leader of Compassionate Friends

"*And a Sword Shall Pierce Your Heart* is one of the most compelling books I have ever read. To read it is a spiritual exercise, like walking along a difficult road that countless others have walked — and in the process found a healing source within themselves."

WILLIAM HAMILTON,
Presbyterian minister, Office of Religious Life, DePaul University

AND A SWORD SHALL PIERCE YOUR HEART

Moving from Despair to Meaning
after the Death of a Child

Charlotte Mathes

Chiron Publications
2006

Copyright © 2006 by Charlotte Mathes. All rights reserved. No part of this publication may be reproduced, stored in a retrieval system, or transmitted in any form or by any means, electronic, mechanical, photocopying, recording, or otherwise without the prior written permission of the publisher.

CHIRON PUBLICATIONS
P. O. Box 68, Wilmette, Illinois 60091

Cover painting, "Mother and Child," Copyright © 2003 by Margaret Humphris.

Copyright © 1968, Yale University Press, Hallo & Van Dike, *The Exaltation of Innanna* (1968) poem "Condemning the Moongod Nanna."

Copyright © 1999 by *Harper's Magazine*, excerpted from "Burning Olivier" by George Michaelson Foy, reprinted from the July issue by special permission. All rights reserved.

Copyright © 1955 by New Directions Publishing (reprinted by Sales Territory; world rights, Frederico Garcia Lorca, translated by Edwin Honig, "Suicide" from *The Selected Poems of Frederico Garcia Lorca*.

Copyright © 2002 by Duke University Press, Karla F. C. Holloway, *Passed on African American Mourning Stories*.

Copyright © 1991 by Diane Wolkstein, reprinted by permission of Harper Collins Publishers, brief quotation from *First Love Stories: From Isis and Osiris to Tristan and Iseult*.

Copyright © 1939 by Harcourt, Inc., and renewed by Dudley Fitts & Robert Fitzgerald, reprinted by person of the publisher, excerpt from *The Antigone of Sophocles: An English Version* by Dudley Fitts & Robert Fitzgerald. CAUTION: All rights, including professional, amateur, motion picture, recitation, lecturing, performance, public radio, radio broadcasting, and television are strictly reserved. Inquiries on all rights should be addressed to Harcourt, Inc., Permissions Department, Orlando, FL 32887-6777.

Copyright © 1999, UCSF AIDS Health Project, Peter Goldblum & Sarah Erickson, *Working with AIDS Bereavement*, "True Story Three: Rosetta Du-Bois Gadson."

Copyright © 1994 by Ann Lamott, *Bird by Bird* by Anne Lamott. Used by permission Pantheon Books, a division of Random House, Inc.

FIRST EDITION

LIBRARY OF CONGRESS CATALOGING-IN-PUBLICATION DATA

Mathes, Charlotte.
    And a sword shall pierce your heart : moving from despair to meaning after the death of a child / Charlotte Mathes.
    p. cm.
    Includes index.
    ISBN 1-888602-34-1
    1. Grief. 2. Bereavement—Psychological aspects. 3. Loss (Psychology) 4. Children—Death—Psychological aspects. I. Title.
    BF575.G7.M385 2005
    155.9'37—DC22

                                    2005013877

TABLE OF CONTENTS

ACKNOWLEDGEMENTS

ALTHOUGH THE FOCUS of this book is mother grief, I would not have been able to write it without receiving help from three great men.

My Husband Mel sustained me with his loyalty, support, calm nature, and practical, technical knowledge. Mel, thank you for your constant loving presence and your ready willingness to help. By your example, you have taught me faith and patience.

I am deeply indebted to my editor Stuart Miller, a talented, tenderhearted scholar who coached and encouraged me to work through successive drafts. Stuart, thank you for your devotion to correctness and accuracy and for always giving good advice.

I am forever grateful to Jungian psychoanalyst Dr. Ian Baker, who introduced me to symbolic life. His compassionate understanding of my connection to the Pieta strengthened my resolve to write. Thank you, Ian, for your patience with my darkness and depression as you led me to the light. The wise way you taught me to see will always be part of my inner experience.

My greatest gratitude is to the women who shared their stories. This book is a compilation of experiences we offer in hope of helping others. What we learned from the interviews was that the coming together of women who mourn their child's death creates a transformative power. We recognize the impact each of us has had on the other. By sharing intimate parts of ourselves, we deepen our compassion and understanding and derive strength from one another. I thank each of you for your heartfelt sympathy over the death of my son Duncan. I share the same profound bond with you, and I pray that your involvement in my work has moved you a few steps farther along your path.

PREFACE

THE NIGHT MY son died, after the police left and friends had shared the burden of our grief, I got into bed with a pounding headache. Holding my husband and sobbing, I felt rage rising as I remembered two of the evening's outlandish condolences: One from my son's Jesuit professor advised, "You can still have a relationship with Duncan, you know," and the other from an old philosophical mentor encouraged, "Some day you will see his death as the transforming moment of your life." Though first received with anger and fear, now, much later, I realize the truth of their statements.

My son's death turned my life painfully upside down, and forced me into places I never dreamed of going, both in my inner and outer worlds. Many years of self-examination and searching led me to become a Jungian psychoanalyst. And when called to do a doctoral dissertation, I chose the approach of "qualitative research." Eschewing a hands-off distance and statistical measurements of this or that variable, I joined myself as participant-observer to other mourning women courageous enough to engage in self-reflection about their mother grief. The causes of their losses ranged widely: barrenness or miscarriage, long or sudden illnesses, accidents, suicides, murder, and even acts of war. For more than a year we met and shared strong emotions and strange occurrences, struggling to put words both to the details and the total import of our experiences. This book reports and reflects on our stories and those of many others in similar situations, with whom I later worked as therapist and researcher. My recurrent themes are the profundity of mother grief and the deep tasks such mourning women must complete to heal themselves.

The book divides into two Parts. Chapter One, Part One gives a fuller account of my own son's death and its circumstances and my reactions to it. In intimate terms, this chapter serves to set the painful problem the book addresses: How does a mother face the aftermath of such a terrific event? The following eight chapters of Part One examine

how any individual mother's turmoil arises not only from her particular personal history but also from universally shared psychological patterns or energies, what C. G. Jung called "The Archetypes." Embodied
in the myths and folklore of every culture, these collective patterns are
unconsciously absorbed by everyone. In turn, they serve to amplify and
structure the individual mother's terrible struggles. For example, she
apprehends her loss not only as that of her own child but also as that
of The Child, the being anciently created in our collective mind, each
of whose living exemplars carries for us such precious values as Beauty,
Tenderness, Promise, Hope, Regeneration, Replication, and Futurity.
An individual mother losing her particular child also feels as though
she has lost these other values as well.

After explaining the concept of Archetype more fully, examining
some of the main ones weighing on the bereft mother, and showing
how Archetypes define the themes and phases of mourning, I pass
on to how death affects family members. Men, women, and young
and older children grieve differently, so all need to cope with these
often painful variations. The succeeding Chapters of Part One also
consider particular challenges attending the different causes of child
death, from miscarriage to suicide. In each case, I use the concept of
Archetype to illuminate mothers' struggles. More generally, by coming
to understand the differing problems, of other grieving mothers, every
woman will be comforted by feeling the solidarity of an immense sisterhood.

Part Two (Chapters Nine to Fourteen) explores practical ways
mothers can use to open themselves to healing and transformative
experiences. After their child's death, women urgently want to know
what they can do to feel better, but I give no pat or simple answers.
Though a quick "getting over it" is often what others expect from us,
no strong will can force away grief. Nothing cures it, and attempts to
bypass mourning pains only postpone healing. Our reentry to full living may ultimately depend on grace, but there is much we can do to
assist it.

As part of illustrating this process, Part Two takes up my own story
again, charting the stages and steps that moved me forward. Adducing
also the testimonies of other women actively engaged in mourning,
I show how insights from Jungian psychology can join with other

complementary approaches to help. We can avail ourselves for aids from family therapy, meditation, journaling, behavior therapy, symbolic action, and transpersonal psychology among other approaches. Most mothers consider their child loss to be their salient life-changing event. Though fear and other strong emotions, together with their own strange behaviors, sometimes threaten to overwhelm them, through dreams, imaginings, prayers, and other means, many mothers feel pulled into suprahuman psychic realities. All the mothers I have worked with over many years also believe they will maintain an inner relationship with their dead child throughout their own lives.

Though this book primarily addresses the vast number of mothers who have lost children, it will also enlighten those more numerous family members, friends, colleagues, and helping professionals affected by child death and mother grief. All those close to the mother are shaken by her loss, and accordingly, need better understanding both of her reactions and their own. Humanity's great circle participates in a mother's mourning work, and many belonging to it will find help here.

This child is destined to be a sign that will be
opposed so that the inner thought may be revealed—
and a sword will pierce your own soul, too.

—Luke 2:34–35

PART ONE:
ARCHETYPAL REACTIONS TO CHILD LOSS

Chapter One

MY TWICE-LOST CHILD

REASONS FOR TELLING

I ALWAYS FEEL DIFFICULTY telling the story of losing my son, Duncan, first to schizophrenia, and then to suicide. I am a naturally private person, and I will not parade intimate events without good reasons. Though I no longer have any need to ventilate past pains or exhibit old wounds, several motives move me to detail my own loss here.

In the first place, I want mothers to know, as the saying goes, "that I have been there." I bring to this book not only my professional expertise, but also personal knowing from walking the path of mother grief. I also need to use parts of my story to establish background to certain ideas I will advance in the second part of this book, concerning aids to grieving. I discovered those not just by studying the work of other professionals and conducting original research, but also by carefully observing the vicissitudes of my own search for healing.

Then, too, I hope some mothers will take particular comfort from an extended retrospective account of how mental illness leads to suicide. It may help them understand that their own child's major depression, bi-polar disorder, or schizophrenia is a possible explanation for their child's death.

Finally, I want to suggest how a woman's previous life, including her relationship to her child, greatly influences her mourning process. Some of us face our child's death without previously experiencing any great loss or pain. As I have said before, the shocking end to these mothers' innocence is tremendous. Others, however, come to their child's death after sustaining many losses or great struggles. Naturally, their grieving will be different.

In the Beginning

When I was just nineteen years old, my half brother hanged himself in his bathroom, leaving behind a wife and three young children. My mother told me there was "something wrong with him, and he had never been my 'real' brother." We never talked about him much after that. In retrospect, I tried to make up for my father's shame by studying seriously and marrying a brilliant young medical student. We were married for seven years before I became pregnant. But two weeks after my son Duncan was born in late November, his father left, declaring he was in love with his nurse. The strains of medical school had broken our marriage. Because I was too ashamed to tell anyone of my husband's departure, Duncan and I spent our first Christmas together alone.

Most of the life decisions I made thereafter centered around my son. I moved to New Orleans so that Duncan would have the support of my sister's family, and two years later, I married a wonderful man who provided love and stability to both Duncan and me. It wasn't long before my husband's nine-year-old son also chose to live with us. Indeed, we had everything to offer him: My husband was a dedicated father, and I was "super mom," planning family outings and birthday parties, baking bread, and teaching Sunday school. In addition, my full time job at an academically prestigious school qualified our boys for a tuition waver. Things certainly looked rosy for us!

Duncan's Childhood: A Shooting Star

When Duncan started kindergarten, he had one of the highest intelligence test scores and showed unusual talent in performing. He was often chosen to read or sing in front of the entire student assembly of grades K through 12. Learning came quickly to him, and he seemed happy, though somewhat impulsive and immature. By the end of the second grade, however, Duncan had trouble making friends. Boys his age shunned him for being small and babyish, and teachers noticed erratic behavior. His differences concerned me enough to have him tested, but a psychiatrist found no abnormalities: "You're overly anxious, Mrs. Mathes. I'll send you to a social worker for counseling."

Looking back at this failed diagnosis makes me wonder whether we can pinpoint which young children are at risk for mental illness. As he grew older, Duncan struggled with flighty friendships and periods of hyperactive and impulsive behavior followed by despondency. Never fearful of authority, spoiled by grandparents, and overly attached to mother, he, on the other hand, was a creative, imaginative child who filled our home with joy by playing music, giving magic shows, planning a party and always, literally, wearing a different hat.

When only in sixth grade, Duncan landed the leading role in his high school's production of *Oliver*. After the school year ended, he was invited to play it at Tulane University's Summer Lyric Theater. The next year, when Paramount shot a film in New Orleans, Duncan was given a speaking part and became a member of The Screen Actor's Guild. We acted on the film's producer's encouragement to come to Hollywood the following summer. There Duncan contracted to appear in several commercials and played a six month run of *The Sound of Music*, and I thought he had found himself. A natural actor, he loved the theater. When the show closed, however, he was very unhappy about having to return to New Orleans. He never adjusted to home again.

I tried different environments, first placing him in an all-male Jesuit high school. There I hoped he would receive the discipline and role-modeling he needed to become a man. But Duncan could never quite fit in. Somewhat desperate, I thought he might do better at a school for creative children and allowed him to attend the Professional Children's School in New York City. He failed to attend class, then blamed me for forcing him to return to New Orleans. I was sadly learning that you can't make someone healthy by placing him in a healthy environment.

Schizophrenia: The Star Burns Out

It may be difficult for outsiders to comprehend how two responsible parents with some community influence can unwillingly lose all control of a sixteen-year-old. One day, Duncan simply moved out of the house. Then came periods when we had no idea where he was living. Immobilized by guilt and others' blame, I had now become too unsure of myself to take any action. Then too, some people encouraged Duncan's flight from home. The headmaster of his new high school gave him a full scholarship and purchased thousands of dollars of musical equipment for his use. Some well-meaning friends, including a psychiatrist, maintained that Duncan needed only to cut the apron strings. The social worker I engaged for him failed to tell me Duncan was experimenting with drugs, and his grandparents relentlessly bailed him out of sticky situations. A master manipulator, Duncan seldom suffered consequences. He also helped cause everyone to think that his overly protective mother was making a mountain out of a separation gap.

During these years family members particularly blamed the theater, New York, and California. But Duncan didn't lose sight of himself in California. There, I was with him daily, playing the ignominious role of stage mother to be sure, but nevertheless reinforcing values, and helping him when he showed poor judgment. There, I offered him the safety of a containing holding relationship, but that relationship gradually became developmentally unuseful because it grew appropriate for him to begin separating from mother. When he turned fifteen, a part of him still needed me desperately, for he didn't have enough inner resource to sustain the healthy part of himself without me, yet like all adolescents he wanted and needed to become autonomous. From the time we first returned to New

Orleans, his inner tension between connection and separateness made our relationship highly conflicted, and I wondered whether he would someday lash out at me physically, as he had become prone to do verbally.

There are various ways in which schizophrenia first manifests itself, but in cases like Duncan's, where the personality slowly deteriorates during adolescence, the period before diagnosis can traumatize the family. Because loved ones do not know they are dealing with a brain disorder, the youngster's disintegration causes them to feel devastating guilt, blame and shame. One day a friend found me sobbing while Duncan was verbally lashing me. She convinced me to see a psychiatrist, and I started psychoanalysis. Unfortunately, four days a week on the couch turned out to be worse than useless. I spent months wallowing in self-pity, recounting each life incident wherein I had been an "unfit" mother and swallowing whole the guilt, blame, and shame I felt, much of which others had heaped upon me. My condition worsened when the physician failed to keep appointments, introduced totally inappropriate material, and mumbled his speech. I finally realized he was intoxicated during our sessions. A year later, I confronted this psychiatrist about his alcoholism and successfully recouped the money I had paid him.

Because of my own bad experience with psychiatry, I wanted to select a good doctor for Duncan, but he refused treatment. He dropped out of his college freshman year to sing and play keyboard and guitar in a rock band. One night he telephoned to say he was appearing on MTV. Watching his performance, I hardly recognized the crazed-looking young singer who was my son, but my hands were tied: He gave me no permission to interfere in his life in any way. Finally one Sunday morning he called for help. "Somebody is trying to kill me," he said, "but I've gotten my suit cleaned, so will you take me to church?" I told him I'd be right over.

I knew that Duncan needed hospital care. We drove to the psychiatric hospital and stood outside for an entire hour while I cajoled him to admit himself. Finally, despite the objections of other band members (who had gathered to protect him from "the myth of mental illness"), Duncan agreed. Now I needed a doctor with hospital staff privileges to admit him. I telephoned a physician I knew, but could only reach his associate on call. In such an accidental way, this man became Duncan's psychiatrist.

Terrible Mother or Caretaker

I telephoned Duncan daily, but on the fourth day a psychiatric aide told me to "stay out of it." Apparently, after talking with me the night before, Duncan had smashed his guitar. Because Duncan's doctor believed in confidentiality for his patients and because I felt guilty and useless, I scarcely saw my son for four months and only received his schizophrenic diagnosis in a curt medical phone call. While at the hospital, Duncan was given no medication, but at last, with his release pending, the doctor told me he had "prescribed antipsychotic drugs to offset Duncan's suicidal delusions. Unfortunately, I must warn you that he probably won't take the medicine." With those ominous few words, though I had never been consulted about his treatment, I suddenly became completely responsible for Duncan's care.

Since there are few long-term facilities for mentally ill persons, those who are not roaming our streets are usually cared for by their mothers. A mother worries about what will happen when she dies, how her adult child will survive. Adding to that weight, until very recently, many mothers, like me, have suffered the humiliation of being blamed for their child's illness. Looking back on my own case and the plight of many other mothers, I have concluded that the most damaging theory about schizophrenia was Frieda Fromm-Reichman's idea of the "schizophrenogenic mother." After studying twenty-five mothers of schizophrenic patients and finding them to be "overanxious, obsessive, and domineering," Fromm-Reichman concluded that the mothers' own warped psychosexual development impacted their children and could very well have caused schizophrenia. Starting in 1949, Dr. Trude Tietze propagated this idea throughout the mental health profession. Later on, Gregory Bateson's 1956 "double-bind" theory also held mothers responsible for their children's schizophrenia. According to Bateson, adolescents adopted the symptoms of the disease in order to overcome the inhibiting and controlling effects from double-binding messages in family communication. Although Bateson's hypothesis was never professionally tested in any way, it was widely taught to psychologists, social workers, and psychiatrists and long remained a major basis of non-pharmacologic treatment.

Nowadays I find it inconceivable that any psychotherapist who has witnessed a full-blown schizophrenic break would believe a child's sane mother has the wherewithal to cause such catastrophic illness. I now view these theories as their inventors' unconscious projections of super-human powers that belong only to the Mother Archetype. Theorists polarized the archetype, projecting the Negative Mother onto human ones.

Chaos and Peace at Last

Although I can retrospectively see that the schizophrenogenic mother era had already started ending by the time Duncan became ill, its still vigorous notions often kept doctors from prescribing medicines he sorely needed and also kept him from taking such medicines when they were prescribed. These theories further contributed heavily to my old feelings of blame and shame. Duncan spent the next two years at home with us, where the inherent chaos in our situation was exacerbated by his band's continuing success. He had quite a following, and many youngsters, themselves often in need of psychiatric help, frequented our house at all hours.

Duncan was sometimes manic, other times dangerously suicidal. One night the police found him sleeping in the park at Monkey Hill. Another night they stopped him from jumping off the Mississippi River Bridge. Yet other days he stayed in his room writing poetry and music, though he was never without a cigarette. On several occasions, he signed himself into the psychiatric hospital. Finally, in desperation, I sought a court order to take Duncan to a famous specialist in New Mexico. For a brief time, the doctor questioned the schizophrenic diagnosis and I felt hope. But Duncan failed to respond to lithium, the drug used for bi-polar disorder, and continued disintegrating. After several more hospitalizations, he finally agreed to come home and faithfully take his prescriptions. At last, I believed my son to be safe.

During those last months he was with us, I came to know him anew as a young man whose kind personality had been altered by a cruel disease. Despite his illness, he showed concern for others and tried to protect his dad and me from his torments. He had great affection for his aunt and his grandparents, and he loved and admired his brother and cousins. I was amazed how much kindness he showed, despite his having to bear an internal flood of intrusive voices and images. He once looked compassionately at his doctor and said, with great concern, "Don't worry, it's not your fault."

Gradually, Duncan began to stare intently at nothing in particular, becoming more and more withdrawn from the social world. I would look at his handsome young face and try to guess what strange movie might be playing behind it. I know from our candid talks that his inner world could be filled with wonder and mystery, bright colors, music, and mystic connection, but it could also be fragmented, cold, and plastic. His conversation often broke off when he couldn't complete his thought or had become stuck on a certain word. In his most psychotic states, he would hear commanding inner voices, particularly telling him that his song, "Circling Round," had "become a malevolent force." He suffered tactile hallucinations, feeling his skin burning again on a childhood scar. But during his more coherent times, he could think brilliantly. In a single interview, he convinced a new psychiatrist to change his diagnosis: there was nothing wrong with him. Sometimes he sounded so wise, like an old soul, an unusually evolved person. At such moments he would regard me sagely as if to say, "Don't worry Mother, this is all just a play we are acting. In some other world, we will all find harmony with each other."

Over and over again I have wondered what internal drama was playing the Sunday he died. He phoned that night on his way home from work: "Can I bring you something, Mom?" Seemingly in good spirits, he greeted us heartily. Then in the safety of home, he climbed into his bedroom loft and shot himself.

So shaken was I by Duncan's death, so lost, that I was led into a sustained search for insight and help. As promised, I will continue detailing the personal aspects of that story in Part Two, but the search also led me into professional study and work with other grieving mothers as a psychotherapist and then a Jungian analyst. In professional endeavor, my most useful discovery was the existence of Archetypes and their bearing on the psyche of a grieving mother.

Chapter Two

UNDERSTANDING
THE ARCHETYPE

*Every time an earth mother smiles over the birth of a child,
a spirit mother weeps over the loss of a child.*
— ASHANTI SAYING

THE HISTORICAL CONTINUITY of mothers' profound grief experiences upon losing a child can be illuminated by applying Swiss psychologist C. G. Jung's concept of "Archetypes" to them. He divided our unconscious mind into a personal unconscious, which contains an individual's subjective life, and the collective unconscious, which houses the Archetypes, innate psychological patterns that we share with all humanity. Over the immense lifetime of humankind, individuals' repeated experiences of these patterns or Archetypes have embodied themselves in symbolic motifs, some universal, some particular to a specific culture. These archetypal motifs take such various forms as representational images, abstract symbols, myths, fairy tales, and folk stories. Symbolic motifs express recurring great human ideas, themes that significantly stimulate and otherwise influence our lives. When we experience these archetypal products, we feel them to have arisen from the deepest part of ourselves and, consequently, make statements like "I was deeply *touched* by that painting," or "I really *identified strongly* with that story," or "I was *so moved* by that piece of music."

We cannot have a personal religious experience without being seized by that mysterious archetypal quality which may be called *"the numinous,"* an impressive happening that at once mystifies and controls us. Not only deep religious experiences are numinous; so are other dark and frightening moments that force us to feel "outside" ourselves. The overwhelming event of our child's death necessarily puts before us images—our child is crying for help, two autos colliding on a highway, the little baby wasted by cancer—that evoke numinous experiences. Unimaginable to us before the tragedy, such moments leave us traumatized in a world turned upside down.

Being overcome by archetypal forces can be dangerous. For example, we may become "inflated" in our self-concept, identifying too much by what belongs only to a Higher Power. Such is often the experience of leaders of cults, chronic gamblers "on a roll," many politicians and ordinary people in certain moods of exaltation, or even despair. We can also be "defeated" when archetypal forces are set in motion following hurts to ourselves or others. For example, some mothers become so caught up in their own mourning that they no longer comprehend anyone else's pain. The archetypal force of the Mater Dolorosa, the grieving Virgin Mary, symbolized in many famous paintings and sculptures, can lead a mother to feel victimized and powerless if she falls into its depressive aspects and fails to recognize the redemptive one also present. Each Archetype has both a positive and a negative pole.

When our child dies, many archetypes intensely move us. Motifs embodying these archetypes—whether symbols, images, patterns of behavior, or ideas—easily become linked to our personal experience. We may suddenly break out in tears when we see a child at play or a mother pushing a baby carriage, for we are reminded of our loss. But beyond that we may also experience to a degree the child loss of every bereft mother—CHILD LOSS in capital letters, so to say. A powerful collective human experience, having gathered up the infinitude of individuals' pain from all times and places, focuses itself on us. Examining some archetypes pertinent to child death can gradually help us understand how their influences, arising from the collective unconscious we all share, evoke intense reactions both in mothers generally and in our selves.

The Child Archetype

The whole human race shares a basic image of the child. Everywhere we discover the child to be both vulnerable and invincible, male and female, enigmatic and wise. Interacting motifs expressive of The Child Archetype show us how much energy is wrapped up in this collective image and idea. Not surprisingly, a bereaved mother takes some of these collective constructs into her heart. She couples them with the personal memories she has of her child and her own experiences as a child. The interconnectedness of all these constructs creates a mother's intuitive knowledge of "the child," and her own child in particular. We mothers understand that our intuitive knowing is linked with very deep feeling and that our experience of what it means to have a child and to lose a child cannot be fully expressed in words.

Having a child or losing her also links us powerfully to the time when we had not yet developed full consciousness, an original state that was one of wholeness. We see vestiges of this wholeness in preschool children's art. Rhoda Kellog has shown that children first take a crayon and scribble at age two, but soon they begin to cross lines. Next they enclose the cross, creating the basic pattern of the *mandala*, a sanskrit word meaning "magic circle" and referring to a geometric figure in which the circle is squared or the square encircled. Mandalas symbolize a state of wholeness we have known already, the original state of an infant before she grows to encounter the tension of opposites, such as the pull between good and evil, between pleasure and duty, or between impulse and reason. It is this earlier state that adults often long for when we grapple with such ambiguities of living, ones that the fact of our being conscious daily presents to us.

The greatest philosophers and poets have tried to explicate certain aspects of The Child Archetype and its power to move us. There is, for example, a tradition dating back to Plato that before children enter the world they choose who their parents will be. In the *Symposium* Plato says that our adult process of earthly learning is only a recollecting of knowledge we had gained earlier when we dwelled in a spiritual realm, but forgot at birth. The child is therefore closer to that spiritual knowledge. We can regain forgotten knowledge by heeding our intuition and remembering our own childhood. Wordsworth's

Ode: Imitations of Immortality from Recollections of Early Childhood celebrates the child, who "trailing clouds of glory," still retains memories of his celestial abode:

> Our birth is but a sleep and a forgetting
> > The Soul that rises with us, our life's Star,
> > Hath had elsewhere its setting
> > And cometh from afar:
> > Not in entire forgetfulness,
> > And not in utter nakedness,
> But trailing clouds of glory do we come
> > From God, who is our home:
> Heaven lies about us in our infancy!

Similarly, when Jesus says, "Suffer the little children to come unto me, and forbid them not, for of such is the kingdom of heaven," he is implying that the childlike qualities of humility, trust and dependence on a Higher Power are what is needed to find wholeness. (Mark 10:14) We know that "out of the mouths of babes" has come to mean that out of innocence, the truth is candidly spoken. Many women also report dreams of a wise baby, able to speak with adult clarity. Often the reaction of the dreamer is to desperately try and remember just what the baby said, for she knows it is important information that would answer questions unanswerable in every day reality.

The Divine Child who spontaneously appears so universally in dreams and visions symbolizes a treasure difficult to obtain. Something new has been born in the dreamer that needs nurturing in order to mature. The Child represents all the future's potential, as we mothers who have lost our child well know. The Divine Child is found in most major religions and in much myth. A son falls helpless into a world full of terrible enemies, but because he is divine, he possesses powers far exceeding those of other humans. He brings light. In the Christian tradition, the birth of baby Jesus is reenacted every year at Christmas time, when believers experience a new beginning, a rebirth within their own psyche.

Nowhere is the idea of the divine and innocent child more vividly evoked than in the novels of Victorian writer Charles Dickens. In *The Old Curiosity Shop* Little Nell's childhood innocence contrasts with the hunchback Daniel Quilp's evil. She is portrayed as unusually wise for her age, willing and able to care for her grandfather, an obsessive gambler who has stolen her money. The illness and dying of fourteen-year-old Little Nell occupies the last two hundred pages of the seven hundred page work. It is said that readers of this novel mourned Little Nell's fictional death by ringing church bells throughout England. In New York, the Battery at the tip of Manhattan crowded with readers waiting for the latest number of the magazine in which the story was first printed. Some twenty thousand persons shouted to the docking crew: "Is Nell Dead?" Men wept over a child-goddess created to teach humanity the value of goodness.

Contemplating all these examples together—Rhoda Kellog's mandalas, Plato's and Wordsworth's recollections, the Divine child, Jesus, and Dicken's Little Nell—we can feel a little of the collective power which aspects of The Child Archetype has over all of us. Reviewing some of these symbols of The Child Archetype can make us shudder at the thought it might be threatened, and when we believe it will triumph, we feel exalted. Such are the strong effects that some symbols of a single pertinent archetype can have on us. But for grieving mothers, there are more archetypes than that of the child which impinge on and condition their experiences.

The Mother Archetype

The Child Archetype is almost always portrayed in image and story as interrelating with The Mother Archetype. After spending nine months in the mother's womb, the human child requires an additional year of mothering before it reaches the maturity of other young mammals at birth. During this time the mother and child live in what has aptly been called a total *participation mystique*, wherein the mother's ego and unconscious intermingle with the unconscious of the child. This symbiotic bonding between mother and child will often resurface during the crises following a child's death. We can say that the unbreakable bond lasts throughout the mother's life.

When we recall that archetypes are structures carrying all earlier experiences of human kind, we begin to grasp why the deepest feelings connected to motherhood have surfaced with such urgency during our grieving. Simply put, what we feel personally is fueled by The Child and Mother Archetypes we have inherited from the collective experience of our race.

Reaching back to prehistory may help us accept our wound with more compassion and understanding for ourselves and lead us to reclaim our regenerative powers. Anthropologists suggest that all concepts of life were manifested in symbols of the mother. The first deity was the Mother Goddess, carrying the mysteries of both birth and of life itself. From Spain to Siberia, dating back twenty thousand years, the female body was replicated in figurines with full, falling breasts or round pregnant bodies. Here was the sacred goddess, mother of the universe, connected with the moon and its phases, and even with the stars. Changes in a woman's body related to changes in the moon's coming to be seen as stages in the Mother Goddess' own life. The crescent moon represented her as maiden; the full moon, as pregnant woman; and the darkening moon, her as the wise old woman whose light was within. In the rhythmical phases of light and darkness was seen a pattern of growing and decaying and rebirth of the crescent moon. Darkness and death, then, were not something to be feared but aspects of the Goddess, who also became the goddess of death and transformation, for did she not receive the dead back into her womb for rebirth?

All of life, then, it is believed, was apprehended by early humans as an expression of the omnipresent Mother Goddess. Moving the tides, she was the water of life and giving birth to herself, she was earth mother. She embraced all nature and her aspects were seen seen in many animals, as when her regenerative powers were found in the snake and the butterfly. Her inherent changeableness and the light-dark play of clouds upon her face caused her to be symbolized, even incarnated, in the labyrinth, itself a figuration of the sacred way to approach life's mysteries. Such goddess manifestations continue alive today and frequently appear in women's dreams. The snake remains a symbol for the power of healing and the butterfly's image represents new life for the Compassionate Friends, a self-help group for parents whose children have died. Throughout the United States there is also an awakened interest in walking the labyrinth as a way to help find one's center of wholeness. The twists and turns of the maze depict the expected and unexpected events of our journey on earth. Such rituals renewed archetypally connect to the Mother Goddess.

We learn more about other ancient rituals concerned with the Mother Goddess because writing was instituted in the Bronze Age. In Iraq, only one hundred fifty years ago, ancient poetic writings of Sumeria were recovered which tell the story of the Goddess Inanna, who goes below the earth to meet her sister Ereshkigal. Inanna is allowed to return when she sacrifices her son-lover Dumuzi, who replaces her in the underworld. A virgin Mother Goddess, Inanna carries her own regenerative power, symbolized in the radiance of the full moon. During the waning moon she weeps for her dying son-lover.

To honor the mystery of death and have hope for new life, humans reenacted the ritual sacrifice of such a divine son or daughter for over five thousand years. We can trace the story from Sumeria to Babylon, where each Spring Istar journeys to the Underworld to awaken her son Tammuz and bring him to light. In the next chapter, we will follow the tale to Egypt, where the goddess Isis grieved for her son-lover Osiris. In all these myths the dying God is both son and lover to the Goddess, for the Goddess encompasses the successive roles of a woman's life—mother, daughter, sister, and wife. We will see the relationship of mother and daughter as we explicate the Greek myth of Demeter and Persephone. We will understand how the pattern of divine mother and child locked in a cycle of death and rebirth continues historically, culminating in the Christian story of the Virgin Mary and the crucifixion of Christ, where the seven sorrows of Mary persist as the subject of contemplation and religious art in the present day. The Mother Archetype abides within us all, focusing motifs from various cultures throughout time.

The Mother Archetype also influences contemporary thought. Psychologists' researches discover the importance of bonding, of mirroring and cooing with our baby. Experts teach us how to enhance each stage of child development from infancy through adolescence, science joining with our own intuitive powers so we may learn how to nurture, when to protect, and when to let go. We learn that in the first few months an infant cannot distinguish her body from her mother's, and we have been schooled about breast feeding, separation anxiety, toilet training, childhood education, the acquisition of morals, and the problems of teen rebellion. All of these messages combine with our personal experience when we contemplate what it is like to be mother. Accepting how large a space motherhood occupies in our psyche leads us to a new, more generous, understanding about the magnitude of our loss.

By exploring the goddess role throughout history, we also gain an appreciation of her earlier worshippers' precocious imaginations. When they observed the habits of animal life, the rhythms of the seasons, the waxing and waning of the moon, and the functions of a woman's body, they did so in a religious spirit, honoring the feminine principles of becoming. We too can be enriched when we live life metaphorically, not always limiting ourselves to a literal appreciation of events. Death without imagination is unbearable, but openness to the invisible world enables us to find hope and acceptance. By seeing life as cyclical periods of transformation, all of nature becomes a subject for our creative musings. We can seriously learn to embrace images and symbols that connect our inner and outer worlds and discover a merging of the mind and heart that brings about the fundamental work of grief. Exploring The God Archetype will further this journey.

The God Archetype

Just as the Mother Goddess is part of the collective unconscious, so is the image of God. Should our shared God image be but an outdated reflection of obsolete philosophy, it may no longer be useful, and it may need refashioning by each of us to develop our own *imago Dei,* our adult concept of God or Divine Power. A picture of God as an old man in the sky with a white beard is seldom helpful to grown-ups. An example of change in the image of God is seen by comparing the Old Testament God with Christians' and Jews' view of God today. Yahweh is sometimes jealous, vengeful, and angry, but today one understands the Divine as centering around love and redemption.

When speaking of The God Archetype, I am acknowledging a biologically inherited tendency that makes humans long for, seek, and create an image or motif for a Higher Power. Our system readiness is active in creating the individual's concept of God. In no way does this way of thinking disallow a Higher Power outside a person; rather

I encourage an understanding of Divinity that validates each person's belief system.

In working with mourning mothers, I have found that their spiritual life changes, becoming more prominent after a child's death; The God Archetype plays upon them forcefully, and they feel a strong need to respond to it. Some women identify more fully with the teachings and rituals of their tradition, reaching a deeper level of faith because of their suffering. Those whose experiences find containment in a personally valuable belief system find meaning in death and life and seldom need psychotherapy. Other women are unable to accept the ways their traditional systems conceive of God, and many are angry with God. Others are enriched by incorporating Eastern traditions such as yoga and meditation. The study of Buddhism teaches some mothers much about suffering and compassion, and the doctrine of reincarnation, once a part of the early Christian tradition, sometimes answers their questions about why good people suffer. Today, also, there is a resurgence of the Goddess in women's searching for the feminine face of God.

In my opinion, the only lasting religious belief for women after child loss is one based on personal experience. The moments we touch the Divine arouse very strong emotions, a stirring of the soul, connections with a greater consciousness, and a feeling of strong fascination. They occur in visions, dreams, and synchronistic events. They may be a result of prayer and meditation or from an appreciation of nature, or they may arise spontaneously as an act of grace. After such a moment, we are filled with awe and humility. What is essential in order for these experiences to take place is a religious attitude, an openness to the mysteries of life. We give credence to transcendent powers and attention to the essential questions of life. We value the numinous experience. We search for meaning so that we are inspired to worship, obedience, reverence and love. Through all of these means, we mold our personal images of The God Archetype.

The Archetype of Meaning

The Archetype of Meaning comprehends our universal need to find significance in an apparently senseless world. It weighs on us most strongly after we have lost a child. In general, we see much evidence of humans' search for meaning in our organized religions, philanthropic endeavors, creative arts, and competitive strivings in the work world. The quest for love can also be such a search. Sometimes The Archetype of Meaning may result in mass movements, which can be good or dangerous. More often, this archetype elicits an individual's authentic personal search.

There are various views as to how one finds meaning in life. Many psychologists and philosophers believe that we are obliged to create our own meaning rather than search for something that we think is outside, waiting to be discovered. They argue that we cannot find meaning vicariously and that meaning must reflect individual values and be born of the inner subjective world.

Victor Frankl, an Austrian psychiatrist who spent three years as an inmate at Auschwitz, developed an existential psychotherapy called logotherapy which holds that we do not invent meaning, but rather detect it. Frankl states that what matters is not the meaning of a person's life in general but rather the specific meaning of a person's life at a given moment. One should not ask what the meaning of life is but rather must recognize that it is she who is asked by life for meaning. She must answer for her own existence and can only respond by being responsible.

In his book *Man's Search for Meaning*, Frankl writes about a young woman in the Auschwitz camp who knew she would die in the next few days. The woman began talking to Frankl:

> "I am grateful that fate has hit me so hard. In my former life I was spoiled and did not take life seriously."
>
> Pointing through the window of the hut, she said, "This tree here is the only friend I have in my loneliness." Through that window she could see just one branch of a chestnut tree, and on the tree there were two blossoms. "I often talk to this tree," she said.
>
> I [Frankl] was so startled and didn't know how to take her words. Was she delirious? Did she have occasional hallucinations? I asked her if the tree replied. "Yes." What did it say to her? She answered "I am here—I am here—I am life, eternal life."[1]

Jung would say that the healing image of the tree brought meaning to this woman in her darkest days. Jung believed that "People become neurotic because their lives are led too rationally," and meaning is found by "living the symbolic life." In addition to fulfilling one's social roles and duties, each person needs to find a role as an actor in the divine drama of existence. Frankl's woman's tree attached her to abiding life, making her an actor in the divine drama that gives peace and meaning. Everything else, even children and career is *maya*, an illusion, as the Hindus and Buddhists saw long ago.

As a pragmatic example, Jung recounts a talk he had with a tribe of Pueblo Indians' master of ceremonies. The Indian was complaining that white Americans were trying to interfere with his religion. Pointing to the sun, the Indian elaborated:

> They should not interfere with us because we are the sons of the Father, the Sun. He who goes there, [pointing to sun] that is the father. We must help him daily to rise over the horizon and walk over heaven. And we don't do it for ourselves only: we do it for the whole world. And if white Americans interfere, they will see that in ten years, Father Sun won't rise anymore.[2]

In the beginning of mourning, we exist without inspiration, what was previously valued has lost its significance, and events are stripped of the importance they once had. All our view of reality has been transformed. We must find a way to recreate ourselves and give meaning to life. In the second part of this book we will learn how we can create a climate that will help bring about the intrapsychic changes needed for healing. Frankl warns us that this search should not be self-serving, insisting that real meaning transcends the ego. This thought brings us anew to the dark sides of the archetypes.

The Dark Sides of Archetypes

As we have already seen, when we examine an archetype we become aware of the multifaceted aspects of the motifs—symbols, images, and so forth—that arise from it. One way to understand this multiplicity is to examine the archetype's polarities. If we engage in interpreting only one pole, we finish with what Jungian analyst Gugenbuhl Craig calls "unhealthy mythologies."

The dark side of The Archetype of Meaning, for example, is fool-ishness. It manifests itself when the inconsequential is treated as meaningful. If we attempt to live the symbolic life, as Jung suggests, we must guard against triviality. A synchronistic event[3] can have great meaning; on the other hand, all events are rendered foolish if every coincidence is interpreted as having some profound significance. We can see examples of giving excessive meaning to too trivial peak experiences in some of the New Age literature. We also know that paranoia is a pathological distortion of meaning. We must carry the sword of discernment as we take our symbolic journey.

Similarly, when we project the divine very long onto a single human child, we are in danger of falling into excessive sentimentality. A household can become too child-centered, becoming one in which no attention is paid to an adult's needs, and the child ends up self-absorbed and spoiled, feeling entitled to anything she wants. She becomes a crippled adult, unable to have lasting relationships or understand the rights of adult others. Speaking psychologically, she develops a narcissistic disorder, for like Narcissus in the Greek myth, she falls in love with herself. On the other hand, narcissism can also result from child neglect. If her basic needs are not met, the child learns by herself to fend for herself, a survival technique that usually includes little regard for others.

The sentimental view of the child in Dicken's Victorian novels resulted in an *enantiodromia,* a psychological law first outlined by Heraclitus: sooner or later everything turns into its opposite. In reaction to Victorian sentimentality, people began to see the child differently. In fact, this enantiodromia drew from the Christian doctrine of original sin, first elaborated in the writings of St. Augustine, who points out that "No one is clean for a day, not even if his life be only for a day. Who can bring a clean thing out of an unclean?" The idea of children being naturally inclined to evil surfaced again when Sigmund Freud formed his theories of childhood sexuality and showed that children had good and evil characteristics like adults. Freud influenced such writers as William Golding, who depicted the savagery of boys stranded on an island after a plane crash in his novel *Lord of the Flies.*

Similarly, The Mother Archetype has its dark side. The idea that women are inferior to men colors the Genesis creation story, where all the life-affirming images of the Goddess are dropped and she is changed to instill fear, blame, and punishment. The woman and the serpent, both Goddess symbols of regeneration now become causes of our expulsion from Paradise. In addition, because Eve's body is created second, it too is considered inferior to Adam's. Becoming more prominent in our collective unconscious overtime, such influences contributed to the dominance of the negative pole of The Mother Archetype in people's thinking. Nevertheless, we must accept the fact that The Terrible Mother is a genuine archetypal part of our psyche.

Today we certainly cannot underestimate such powers of darkness when we read about teenage mothers stuffing their infants in trash bags or drowning them in bathtubs. To prevent such atrocities, crimes against children are punishable, and laws require teachers and doctors to report harm and neglect. Advocates for children have rightly brought family violence to public attention, and child protection agencies closely monitor suspected offenders.

In medieval days such protection for children was not so prevalent. Infanticide was not punishable by law until the sixteenth century. Nevertheless, moralists and clergymen condemned women who killed their infants, and European researchers have been unable to find evidence that infanticide was widespread. The Terrible Mother Archetype manifested itself in crazed individuals then just as it does today, and records exist of some mothers killing their infants by leaving them exposed to the elements or stuffing them down latrines.

What is more commonly true for all times is that a degree of ambivalence, a vacillating between the negative and positive pole of the Mother Archetype, typifies the experience of most mothers. Certain lullabies reflect some ambivalence in medieval mothers. One nursery rhyme, later lyrics for a Brahms cradle song, was sung to generations of infants:

> Rock a-by baby
> On the tree top
> When the wind blows
> The cradle will rock
> When the bough breaks
> The cradle will fall
> Down will come baby
> Cradle and all.

These lines may merely reflect medieval mothers' dread anticipation of an infant's early death from disease or accident. But the words, like those in other early lullabies, may also express unconscious desires for relief from the frustrations of motherhood.

In the United States today, many women admit to mixed feelings about motherhood. Further, several new baby-advice books reject conventional, nurturing tones about the experience of mothering and frankly point to stay-at-home moms' isolation and loss of identity. Generally, the drudgery of child care, now discussed by women who struggle with ambivalence, is out of the closet. But mothers who have lost children may remember with remorse moments when we were in the grips of the negative mother. Perhaps we were able to admit that sometimes our child was really bothersome, so that when we spontaneously expressed our anger we rid ourselves of frustration and impulses to vengeance. On the other hand, perhaps we became highly ambivalent and gave mixed messages. Frequently, when she allows resentments to build up, the negative mother holds on to hurt feelings and acts like a martyr. Then she often uses guilt to control her child, even as she is trying to be the perfect caretaker.

In children's fairy tales, we also find the negative pole of The Mother Archetype. It is believed that the Grimms changed "Mother" to "Stepmother" in the tales they collected. They apparently wanted to protect children from thinking that their birth mother could be envious, vengeful, and cruel, for in fairy tales the children suffer greatly at the hands of a wicked one. Hansel and Gretel are left to starve in the woods by a mother who is herself starving and unable to provide for her children. Cinderella suffers terrible abuse from a mother who loves her other daughters more, and Snow White is the target of her stepmother's envy.

Like the negative Mother Archetype, the dark side of the God image is a force that all grieving mothers encounter and must come to terms with. Like Job, who protests against God's injustice in allowing Satan to kill his ten children, we wait patiently to allay our suffering. Although other religions contain gods with both good and evil aspects, in the Judeo-Christian religion, evil has been assigned to Satan. Evil is a difficult issue that arises in any monotheistic religion affirming God as omnipotent, omniscient, and all good. If an all benevolent God has complete control, then why does evil exist in the world? Mothers who have lost a child know that evil is not just an absence of good. Part of grief work is to come to terms with the question of evil coexisting with the Almighty's power.[4]

NOTES:

1. Victor E. Frankl, *Man's Search for Meaning,* New York, 1969, p. 109.
2. C. G. Jung, *The Symbolic Life,* vol. 18, Collected Works, London, 1993, p. 274.
3. See chapter 13 for discussion of synchronicity.
4. For an exploration of the wrath of God, see Greg Mogenson, *God Is A Trauma: Vicarious Living and Soul-Making,* 1989, Dallas, pp. 18–22. Morgenson shows how trauma may release a person's creative, soul-making powers.

Chapter Three

HOW WE MOURN:
THEMES, PHASES, AND A MYTH

Grief fills the room up of my absent child
Lies in his bed, walks up and down with me,
Puts on his pretty looks, repeats his words,
Remembers me of all his gracious parts
Stuffs out his vacant garments with his form:
Then have I reason to be fond of grief.

— SHAKESPEARE, *KING JOHN*

WOMEN DO NOT mourn their child losses randomly. Common themes and phases exist, often reflected in myths. One recurring theme is a woman's need to know how other women mourn.

The Need to Know

Most mothers have never been close to someone who has suffered such a life changing event, and even when they have, they could not have then understood its magnitude. Consequently, women now feel an urgency to find out everything they can about other mothers' reactions. They search relentlessly for information that will help with their immediate pain. Hungry for facts and statistics, they look for books to guide them through grief and find solace in hearing another stricken mother speak of a reaction similar to their own. Because they fear their grief will not abate or that things will only get worse, they search for help that will give hope or enable them to fend off further disaster.

They want some predictability restored to their lives. Though nothing takes away their pain, many mothers later point to a bit of useful information or wisdom that made a positive difference.

About two weeks after Martha's death at age thirteen, Eugenie started what seemed an unending search for books on child loss:

> They all said about the same thing, but I devoured them. I just had to find out all the facts. I guess in the long run, they did help me, but at the time, I was just so obsessive in tracking down whatever I could.

From her reading, on the other hand, Mary seemed to find immediate relief:

> I had so many things wrong with me from the start. I couldn't eat or sleep and I was always so irritable and flying off the handle at everybody. I learned that other people had the same things going on with them.

Kate rushed to find books that would take away a particular fear.

> We had always had a good marriage, but when my husband heard that people get divorced after a child dies, we ran out to get books about that. We found out that we had to keep talking to each other.

The kind of books women choose to read vary as they move deeper through grief. About a year after her son's death, Ruth was able to change her attitude. The works of one author, Harold Kushner, really helped her.

> I read *When Bad Things Happen to Good People*, and after that I didn't ask so much about 'Why me?' So I went and got his other book.

Unexpected / Unprepared

When a child dies, we lose our commonsense faith in life's predictability. The unanticipated early death cuts through what we have formerly assumed is a natural order of things, shaking the very foundation of our living. All we believed comes into question, and we feel as if we have no standpoint.

There is a saying to the effect that we only understand our lives after we have suffered disappointment: "Life is what happens to you after you make your plans." Once we had ideas about what coming years would bring to our family. After the death of our child, however, we find ourselves thrust into a period where, while there is no foretelling the future, we suddenly have no plans, and our dreams have been shattered.

How different this is from the sadness we feel when an older person dies. If she has lived a full life and dies naturally, we may miss her, reminisce about all she meant to us, and perhaps wish that we had taken more time to appreciate her. We also come to acknowledge that life brings a series of losses, and we may even understand that they are somehow necessary, or at least part of everyone's experience. But the death of our child attacks our understanding of life's rhythm and purpose, leaving us wandering in unmapped territory.

After John Kennedy Junior's plane crash, Lauren Basset's parents and Carolyn Basset Kennedy released the following statement: "Nothing in life prepares you for the death of a child." Though it had been twelve years since my son's death, I wept when I read those words, for they brought me back to when I was unprepared for my struggles with his illness, for his death, and for the challenging grief work required to once more be fully alive.

Today's women mature knowing much about how to deal with expected milestones: sexual experience, marriage, professional life, working motherhood, and even divorce, remarriage, and menopause. That which we don't already know, we feel reasonably confident of learning from abundant resources which are easily available to us. Consequently, we don't anticipate a life-changing event that puts the core of our being in doubt. Even those who have experienced much tragedy in their lives are unprepared for a child's death. Without self-pity, Ruth first summarizes her many losses before coming to her stark conclusion.

> My life has been full of pain. As a child, I experienced coming from 'the wrong side of the tracks.' My father and mother left me when I was thirteen and I had to find other caregivers. My little sister died when I was eight; my father died when I was twenty-two. My oldest son had cancer of the bone at age

eighteen. My first and only grandson was born with Down's syndrome. He had open heart surgery and was in critical condition for two weeks. My husband had open heart surgery and died two years after Tom committed suicide.

None of this has been as devastating as my son Tom's death.

The Intensity of Our Reactions

As they seek guidance, grieving mothers come to know other women's dramatic changes in body, behavior, and inner life. We learn how common are sleepless nights and changes in appetite as well as other such physical symptoms as allergies, migraines, stomach pains, shortness of breath, and irregular heart beat. The physical stress of child loss also makes women fear long-term health effects. Sesley says:

> I was always so stressed out and sick, catching the flu, being exhausted, and my back wouldn't stop aching. I became convinced that I wasn't going to live very long. And it was true, if I hadn't started to feel better, I wouldn't have lived long. But the third year I got stronger and stopped being sick.

The body mirrors our strong emotions, and we will later see how to care for our bodies.

What most worries us about our feelings, however, is not the central fact of sadness but the many psychological reactions and symptoms surrounding it. Women become frightened when they are unable to concentrate, remember details, control tearful outbursts, mitigate anger, and engage fully in routine responsibilities. They are also plagued with haunting thoughts and images. In all such states, they sometimes wonder if they are going crazy. Others feel they are falling into a dark hole of depression from which there is no escape. Mothers naturally try to gain some control over these experiences by asking, "Is it normal that I feel this way?" The answer is "Yes," witness these other experiences mothers have had in the extreme trauma of child loss.

> After our baby Sophia died, we finally got home from the hospital. Because I was in so much physical pain, I had a hard time getting up the steps to our apartment. All her things were everywhere, and we didn't know what to do. When I wasn't

looking, Ben started to throw things away, but I pulled the pacifier out of the garbage. Ben poured the breast milk we'd bottled and refrigerated down the drain. We got in bed and just lay there crying, and then at some point I said, 'I have to call people and let them know.' I had a list. This seemed perversely organized but what else was I going to do with myself?

Natasha

One day when I was alone I took the gun and shoved the barrel in my mouth down into my throat, but not to kill myself. I was just trying to see how it felt.

Rhonda

On the anniversary of my daughter's death, I called the doctor and reminded her that it was a year since my girl had died. 'You Goddamn killed my baby! Why didn't you intubate?' I yelled.

Wanda

I know when the photo album is in my head again. The images flash by—all that happened to Marcia. The tubes hooked up all over and labored breathing and all the swelling in her face. The courage she had, and how she wanted to take care of us—*us*, mind you!

Connie

In the end we had to make the difficult decision to withdraw the life-support systems. This traumatic decision plays again and again in my mind.

Rheba

It's been three years and I still haven't wall-papered the kitchen. The walls are just there with the old paper torn off. I can't finish it because Anna was going to choose the paper. To select it myself would be, I don't know what it would be, I just don't want to do it.

Carmen

None of these women were so dangerously over the edge that their grief should be considered pathological. They are merely describing some of the turmoil inherent in maternal mourning. Moreover, their willingness to withstand confusion rather than retreat into numbness or denial is a healthy response to grief.

Discovering Phases in Women's Mourning

Generally speaking, the progress of a woman's grief work cannot be measured by the intensity of her symptoms. The word symptom itself denotes pathology, and our journey should not be considered a disease. There is no list of linear stages that mothers go through, such as the denial stage or the angry stage, but generally mothers move from shock and numbness into a long period of acute suffering, eventually finding some way back into life. Although completion of the mourning process may be possible with other deaths, mothers never "recover" from their child's death. Looking at the grieving process archetypally affords an opportunity to embark on a spiritual journey, moving mothers to deeper self-awareness. For example, two great archetypes, Chaos and Time, play central roles in mourning, and the myth of Isis, whose grief reactions were reenacted by Egyptian initiates for thousands of years, clearly delineates a way of mourning leading to regeneration.

Chaos: Destroyer and Reformer

Depicting Chaos in "The Creation," at the beginning of his *Metamorphoses,* Ovid creates a metaphor for the warring parts within us.

> Before the ocean was, or earth, or heaven,
> Nature was all alike, a shapelessness,
> Chaos, so-called, all rude and lumpy matter,
> Nothing but bulk, inert, in whose confusion
> Discordant atoms warred: there was no sun
> To light the universe; there was no moon
> With slender silver crescents filling slowly;
> No earth hung balanced in surrounding air;
> No sea reached far along the fringe of shore.
> Land, to be sure, there was, and air, and ocean,
> But land on which no man could stand, and water
> No man could swim in, air no man could breathe,
> Air without light, substance forever changing,

Forever at war: within a single body
Heat fought with cold, wet fought with dry, the hard
Fought with the soft, things having weight contended
With weightless things.
Till God, or kindlier Nature,
Settled all argument, and separated
Heaven from earth, water from land, our air
From the high atmosphere, a liberation
So things evolved, and out of blind confusion
Found each its place, bound in eternal order.

Ovid's Chaos evokes the abysmal formlessness into which a mother falls when hearing her child has died. There is no light, no ground to stand on, and like all things, all beliefs and feelings are at war with one another. To end the chaos and regain control is the *implied* work of the mourning process, but to *enter into the chaos fully* seems the necessary first step on a path to transformation and wholeness. Only then will each conflicting part of our psyche come to rest with some sense of renewed order. Chaos is the original substance, the *prima materia,* but it is precisely this uncontrolled state which holds the possibility for personal change. "God or kindlier nature" eventually changes the chaotic into form. So too the psychological *masa confusa* arising from the shocking separation of mother and child mysteriously contains our as yet unknown pattern of transformation. New life evolves from it.

In short, mourning begins a dynamic process. Those who refuse the journey, who keep their grieving motionless and fail to attend to their feelings, obsessionally insist that things are "quickly coming back to normal." Mothers of this sort pride themselves on being strong. But they thereby deny their own needs, and as a consequence, their attempts to protect their loved ones from the work of grief usually fail. They may initially appear to be handling everything in an admirable way, however, as was Stacey's case:

> You don't spread your troubles for the world to see. You have to just suck it up and move on. I never cried as a kid and I didn't cry much when Sandy died. I just stayed busy, running car pools. Tom (her husband) and I didn't talk much. He wanted me to get back to all our friends and stay active. Everything sorta just went on as normal.

Perhaps others' needs, sheer duty, made Stacy's solution—suppression, repression, denial—best in her circumstances. After all, other children had to be cared for. Or perhaps, she could have found a middle path.

Sally took a different route, never losing sight of her loss but finding her way to new meaning and personal depth.

> It's been four years since Chip died, and I found myself crying all the way to this interview. I still can't get hold of myself sometimes. I think how Chip would be at this age, just starting second grade. But I think there were lessons I somehow had to learn. I just have to learn and take the good out of it and work with that.... I would say this: there has been good coming from the death, but I would trade it in a second to have my son back. I'd live in ignorance the rest of my life to have my son back.

Recent discoveries have created a suggestive parallel between physical and psychological chaos. The ability to analyze complex dynamics has improved. Physicists once believed that chaos contained no patterns. With the development of computerized technology, however, scientists now discover that much (and perhaps all) of chaos is best described as "deterministic randomness." In short, it obeys certain equations, though complexity makes it appear random. Chaos has the ability to self-organize, generating greater complexity. Within a dynamic, in other words, physical chaos can actually lead to higher levels of order.

If we make parallels between this new chaos theory of physics and the traumatized soul, we open ourselves to the possibility that a descent into psychological chaos has the potential to lead to increased functioning. Because all our psychological being can be seen as a manifestation of psychic energy generated by tension produced by pairs of opposite qualities, one can make choices: yes or no, right or wrong, reason or heart. There exists then an alternative to the status quo. But if we refuse or don't know which choice to make, the oscillation can accelerate and chaos comes to us. An alternative is to wait for a third solution which arises from the unconscious and brings the two opposites together. In religion this resolution is called a state of grace. Much of our mourning time is spent in an apparent war with the opposites, awaiting resolutions that will enable us to transcend the havoc within.

Time: How Long Will It Take?

Waiting? OK. But will a lightness of heart ever come? Does time really heal all wounds? Mothers who have experienced child death assure us that "it will get better." Friends and loved ones may tell us that "it is time to get over it and get on with life." We hear about closure, but researchers say that a mother never ceases mourning the death of her child. The truth is that there is no set chronology for mourning mothers.

In mythology, Father Time is sometimes depicted as helping Truth out of a cave, symbolizing that in time all things come to light. We cannot hurry Truth along. Like the ancient alchemists, we must wait for *kairos*, the astrologically correct time, or God's time, for allowing things to turn out right. Our questions about how long it will take to heal may long remain unanswered.

Changes in One's Sense of Time

The grieving process alters our personal sense of time in several ways. During the traumatic hours after the death, everything in our other life comes to a halt, and our time stops. It takes a number of days before we realize that, although our world has changed forever, the rest of the world continues its usual operations.

> At my daughter's funeral, I was amazed when a friend told me he had to go back to his office. It dawned on me that people were going about their business. The world went on, though my world had ended.
>
> Emily

> After the service I stood at the grave site, holding a rose from the casket. Time had stopped. My sister came up and said I had to leave because other people wanted to go home.
>
> Annie

For the rest of our life, however, the moment of our child's death continues frozen in time. We remember every detail of the event as if it were yesterday, and we continue to mark the chronology of our experiences with that dreadful date. Paul Newman, whose son died of a drug overdose, said that everything in his life was divided into two periods, time before his son died and afterward.

As we continue to mourn, our normal sense of time alters in another way: we mark time carefully. We count the number of months we have lived without joy, since the light of our life has been extinguished.

Dear Andrew,

It's been nine months. It took me nine months to bring you into the world and now you have been away from this world for nine months. Today the grief washes over me and I hear myself crying 'Mama.' I am a child myself, and I long for comfort. I don't know if comfort exists when you are gone.

Kate

Part of our altered sense of time arises from knowing that the death of our child also means the death of part of our future. Holidays and family traditions will never be the same. Now we will always remember the birthday of the one who is gone, and the anniversary of her death is forever branded in our heart, marking our time. We mourn not only losses in our own future but the unlived future of our child. When we attend a graduation or a wedding, we ache for our child who was deprived of these rites of passage. How can we attend these ceremonies without feeling victimized? The way out of victimization I know is this: we must eventually come to see our own mourning process as a personal rite of passage. We are being initiated into a different life with new perspectives.

Rite of Passage: A Time of Liminality

Throughout the world, rituals of rites of passage are performed at every major transition in a person's life. First the initiate is separated from the community because she is entering a new phase. Then she lives, along with other initiates, in a so-called "liminal" period, meaning time "on a doorstep," a time of ambiguity that has few of the attributes of her past life and only a glimmer of her life ahead. After the liminal period, she is reincorporated into the community but with a different status.

The period of liminality is a marginal phase, a period when we cannot go back in time and we cannot move forward. It is an emotionally chaotic time, but also a time for self-reflection; a time of isolation coupled with a need to reach out to others; a time of lamentation but the beginning of acceptance. Barely perceptible changes begin to take place. Borders between the conscious and unconscious realm become permeable, and we have greater connection to the spiritual world. We mothers are able to access intuitive and imaginative powers.

Liminal time is paramount for grief work. It is the period when we work our way through grief rather than busying ourselves to avoid its pain. Naturally, it can be a long period, some of it lived in recurring snatches of days and months. This transitional time is when we have lost our innocence and remain at the threshold which, when passed, eventually brings renewed life:

> I have taken the bite of the apple and have been thrown out
> of paradise and that is true to the marrow of my bones. I still
> think Eve may have a good place to live, but it won't be paradise
> anymore. Before I lost Andrew, it was paradise.
>
> Kate

Symbols of the liminal phases of her mourning can be seen in the memorial that Rheba created just after her son died. She purchased two photographs taken in a Venice cemetery by Sandra Russell Clark. She named the photograph of the woman weeping at the tomb "Despair," and she called the photograph of the angel "Hope." Placing these pictures side by side in a quiet place in her home, she would go to meditate there. Her poem beautifully expresses her struggle.

> I felt a little piece
> Of myself fall away
> As I climbed the rocky
> Craggy face of Mammoth
>
> It was a treacherous climb
> Ambition was my holding cleat
> Survival my pickax.
>
> The Struggle became so great
> The gear so heavy
> I knew myself to be weak
> Faint of heart and spirit

No fierce rapture came
My soul dark, pulling
Upward toward the heights

I felt no lightness as
I moved into the first
Resting Place.

Rheba realizes she has reached only the first resting place. Her heart is still heavy as she continues her climb.

The time of liminality is a time for working one's way through such recurring themes and phases as:

> weeping
> searching
> solitude and incubation
> nursing and compassion
> dismemberment and separation
> reconstruction

We find these acts, these states of being, not only in experiences of bereft mothers but also in importantly redemptive mother myths. One myth concerns the Mother Goddess Isis and rebirth. As we do our mourning, we can come back time and time again to study its various phases and meaning, and if we pay careful attention and are lucky, we will find bolstering inspiration for our journey. From Egypt to Greece to Rome, her myth gave meaning, peace, and hope to initiates and was reenacted by them for thousands of years.

According to the myth, Osiris became king of Egypt, but his brother Seth was so envious that he plotted Osiris' murder. Seth ordered a coffin to be built to the exact measurements of his rival Osiris. Then, at a banquet, each jesting, drinking man was asked to lie in the coffin, trying it on for size. But when Osiris lay down, Seth and his conspirators trapped him inside, nailing the top and pouring melted lead over it. Then they launched the coffin into the mouth of the river Nile.

When Isis heard of the betrayal, she wept. She cut off a lock of hair, dressed herself in mourning clothes, and searched up and down the river, asking everyone whether he or she had seen the chest. Only months later did children inform her that the coffin had been carried out to sea to Byblos in Phoenicia. There the waves had thrust the coffin into the trunk of a tamarisk tree, and the bark of the tree had enfolded it. So beautiful was the tree that the king of Byblos had it carved into a pillar to support his palace.

Isis came to Byblos, veiled in mourning clothes so that no one knew she was divine, and sat by the well of the city. Some of the queen's maidens invited her to the palace to become nurse to the queen's son. Isis did not reveal to the queen that she was a goddess. She gave the infant son her finger to suck ambrosia instead of milk from her breast. Every night, as she continued to mourn for Osiris, she placed the queen's son in the fire in order to make him immortal. Then she changed herself into a swallow and flew around her own son's pillar, lamenting and wailing.

One night the queen saw her little son lying in the flames. She shrieked dreadfully, and in that very moment she deprived her child of the treasure of immortal life. Then Isis revealed herself as a goddess. She asked for the pillar containing the coffin, cut the bark surrounding the casket, and uncovered Osiris' sarcophagus. Then, taking the casket, she set sail for Egypt with the casket. As soon as Isis found a private place in the desert, she opened the coffin and embraced her dead boy.

Later she hid Osiris' coffin in the swamps of the Nile Delta. While hunting, Seth found the coffin, he opened the casket with great fury, cut the body of Osiris into fourteen pieces, and scattered them throughout the Delta. Isis collected each part of Osiris' body except for the phallus, which a sea bream had swallowed. Then she made a replica of the phallus and joined the body together. She hovered over the body as a swallow, breathing life into her son. She was able to revive his spirit, and he then became king of the underworld. As she hovered lovingly over Osiris, she also become pregnant. She called on the gods to protect her unborn child. Then she buried the empty coffin.

The hymns of Egyptian funerary texts show that through ritual, Isis' deeds remained ever-present to the worshippers, who dramatized them repeatedly each year. The single thread that runs through the centuries of worship of Isis is her endurance throughout her process of mourning and her *transformation* as a result of her loss and suffering. Isis can speak to our own mourning.

WEEPING

When Isis first hears of the death of Osiris, she weeps.

Like the nourishing waters of the Nile, Isis' tears nurture the waste-land that her life has become. Weeping is a universal human response to death, yet how we weep is very personal: many of us are unable to control the flood of tears that gush forth, others limit their crying to a time when they are alone, and most mothers are familiar with the sudden burst of tears that comes over them when they least expect it.

> I looked over at the next table and I saw the twins that she had played with as a child. They had been our neighbors, and now they were already teenagers and having lunch with Mom. I just started crying, and I couldn't stop. It had been six years since she died, and here I was unable to control myself in a restaurant. What is wrong with me?
>
> Merna

For the most part, Merna was successfully living her life again, managing fairly well, the pain having lessened. In the restaurant, however, triggered by a memory, she becomes inundated with tears. Strong emotions are attached to our memories, and many of our tears flow from such unexpected reminiscences. When something outside us calls forth a loving memory, we weep, as if we have to bring up each fond image and nourish it with our tears. In this way we are finally able to remember our child with joy.

Judy cries each day just as Isis continued to mourn each night for Osiris.

> What I do when I get home from work each day is go in my bedroom and cry. I almost look forward to a time when I can sob and sob until there's nothing left.

Crying is a way of releasing the overload of emotions accompanying our grief. We empty ourselves and thereby create room for God to come in. Without the Divine, we feel powerless and cry out in protest at the unfairness in life; our anger turns inward, we may sob in self-loathing. Crying helps us cleanse away our feelings of guilt and shame and the negative thoughts about ourselves. We weep until we are all washed out, and afterward feel some relief. The old adage "Have a good cry" reflects the humbly healing nature of our tears.

Looked at only from a biological standpoint, the human body needs continuous tears to keep the eye lubricated and to flush out foreign elements. Emotional tears have an additional biological function, cleansing away harmful chemicals. Tears contain the chemical prolactin, a hormone also residing in the mammary glands and essential in mother's milk. In times of stress, an excess of prolactin is released by the pituitary gland, and crying serves to rid the body of toxic amounts of this hormone. Women tend to cry more during menstruation, and this lowering of the tear threshold may also help excrete excess prolactin. When we chasten ourselves for too much crying, we should be mindful that emotional tears benefit good health.[1]

Crying also helps in other useful ways. As we weep, we are forced to slow the pace of our busy days, thereby helped to accept a period of purging and purification we need, and our tears become a water of life.

On the other hand, a woman who doesn't experience the self-reflection that should accompany weeping may cry too much. The mourning mother who only floods herself with self-pity and maudlin sentimentality may end by drowning in solitary sorrow. Emotionally inundated by the waters of her personal grief, she will be unable to rise to the surface of objective reality, and there to participate in the flows of new life.

Each of us has her own threshold for tears, but what about the woman who is unable to weep? Perhaps as a youngster she was taught not to cry, or she thinks doing it is a weakness, or her despair is so deep that she finds no tears inside her. Because mothers weep in almost every culture around the world, we are right to surmise that those who don't are likely to be emotionally stuck and consequently cold and distant.

This type of woman appears in the film version of Judith Guest's *Ordinary People*. When the film opens, we learn that Conrad (Timothy Hutton) has been hospitalized after his attempted suicide. His mother Beth (Mary Tyler Moore), however, has avoided her work of mourning earlier the death of her favorite son Buck, making her generally unable to express her love and even be hostile to her surviving son Conrad. Though both he and his father Calvin (Donald Sutherland) find a way to weep and then to connect emotionally, the mother remains unfeeling. She becomes inwardly hardened to stone, and in the end, we see her stiff body packing her bags and leaving her family.

Searching

> *I grieve that you are alone. I stretch out my arms to greet you. Isis wanders over the Delta, asking everyone she meets, even the children, if they have seen Osiris' casket.*[2]

As we have already noted, the early days of mourning are characterized by many kinds of searching: the most wanted books, perhaps self-help organizations such as Parents of Murdered Children or Compassionate Friends. Like Isis, we search. Typically, a mother unconsciously believes from time to time that she sees her deceased child standing on a familiar corner, solely to be disappointed or she unconsciously sets a place for her child at the dinner table. Such altered defense our altered ego deploys to combat despair.

> In the beginning I woke up every morning, and I had forgotten he was dead. I had to remember all over again and it would come to me as such a shock.
>
> Rheba

> In the evening, standing at the sink, I would look out the window and see Tad riding up the driveway on his bike. Then I'd remember he was dead.
>
> Dianne

In the first weeks of our child's death, our mind plays tricks on us. It's as if we must expect to see our child in order to hold on to hope. Without any we could become so despairing we might kill ourselves.

Every year in Mexico, around Halloween time, the Good Trickster attends the festivals for the Days of the Dead. At a cemetery, friends of a newly dead child come to play with her toys as she lies in her coffin before burial. On October 30 each year, a time is set aside for communing with such a child. The family also searches the cemetery for their other dead. The family candles and fresh flowers bring light and color to the grave, and they put out food for the deceased. Eating, drinking, and praying, a family may commune all night with the dead child among his other deceased relatives.

After death, we seek the body of our beloved or simply turn our backs and hand it over to an undertaker. Holding the body reassures some mothers. Bearing witness to the passing, they give it their blessing and more easily feel that the child has moved somehow into a spiritual realm. Even in the case of violent death, many mothers seek out their son's or daughter's body. Painful though it is, they receive greater understanding of their child's last moments, and the viewing also confirms death's reality. Mothers also come face to face with death's finality when they either watch the body being put in the ground or receive the ashes from cremation in their hand. More and more people are choosing cremation, because they can scatter the ashes in a place sacred to their beloved, helping to fulfill the part of our searching which seeks continuity.

No matter how we decide to dispose of the body, most of us think that the soul has been released. Yet we continue imagining the child as she was in life and we search for additional connection. We treasure family photographs, holding each picture close to our heart. We need to be near our child, to hold her. Sometimes a certain smell will bring her home, but only for a moment. Mothers want to know "Where is my child now? Is she safe in heaven? Will she come to me in a dream? Is her spirit close to me?"

Solitude and Incubation

> In Byblos, Isis came to love the queen's children and wanted to make her infant boy immortal. Every evening she set him over the coals and recited a spell. As part of the body burned, she changed herself into a swallow, and wailing and lamenting, flitted about the pillar which held Osiris' casket.

This seems at first a strange interlude, akin to another one in Demeter and Persephone's story. Analyzing her act symbolically, however, we can see Isis' actions as a metaphor for several elements in mourning: the need for a period of incubation, a continuing lamentation connecting us with the spiritual realm, and the deepening of a woman's compassion after personal loss. Putting aside her usual self and activities, for a time, Isis has disguised herself as a nurse. Except when caring for the infant, she spends her time in solitude, brooding over the murder of Osiris. Becoming a nurse creates a way to nurture both herself and the queen's son.

Part of the liminal time of healing should be spent in a period of incubation where we slow the pace of life in order to restore the soul. We need to be away from excessive distractions and interruptions. Now we come to see the grieving process as an inward journey. We anticipate alterations in attitude and shifts in perception, and these changes require time to brood over memories and possibilities in order to give them form and substance. As we become less ego-centered, we achieve greater connection with the spiritual realm, becoming more open to the Divine.

Though wanting time alone is a very natural part of grieving, our extroverted society negatively views solitude. Even in mental hospitals an attitude prevails that isolation is always unhealthy, and patients should be forced to participate in group activities. By contrast, D. W. Winnicott, British pediatrician and child psychologist, believed that the capacity to be alone is precisely what enables an individual to live creatively. This capacity in adult life originates with an infant's early experience of being alone in the presence of the mother. The child plays by herself while knowing that mother is available whether immediately thought of or not. Only when the child is alone in such a way can she begin discovering her own personal life. Otherwise she develops a life built on reactions to external stimuli, which Winnicott calls the "false self."

Alone time is a valuable resource in the mourning process. Mothers in mourning intuit the significance of solitude, but sometimes allow themselves to be pulled away from it. Lucy came to me four years after her son Ken was murdered. She worried that her marriage had broken.

> Going down to court so often has been horribly draining and I keep thinking that when the trial's over things will be different. But John (her husband) and I aren't communicating. I am so angry with him because he made me go on with life too fast. He wanted to be back with our friends, and I had to keep on with his clubs. None of my friends talk about Ken much since he died.
>
> Lucy

Failing to listen to her intuition about her need for solitude and resuming activities too soon, Lucy has delayed her necessary and inevitable mourning.

Solitude derives some of its importance from allowing us time and space to regress. Regression is reverting to childish ways, that is behavior characteristic of an earlier developmental stage. Isis "turning herself into a swallow" and "wailing and lamenting" are degrees of regression. Unfortunately, many psychotherapists solely view it as a defense mechanism used by people threatened by external problems or internal conflicts. An example would be an adult who resorts to sulking because she can't have what she wants. But we are all tempted to retreat into immaturity at times, and in some situations it does no harm to yield to that temptation. For example, when we are sick, we may want to be "babied" a little. Jung, however, warned against a person's falling into a trap of regularly dealing with a present reality by wishing a return to former conditions. Though we mothers want our child back home, alive, it is futile to plea very long for what cannot be. Slowly, we must move toward accepting our loss.

We should also note that Jung saw how regression can be a basic condition for creation. He did not believe we need stop with our wanting to be back in the womb's security. In his *Symbols of Transformation*, he suggested that regression, left undisturbed, could go further back, pass through our earliest behaviors such as sucking at the mother's breast and then beyond mother to the world of archetypal possibilities. There one can see the mysteries of life and find that treasure hardest to attain: our inherent potential for spiritual life. Perhaps you have worked psychologically with "the child within," the part of yourself that needs soothing and safety. Therefore, you may have already glimpsed that the child within is also The Divine Child, an archetype patiently waiting to be born into the fullness of your life.

Even though months have passed since Osiris died, each night Isis continues her weeping and wailing. Though this crying is itself a regression, we also see her lament is a spiritual cry, for she flies through the air, changing herself into the swallow that soars and flutters around the pillar holding her beloved's casket. Moreover, because the swallow is thought to be always hungry, it is a traditional symbol of suppliant prayer. Fanning her wings, Isis later revives the dead body. Herself spiritualized, she gives a new spiritual life to Osiris, who becomes, as we have seen, the Ruler of all Eternity in the Underworld. So it is that as part of the mourning process and shielded by darkness and solitude, our nocturnal cries bring us closer to the Divine. As Thomas Moore explains in *Care of the Soul*, we become able to wed spirituality with soul.

> In our spirituality, we reach for consciousness, awareness, and the highest values. In our soulfulness, we endure the most pleasurable and the most exhausting of human experiences and emotions.[3]

In this passage, Moore uses "soul," not in its usual religious sense of having to do with immortality, but in another common understanding of the word to mean a quality of earthly human experience. So we sometimes call music "soulful" or enjoy " soul food." Soul has to do with heart and personal substance and how we relate to life. Spirit, on the other hand, in Moore's meaning, comes from another world and lives of itself. Though it is detached from our body, we react to spirit with strong emotion.

The image of Isis as swallow flitting on her wings as she wails in grief is a beautiful symbol of the unity of soul and spirit. We cannot embrace spirit alone, for we would fly away from life's problems and avoid life's complexities. Many have known people who use a spiritual "high" to skirt the challenges of ordinary living. These people have lost contact with soul, that quality which connects us to all that makes us human.

Nursing and Compassion

She gave the infant her finger to suck ambrosia, instead of milk from the breast. Every night as she continued to mourn for Osiris, she put the queen's son in the fire to make him mortal.

Isis continues her mourning as she nurses the infant. In grief many of us are overwhelmed with the demands of our family and have no desire to assume more responsibility. Paradoxically, however, others who mourn feel a stronger need to nurture while not totally invested in the child. This is particularly true for those of us whose only child has died. Being with another person's girl or boy enables us to love and nurture. Because we are not so caught up in what has happened or what will happen to him, we feel protected from another great loss. We attend to the little one's matter of fact needs and feel the joy of interacting and maintaining a safe distance.

As a nurse, Isis goes beyond the earthly needs of the queen's child, trying to make him immortal by placing him in the flames. Fire is a symbol of divine love and eternity. The interlude often baffles today's readers, but its symbolic function is to show that in her wanting to make the infant ageless, Isis enacts her compassion for him. She hopes he will escape the suffering of mortals. Researchers say that mothers whose child has died report deepening empathy and broader compassion. From their great loss, mothers I interviewed have a different understanding of another's suffering than formerly. Many mothers report a commitment to help others is an important part of their healing.

> I do think that anytime I'm a little depressed or blue, I feel better if do something for somebody else. Like I love to take pictures. I love capturing life in pictures."
>
> Kate

> If I couldn't help out in the world, I wouldn't want to live. It's the only way to make some sense out of the tragedy.
>
> Annie

> The most important ingredient in my healing has been giving to others. Reading to schoolchildren and having them greet me with hugs and smiles lets me know I make a difference in their lives. I also do volunteer work with retarded children, and I give a lot of love to my grandson.
>
> Ruth

> I have found a new career that enables me to give to others. I make sure that kids from divorced homes have access to both their parents.
>
> Dianne

The Dalai Lama defines compassion as a state of mind that is "nonviolent, nonharming, and nonaggressive. It is a mental attitude based on the wish for others to be free of their suffering and is associated with a sense of commitment, responsibility, and respect toward others."[4]

The Dalai Lama differentiates between the love tinged with "attachment" and true compassion. When we are "attached" to someone, we love them so that they will love us back; there is an element of our controlling the other. With true compassion, on the other hand, we take on another's suffering, and though we feel emotionally connected to them, our experience is one of freshness and warmth. Therefore, rather than feeling burdened, we are truly willing to reach out and help.

It may be surprising to learn that increased compassion not only facilitates mourning but is also generally good for you! Recent studies support the idea that developing compassion and altruism has a positive impact on physical and emotional health. Feelings of compassion increase immunoglobulin A, increase energy, enhance feelings of calmness and self-worth, and prolong life. Researchers in the new field of mind-body medicine have demonstrated similar findings.[5]

Dismemberment and Separation

Seth found the body of Osiris while he was hunting. In great fury he opened the casket, cut the body of Osiris into fourteen pieces, and scattered the body parts throughout the Delta.

Many myths suggest that one must pass through what may be called "dismemberment" before transformation is possible. "Dismemberment" can be viewed as one more metaphor for the transitional period of chaos described earlier in this chapter, a time of intense disorientation and suffering. Mothers feel torn apart and themselves experience a partial death. Osiris' dismemberment should be taken as being empathetically reflected within his mother Isis.

In many myths about mourning, we also find the archetypal reaction of rending a garment. When the mourner hears of the death of a loved one, she tears her clothes in anguish, symbolizing that she herself is torn asunder by the news. In the Jewish tradition, a ritual called *keriah* is based on Jacob's actions when the body of his son Joseph was brought to him:

Jacob rent his clothes, put sackcloth on his loins, and observed mourning for his son many days. (Genesis 37:34)

Still practiced today, *keriah* takes place before a burial. Mourners are given black ribbons to tear, and when the cloth is torn, they recite a blessing that praises God as the True Judge. The implication is that mortals are not wise enough to understand the ways of the Divine. By tearing the garment, the heart is exposed and the vulnerable mourner shows that she has been mutilated. She stands naked in the eyes of God, humbled and rendered helpless by the reality of death.

In the Christian tradition the metaphor for dismemberment is Christ's broken body. At the celebration of the Eucharist, believers commemorate the Last Supper with drinking wine and breaking bread. They arrive broken and know they will be mended because Christ's body was broken for them. Christ offers the body and blood of the Lord to anyone who believes in Him: "Take, eat, this is my body which is broken for Thee. Do this in remembrance of me." (Cor.II:24)

Dismemberment and brokenness, while literally applying to some dead persons, are also symbols of the bereaved's inner life. Myths, like poetry, straddle such rich ambiguities, facing two ways or more at once. At the same time she experiences her inner fragmentation, a mother must adapt to the complexities of her outside world. Social relationships become clouded with misunderstanding, leaving mothers feeling very much alone. All of the women I interviewed expressed feelings of having been "set apart" from others.

> It's not the same life that you had before and you have to learn to live with each other differently and with your family differently.
>
> Dianne

> It's always underlying. No matter what I'm doing. If I'm having lunch with my friends, things can seem great, the nicest restaurant. I'm enjoying their company, but it's always there. And I think that's why we can never wholly be in the world—ever … as if I divided up the world in the last two years between people who've lost children and people who haven't.
>
> Kate

In a recent TV show, her best friend has died and the girl won't leave her room. A guy comes in who has lost his sister. "Just tell her I am a member of the club," he says, and she comes out. And I thought, That's it: we are all members of the club; we are different.

Jane

When you lose your parents, you lose your history. When you lose your child, you lose your future. It's still to come, of course. What I mean is there a zillion times when we will have milestones in life, where we're gonna be grieving over again cause our kids weren't there to see this or experience this. You know, so it's never over.

Dianne

Because mothers' values change after their child's death, they often report forming a new circle of friends who are more down to earth and less materialistic. One thing they cannot tolerate is superficiality. They have trouble making small talk, and have no use for trivia. Conversely, mothers remember every detail of a friend's reaction to their child's death. They cherish friends who have remained loyal throughout their ordeal, but feel sad about broken relationships and misunderstandings they are unable to repair. In time, a mother may look back and understand how she herself contributed to the separation.

> I lost one of my lifelong friends after Paul died. I was so angry all the time, and she couldn't tolerate it. One day she said the only reason she stayed by me was she thought I was going to kill myself. It made me even more furious. I wish she knew what kind of person I've become now.

Annie

We have seen how the grieving process is a transitional phase of life, when the bereaved develops different perspectives and attitudes. She will never be the same person that she was before. Because she has changed so much some of her friends may experience their own loss. There is no more connection.

> My best friend and I worked together for the Republicans. Now I am no longer interested in politics so I don't see her. We have nothing to bring us together.

Lucy

Many friends just can't deal with the rampant emotion surrounding a child's death. Uncomfortable with passion, they vainly try to make the grief go away.

> One friend said to me, 'I'm so very sorry and want to tell you that now, but I'll never mention it again.' I was able to keep on loving this man, because I knew he was too fragile inside to tolerate anything out of his control. Ironically enough, ten years later, he lost his own son and he had to talk about it.
>
> Annie

More hurtful are the people who sever relationships because they can't face the possibility that the same tragedy could happen to them.

> Rheba became pregnant two months after my baby died, and I haven't seen her since. First she said she had morning sickness, but that's over. I've called her a lot and she just makes excuses. Our husbands still get together to play golf, but I'm home alone. It feels like I have some contagious disease.
>
> Naomi

Amazingly, many people are highly critical about a mother's reaction to death. One remark I hear constantly is "She hasn't gotten over it yet." Women watch and gossip:

> "I wonder when she will have another baby."
> "She's just trying to be a super woman since he's gone."
> "She looks terrible."

Since bereaved mothers have suffered an injury to the self, they are more than usually vulnerable to criticism. It's as if they are wearing antennae that pick up every nuance of someone judging them negatively. Often when there has been a violent death or an accident, many blame mother. Salt is added to her wound because, no matter how innocent she may be, she is also still blaming herself.

> "She should never have let that child go alone."
> "He was into drugs and she always denied it."
> "The family was already pretty mixed up."

Mothers experience social separation for yet other reasons. There are well-known litanies made, now by well-intentioned people, that bereft mothers find hurtful. At meetings of the Compassionate Friends, parents routinely share the alienation they feel in social situations when the same old clichés are repeated. Unsolicited advice about how to mourn is cheap.

> "Just pray."
> "God works in mysterious ways."
> "You can have other children."
> "Be thankful that she's up in heaven."
> "It's time to move on with your life."

Finally, mothers commonly report a single question that alienates and hurts. "Why?" Even when there is no clear answer, we all want to know why a child died. Happenings beyond our control are hard to accept, so we need a reason for death. Dianne talks about the death of her son Tad, who drowned in the family swimming pool when he was thirteen years old.

> Tad's death was almost impossible for anyone to accept. It is so illogical that a child that age would die, innocently, by drowning in a swimming pool. It's ... you know, people can't accept that. They have to have a reason why, because if it were just fate, it could happen to them and that's unacceptable. I remember that one woman called me to suggest that the death had been suicide.

Reconstruction

Isis collected each part of Osiris' body except for the phallus, which a sea bream had swallowed. Then she made a replica of the phallus and joined the body together. Then she hovered over the body as a swallow, breathing life into her new son. She was able to revive the spirit of Osiris, who became king of the underworld. As she hovered lovingly over Osiris, she becomes pregnant with her son, whose spiritual father is Osiris. She calls on the gods to protect her unborn child.

There comes a time when we must reconstruct our lives, just as Isis was able to reform the body of Osiris. When we begin to notice that the unbearable pain has become a dull ache, we can slowly and selectively resume activities. One day we may be surprised to catch ourselves laughing.

Throughout this process we need to keep in touch with our inner life in order to become the person we truly are meant to be. Psychologists variously call the process self-realization, individuation, or self-actualization. Whatever we may call it, working through grief enhances the changing. One way or another, crisis forces us to change, but we have a choice: to remain stuck in grief and feel victimized, or to move courageously along the path of individuation.

In this chapter, we have walked with Isis in her grief. As we leave the myth, her new baby is not yet born. All of us hope that we will experience some positive transformation after we step back from the threshold of liminal time back into our community. What we long for is a rebirth, a joy of living full of vitality. In Part Two of this book we will examine ways to enrich the grief work which enhances both our post-mourning transformation and, at the same time, our process of individuation. We turn first to the family, however, and the consequences child death has on it and the mother, for it is through family intimate relations that we learn to know ourselves.

NOTES:

1. Tom Lutz, *Crying: The Natural and Cultural History of Tears,* New York, 1999, pp. 101–107.
2. For a beautiful translation of the Isis-Osiris myth, see Diane Wolkstein, *The First Love Stories,* New York, 1991.
3. Thomas Moore, *Care of the Soul,* New York, 1992, p. 231.
4. The Dalai Lama and Howard C. Cutler, *The Art of Happiness,* New York, 1998, p. 114.
5. Ibid., pp. 126–128.

Chapter Four

GRIEF IN THE FAMILY:
UNDERSTANDING DIFFERENCES

The Bustle in a House
The Morning after Death
Is solemnest of industries
Enacted upon earth —

The Sweeping up the Heart
And putting Love away
We shall not want to use again
Until Eternity.
— EMILY DICKENSON

A DIVERSITY OF GIFTS

ONE MOTIF EMANATING from man's archetypal quest for meaning affirms that each of us is unique, created for a purpose or has a calling and a destiny to fulfill. For fulfilling this purpose, we are given different gifts. In Corinthians I:12, for example, St. Paul describes the diversities of talents bestowed on his followers: "For one is given by the Spirit the word of wisdom, to another the word of knowledge ... to another faith ... to another prophecy; to another discerning of spirits; to another the recognition of tongues..." Paul concludes that, in spite of their diversity, these gifts all come from the same divine source—the Holy Spirit.

A contemporary expression of the idea that people have different gifts is the notion of "personality types," which describe the several basic attitudes of individuals and their various ways of functioning. For one person, the gift may be a strong intellect, for another a contemplative attitude. Exploring personality typology can help us understand differences in grieving among individual family members. What we discover is that no one way of grief is better than another. Perhaps, then, we can conclude with St. Paul that, however we may differ in our attitudes and functions, we are all of the same spirit, united both in that spirit and our mutual grief.

While many schemes of personality type exist, I find the Jungian one easy to comprehend and practically useful. Most of us, for example, can identify whether a person is an *introvert* or an *extrovert*. *Introversion* and *extroversion* are two attitudinal tendencies, present from birth, characterizing how we usually respond to the world. An extrovert's energy tends to be directed from herself to the outside world, while an introvert brings the outer world into herself for contemplation. Although no one is either completely extroverted or introverted, identifying individuals' preponderant attitudes helps us understand them.

Though introverted and extroverted tendencies are of equal psychological worth, various social groups accept one attitude more readily than another, giving rise to communication problems between them or even between spouses. Because an introverted husband works inwardly on what he encounters outside, he may be slow to answer questions or offer opinion. In fact, he is exploring the issue inside his head and heart, having a debate within himself. The extroverted husband, by contrast, relies on others to help integrate experiences. He will react outwardly to an event, throwing forth an idea, listening to what he said and what others replied, and then, developing a new reaction, changing his mind. He examines the issue by using other people's responses. During a time of grief, if he is extremely socially oriented, he may give his wife the impression that he is not mourning at all, just talking, frequently about subjects that seem to have little to do with his loss.

In addition to being understood as more or less introverted or extroverted, people can also be seen to have two distinct ways of *perceiving*. One is *sensing*, a process by which we become aware of things directly through our five senses. The other is *intuiting*, with which we blend ideas from the unconscious with perceptions coming from outside. If a person's dominant perceiving function is sensing, she will tend to see things realistically as they are, but if she is more intuitive, she will have an overall impression that includes possibilities of greater meaning but accords less importance to concrete details.

After information is taken in, either by sensing or intuiting, people tend toward two distinct ways of coming to conclusions. One way uses *thinking*, a logical process aimed at an impersonal finding. The other proceeds by *feeling*, that is by bestowing personal and subjective value on things. As children, we begin to favor one way of perceiving and more or less neglect the other. Similarly, children who prefer reaching conclusions through thinking develop along different lines from the child who prefers feeling.

The way an individual grieves is also influenced by her type of perception and the way she draws conclusions from the information she receives. If she relies heavily on feeling, she will have strong emotions which she needs to express, suppress, or transform. If she relies on thinking to come to conclusions, she more easily masters her feelings and expresses them in activities leading to goals.

Confronting death, however, involves not only our reactions to the visible world but also our ways of understanding the invisible. A grieving person with a high sensing function may bridge the gap between the visible and invisible world by contributing great significance to natural phenomena, seeing something beyond what is there. For her, being in the mountains may bring forth a spiritual awakening. An intuitive person, by contrast, will have moments of direct and immediate understanding without reflective thinking. She may meet a person by chance and believe she has found a supportive soul-mate. A feeling type will value her emotions and use them as a guide into the mysteries of life, while a thinker may rely on philosophical or religious systems that have proven true.

Let us remember, however, that no model of personality, no matter how good, completely describes an individual's uniqueness: we do not conveniently fall into prefabricated slots no matter how good the model. In *Talks To Teachers*, William James rightly cautions about overly categorizing even such apparently simple matters as different types of apperception.

> Every impression that comes in from without, be it a sentence which we hear, an object of vision, or an effluvium which assails our nose, no sooner enters our consciousness than it is drafted off in some determinate direction or other, making connections with materials already there, and finally producing what we call our reaction.... It is the fate of every impression thus to fall into a mind preoccupied with memories, ideas, and interests, and by these, it is taken in.[1]

Though we can see from this discussion how complicated the individual grieving process is, typical patterns exist that, deftly applied to an individual case, will help us understand our husbands, surviving children, and other persons significant to us.

How Men Grieve

While remaining aware that socially constructed gender identities change and the grief process is an individual experience, we can safely say that at the present time most men in the United States grieve differently from most women. Although some identical archetypal forces influence both genders, The Hero Archetype and The Father Archetype also strongly evoke and structure many grieving men's reactions.

The Hero Archetype finds embodiment in similar figures of legend and fairy tale cherished by nearly every culture. Joseph Campbell describes the mythological journey of the hero as including his divine birth, call to adventure, descent into the underworld, performing dangerous tasks, and encountering the feminine temptress or helper. The overall pattern of the hero's journey also includes defeat, death, and rebirth. Campbell defines the hero as "the man of self-achieved submission." How to submit is the riddle each individual must answer for himself. Within the soul there has to be "a continuous recurrence of birth to nullify the unremitting recurrences of death."[2]

Nowadays, most of us have a somewhat truncated view of the hero's journey. We think of hero, villain, and victim as principal characters in a hero's story where good triumphs over evil, if men only have the courage to fight for their beliefs. Many young men, when they enter the work world, feel a need to fulfill this warrior aspect of the hero, slaying the dragon and rescuing a princess. To act such role, however, the young man must repress and suppress any awareness of previously wounded or fragile parts of himself. Attempting to become invincible, he divorces himself from softer, dependent, and even charitable feelings and, therefore, from essential aspects of his full self. Edward Whitmont describes the hero prototype of today's male psychology as an outgoing man who is a "go-getter." He fights, strives, and accomplishes in order to establish himself in society.[3]

Although such a hero may accomplish much good for himself and others and may even be essential to social safety and prosperity, there is danger when men identify too narrowly with the hero's warrior aspect. When the warrior doesn't win, as no one always can, a man may gradually find his belief system shattered and himself alienated and powerless. Though all our husbands are not captive to this aspect of the hero archetype, almost every man in Western society is under its influence. Therefore, we wives must try to understand the devastating impact that child death has on a husband who models himself on the warrior hero. On the other hand, the death of a child may offer a man an opportunity to renounce some of the warrior hero's dictates, thereby liberating him to discover deeper meanings for his life. Often a man is led to this deeper understanding by his wife. When a woman finds her own regenerative spirit, like Isis, she is able to breathe new life into her husband, helping him to see through spiritual eyes. She opens him to new depths, but at the same time she should honor his position as father and support his authority in that role.

The Father Archetype embodies such fundamental aspects of male psychology as authority, law, and reasoning. The Father is a leader concerned with maintaining the established social order. Most important, the Father is the protector of his children. Many women are drawn to father types for husbands because we value their stability. Such men, generally thinkers rather than feelers, can provide welcome structure and discipline to family life.

A man influenced by The Father Archetype but unable to protect his child from death, however, will try to maintain the same life he and his family had before his child died. Distancing himself from emotions of raw grief gives him the strength to continue to protect and provide for his family. Although he needs the emotionally connecting love of his wife in order to feel related, he brings clarity in a time of chaos and lends stability to the grieving family. Most often, however, he has difficulty experiencing and expressing his feelings.

Considering the hero aspect of male psychology, it is not surprising to find that even without the tragic loss of a child, many middle-aged men coming for psychotherapy complain of "general malaise," an undifferentiated "cloud that hangs over them," or a "feeling of numbness." Having lived so many years divorced from their emotions, they say they have no feelings at all, or can express only anger. Trained mainly to produce and achieve, many men previously considered feelings impediments to their life goals. But what worked for them in the past, works no longer. Now they must confront childhood wounds they have repressed and clarify their values, giving attention to their own deepest nature.

Because our society typically devalues "feminine" aspects of a man's personality, a father whose child dies, like men in mid-life, often lacks the capacity to connect with his emotions. Even men who experience emotional grief feel constrained to suppress feelings that others may perceive as less manly. Not only are they reluctant to talk about their feelings, they also spend much energy mastering them. Many men have been programmed not to show emotional pain and have no language for grief. They have been taught that vulnerability, sensitivity, and tenderness are weaknesses. Recognizing that such dictates restrict personality growth, many therapists are helping men move toward greater wholeness. The poet Robert Bly envisions a male role that is vigorously masculine, yet strongly emotionally rooted. In one book, he recounts how he has rid himself of numbness after having decided as a child not to feel.

> If I accepted my mother's protection, I would have to learn to feel as a woman feels. But I was a man, and so I decided to have no feelings at all.[4]

We must conclude, that, in itself, a man's reticence about his feelings is no indication he is not grieving. Women frequently make the mistake of expecting their husbands to grieve the way they do. They do not always understand how gender and the archetypes that fight it influence patterns of grief. Becoming aware of typically masculine modes of grieving can help women respect and support their husbands' more muted reactions to loss.

Above all, we women must realize how often we make contradictory demands on the grieving fathers. We may require men to be strong and criticize them at the same time for not showing more emotion. Grieving males may quietly seek support and be given little: they are expected to support others. Women want them to keep control in the family; employers give them a few "consolation days" and then require them to return to work. Men are expected to solve problems—their own and others'. It is certainly true that, because they often find the repetitive and chaotic emotional aspects of mourning problematic, men are likely to seek activity when they grieve. Masculine energy, by its very nature, is goal-oriented, and men tend to see themselves as problem solvers who work to find solutions to whatever impedes progress toward their goal. As household provider and protector, a father may often find his primary goal is to restore family normality. He will plan family outings, for example, or otherwise move in directions that somehow make life the way it was.

Because of feeling inwardly stripped of all control, grief-stricken fathers also seek to renew their confidence by showing competency. Many men find the workplace a safe harbor for reestablishing a sense of control and releasing pent up energy from feelings they are unable to verbalize. There they can feel a sense of accomplishment and mastery. Because much of their identity is closely tied to their work, they can help restore their injured self-image by gaining their colleagues respect for jobs well done.

In order not to become too one-sided though, a grieving father should also plan for his leisure-time activity. He could become involved in team sports or enjoy a fishing trip with his buddies. For most men, friendship bases itself on shared activity rather than self-disclure. To regain confidence, a bereaved father requires the world of men. He also needs to be physical, to feel his body working. Even if done alone, activities like jogging or biking help a father validate his manhood.

Many men also find strength devoting energy to causes related to the tragedy of their child's death. They may organize a benefit golf game, educate against teenage suicide, or start a neighborhood crimewatch. Paradoxically, involvement in such goal-oriented activities slowly allows them to let go of the deceased child, while staying connected to her in ways leading back to a fuller life.

Some men will try an activity new to them: joining a church choir, starting a band, or taking a painting class. Another creative way to renew faith in life, working with wood, builds something tangible, something he brings to completion. All these activities can be constructive responses to grief because they involve a man in action.

The true story, "Burning Olivier," movingly illustrates a bereaved father's need to respond to loss with goal-oriented action. George Michelsen Foy's decision to personally bury his deceased month-old boy was prompted by the inhuman ordeal the child endured while hooked to life-support systems. Foy saw his son as a battler for life, a two-pint warrior, finally laying down his sword and accepting defeat. For the admiring and grieving father, there was no question of abandoning the dead warrior now. Always having distrusted morticians, Foy vowed his heroic son would not be placed in the hands of those who must manufacture grief emotions for business.

Foy learned earlier that in all but five states—Connecticut, New York, Indiana, Louisiana, and Nebraska are the exceptions—it is legal to handle and bury your own. Where he lived in Massachusetts, the funeral industry had tried to tighten the burial law, but there was still a loophole: "A permit for burial may be issued to a funeral director *or other person.*" If Foy could obtain such a permit, he would have the legal right to transport Olivier's body from the hospital morgue to a cemetery or crematory.

Foy pursued his mission. At the cemetery office he learned, besides the burial permit, he would need a $105 check for that business and a $50 check for the state medical examiner. After a complicated bureaucratic ordeal, he obtained the permit. Then, with help from a carpenter friend, he built his son a coffin. Knowing his wife was not interested in this part of Olivier's journey, Foy hid the coffin from her view. On the final night, unable to sleep, he ruminated about the box. He felt it wasn't quite good enough for Olivier. The hero who had fought so hard to live didn't even have his name on it. So at midnight, Foy drew a red tugboat on the coffin and carved Olivier's initials on its side. Red was for his son's great heart—akin to that of his namesake, one of Charlemagne's legendary paladins, a mythic hero, an archetypal symbol of courage. The tugboat, as modern as Charlemagne's warriors were ancient, symbolized his son's strength and determination in recent battle, as well as his passage from life to death. Foy stood back to observe the finished product. At last feeling satisfied, he thought to himself, "We have a pine box that to my eyes is strong and workmanlike, elegant in color and simplicity, a box good enough to carry Olivier."

It was over a month before Foy, carrying the coffin with him, went to the hospital morgue for Olivier. Taking the cold body from the hospital's medical examiner, he placed his son in the coffin and leaned over to kiss him one more time. Then he tapped in the nails that closed the box and drove Olivier to the crematory.

Foy had advanced his work, a mission guided by the heart. Foy explained, "All I could remember was a code of conduct for which I could barely recall the rationale but which summarized itself in these words: *taking care of Olivier*." Because of its unconscious archetypal underpinnings, the full meaning of his mantra, which Foy had repeated since his son took ill, could not be rationally stated. Nevertheless, moving his task toward completion brought great comfort to Olivier's father.

Foy was always well aware that his way of grieving Olivier was distinctly different from his wife's. In this marriage, each partner accepted the other's reactions with respect and with no requirement that both be alike.

> Ever since Olivier's operations, my wife, Liz, had resolutely withdrawn into an emotional cloister, which was her determination to remember our boy in the first days of life...I understood her perfectly. Because if people are the stories we make up about them—if we are stories we make up about ourselves—then this was the one she had chosen to craft about our son. Just as my tale of Olivier was a male version of a fighter dealing with spatial relationships and the practicalities of battle, hers was a female fable of a baby who when he was healthy possessed

a shining curiosity, an almost solid lust for the attention and milk that made life good.[5]

Liz didn't choose to take part in decisions Foy made after Olivier's death. She was happy to accept her husband's way of taking care of Olivier and participated only in the final burial, the end of her husband's mission and of her own quiet difference. On that day, Foy picked up his son's ashes and he and Liz drove with them to Cape Cod. She took the last bags of her breast milk, defrosted now, and poured them into the hole Foy had dug in his grandfather's garden. Then, together, they buried their son "in the midst of blue myrtle and dogwood and white pine, within sight of Nantucket Sound." Each of them had responded very differently after Olivier died but this couple remained connected to each other and shared their sorrow in a final, ritually meaningful, sacrament.

Couples Estranged

Unlike Foy and Liz, however, some couples losing their child are unable to maintain mutual respect and understanding for each other's grief. The most frequent complaint I hear is, "We don't communicate." It is so unfortunate that many partners just stop talking when they are unable to understand each other's reactions to loss or when they have rigid expectations about how the other spouse should be grieving. There is no more poignant portrayal of this problem than Robert Frost's "Home Burial."

Home Burial

He saw her from the bottom of the stairs
Before she saw him. She was starting down,
Looking back over her shoulder at some fear.
She took a doubtful step and then undid it
To raise herself and look again. He spoke
Advancing toward her: "What is it you see
From up there always—for I want to know."
She turned and sank upon her skirts at that,
And her face changed from terrified to dull.
He said to gain time: "What is it you see,"
Mounting until she cowered under him.

"I will find out now—you must tell me, dear."
She, in her place, refused him any help
With the least stiffening of her neck and silence.
She let him look, sure that he wouldn't see,
Blind creature; and a while he didn't see.
But at last he murmured, "Oh," and again, "Oh."
"What is it—what?" she said.
"Just that I see."
"You don't," she challenged. "Tell me what it is."

"I never noticed it from here before.
I must be wonted to it—that's the reason.
The little graveyard where my people are!
So small the window frames the whole of it.
Not so much larger than a bedroom, is it?
There are three stones of slate and one of marble,
Broad-shouldered little slabs there in the sunlight
On the sidehill. We haven't to mind those.
But I understand: it is not the stones,
But the child's mound——"
"Don't, don't, don't, don't," she cried.
She withdrew shrinking from beneath his arm
That rested on the banister, and slid downstairs;
And turned on him with such a daunting look,
He said twice over before he knew himself:
"Can't a man speak of his own child he's lost?"

"Not you! Oh, where's my hat? Oh, I don't need it!
I must get out of here. I must get air.
I don't know rightly whether any man can."

"Amy! Don't go to someone else this time.
Listen to me. I won't come down the stairs."
He sat and fixed his chin between his fists.
"There's something I should like to ask you, dear."

"You don't know how to ask it."

"Help me, then."
Her fingers moved the latch for all reply.

"My words are nearly always an offense.

I don't know how to speak of anything
So as to please you. But I might be taught
I should suppose. I can't say I see how.
A man must partly give up being a man
With women-folk. We could have some arrangement
By which I'd bind myself to keep hands off
Anything special you're a-mind to name.
Though I don't like such things 'twixt those that love.
Two that don't love can't live together without them.
But two that do can't live together with them."
She moved the latch a little. "Don't—don't go.
Don't carry it to someone else this time.
Tell me about it if it's something human.
Let me into your grief. I'm not so much
Unlike other folks as your standing there
Apart would make me out. Give me my chance.
I do think, though, you overdo it a little.
What was it brought you up to think it the thing
To take your mother-loss of a first child
So inconsolably—in the face of love.
You'd think his memory might be satisfied———"

"There you go sneering now!"

"I'm not, I'm not!
You make me angry. I'll come down to you.
God, what a woman! And it's come to this,
A man can't speak of his own child that's dead."

"You can't because you don't know how.
If you had any feelings, you that dug
With your own hand—how could you?—his little grave;
I saw you from that very window there,
Making the gravel leap and leap in air,
Leap up, like that, like that, and land so lightly
And roll back down the mound beside the hole.
I thought, Who is that man? I didn't know you.
And I crept down the stairs and up the stairs
To look again, and still your spade kept lifting.
Then you came in. I heard your rumbling voice
Out in the kitchen, and I don't know why,

But I went near to see with my own eyes.
You could sit there with the stains on your shoes
Of the fresh earth from your own baby's grave
And talk about your everyday concerns.
You had stood the spade up against the wall
Outside there in the entry, for I saw it."

"I shall laugh the worst laugh I ever laughed.
I'm cursed. God, if I don't believe I'm cursed."

"I can repeat the very words you were saying.
'Three foggy mornings and one rainy day
Will rot the best birch fence a man can build.'
Think of it, talk like that at such a time!
What had how long it takes a birch to rot
To do with what was in the darkened parlour.
You couldn't care! The nearest friends can go
With anyone to death, comes so far short
They might as well not try to go at all.
No, from the time when one is sick to death,
One is alone, and he dies more alone.
Friends make pretense of following to the grave,
But before one is in it, their minds are turned
And making the best of their way back to life
And living people, and things they understand.
But the world's evil. I won't have grief so
If I can change it. Oh, I won't, I won't!"

"There, you have said it all and you feel better.
You won't go now. You're crying. Close the door.
The heart's gone out of it: why keep it up.
Amy! There's someone coming down the road!"

"You—oh, you think the talk is all. I must go—
Somewhere out of this house. How can I make you—"

"If—you—do!" She was opening the door wider.
"Where do you mean to go? First tell me that.

I'll follow and bring you back by force. I will!—"[6]

Frost scholars tell us that he based his poem on his sister-in-law's estranged marriage after the death of her first-born child, but the poem cannot be separated from his losing his own four-year-old child. Frost once commented that his wife, "knew that this world was evil, " after she experienced that tragedy. In spite of her pessimistic view and both parents' sadness, however, the couple remained married for forty-three years. Neither one of them fully recovered from the death, however, and Frost was never able to read "Home Burial" in public because he thought it was so sad. The poem begins with the wife Amy pausing at the top of the stairs to "look back over her shoulder at some fear." The husband, at the bottom of the stairs, wants to know what she sees, for he has seen her standing there many times before. The cryptic dialogue makes us wonder what has gone on before in their lives together.[7]

With kindness, the husband in the poem tries to find out what is so devastating to his wife, but she refuses his pleas and stiffens in silence. She has already decided he is blind to all that matters in *her* world. This time, however, the husband climbs the stairs to see what he has always failed to notice from that viewpoint, the graveyard where the child is buried among others of the family. He understands that the others' deaths are not so horrifying, but that the child's mound is unbearable to look at. Now he tries to console her, but in protest she sobs, "Don't, don't, don't, don't."

"Can't a man speak of his own child he's lost?" he cries.

All communication has broken down in this couple. Amy is convinced that her husband hasn't grieved the death of their son. Long ago he dug the boy's grave himself, but unable to verbalize his sorrow, he spoke instead of fences men can build on a farm and how they rot from the moist soil. We feel alienation arising from the husband's inability to find words for the awful experience of digging his son's grave.

Fences play a key part in such other Frost poems as "Mending Wall," and his using that metaphor here further emphasizes how easily man and wife can build barriers in time of crisis. Unwilling to bear any intimacy with her husband, Amy seeks solace from others outside her marriage. Because she is so embittered, however, it is doubtful that she can find help anywhere, for she blames even her friends for being unwilling to walk with her through death.

Friends make pretense of following to the grave,
But before one is in it, their minds are turned
And making the best of their way back to life
And living people, and things they understand.

The husband begs Amy to let him into her grief, to give him a chance. He implies, however, that he may not be able to follow her completely. Suggesting that she may "overdo it a little," he alludes to her desperation as being "something more than human." Even in the face of his love, Amy remains totally inconsolable and unwilling to see the world as it really is. For salvation, Frost believed, one must recognize and accept the suffering and unfairness that exist for all of us; in spite of the inevitable tragic quality inherent in our existence, we have to reach out for love and life. Amy and her husband are unable to make the connection each of them needs. In the end, the husband's anger increases with her every accusation, mounting to a threat of physical force.

TYPICALLY, WHEN A CHILD DIES, all past grievances between a husband and wife emerge. Grieving couples often hear warnings, based largely on unsubstantiated statistics, about the high number of divorces occurring after a child's death. Some of these divorces, in fact, occur years after the tragedy, but in other instances couples remain married and live separate lives. It is probably inaccurate to say that child loss causes divorces. Rather, the death serves to catalyze the ending of an already troubled union. Sometimes, there is nothing a person can do if a spouse shows dangerous signs of pathological or unresolved grief. Women become unavailable because of deep depression; men may hide behind their work or escape with alcohol and drugs. The parents' absence or inability to communicate falls on the remaining children and disunion inundates the home. Then, the rest of the children's lives can be dramatically affected by their sibling's death.

In Sylvia's family, her husband Bart was definitely the head of household. Sylvia acquiesced in whatever her husband demanded, even when she thought he was being rough on their two sons. When their oldest son Kevin became severely depressed, Bart refused Sylvia's suggestion that they seek psychiatric help for Kevin. The younger son Mark was aware of Kevin's difficulties, but his family's style was not to express emotions or ask probing questions. Mark kept his concerns to himself. Finally, in desperation, Kevin asked to see a psychiatrist. His mother made the appointment, and his father agreed to drive there. Along the way Kevin and his father lost their way, an argument ensued, and they were too late for the appointment. That evening Kevin put a gun to his head and took his own life.

After the death Bart refused to talk about his deceased boy. He insisted that the family return to normal activity immediately, particularly to avoid feeling shamed in the community. Mark began experimenting with drugs and alcohol. Less than two years later Bart died from a heart attack. Sylvia says her husband died of a broken heart, and now she struggles with her surviving son, who has become a chronic alcoholic.

The Family as an Archetypal System

Sylvia's and Bart's is a sad story of unresolved grief in a family that was fairly functional before tragedy. Families can be seen as systems; when a child dies, there is a disruption of the system requiring its restructuring to reclaim equilibrium. For many years, Sylvia's decision to allow her husband to make all major decisions worked fairly well. With her older son's depression and subsequent death, however, the old way of functioning lacked flexibility necessary for family survival. Their heart wrenching loss could not be integrated into a new way of relating to one another.

When a child dies, each person must cope not only with his own acute *intrapersonal* stress, but also with the novelty and pain of altered family relationships. A person's intrapersonal stress arises from her inner conflicts, all the strong emotions accompanying great loss: denial, grief, anger, depression and so on. One particularly painful cause of personal turmoil, though rarely discussed among family members, is "survival guilt," the guilt survivors feel merely being alive. Grandparents, having lived complete lives, wonder, "Why didn't God take me?" and mothers know that they would willingly die if death would bring their child to life. Among all family members, however, siblings suffer most the question, "Why her and not me?" It may haunt them throughout life.

In addition to enduring their own inner turmoil, then, all family members must learn new ways of relating to one another. Frequently, however, the interpersonal stress arising from crisis brings disunity rather than cooperation, not just to the couple but to the total family system. A mother whose "favorite" child has died may unconsciously shun one surviving. A daughter will suddenly feel imprisoned by an overprotective parent, or a son may feel pressured to live out a dead sibling's ambition.

A key mechanism transmits problems between two family members to the larger group: the breakdown of preexisting "triangulations." Complex interlocking "triangulations" occur normally and usefully in all families, but in times of traumatic stress they can dissolve into both deadly silence and chaos. (Normal triangulation was first documented by Murray Bowen, who believes it is a universal, multicultural, and multigenerational phenomenon.) Triangulations function by binding family members together to reduce anxiety. Simply stated, triangulation occurs when two family members who are experiencing excessive anxiety between themselves come to involve a third person. They may bring the third person into the triangle themselves, or the third person may move in of her own accord, or both. The new triangle diffuses the anxiety between the first two members by redirecting interactions to include the third person.

What happened to Mary and Donald is a good example of triangulation breakdown. Their marriage had been strained even before eleven-year-old daughter Katie was killed in an automobile accident. As both he and his wife later admitted, Donald began staying out late after the death, "drinking and womanizing." In the beginning, however, they wanted help for their older daughter Kindred, who was "unmanageable." The parents distanced themselves from their marital strain by focusing all their worries on their surviving daughter. "If only she would straighten out," they said, "things would be all right."

Fortunately, they engaged in marital therapy for several months and even though Kindred did not attend the sessions, her behavior improved. Mom and dad "began to lighten up on her," and Kindred felt relieved of emotional pressures she had experienced in the triangle.

To be sure, when acknowledging their marital problems her parents felt much anxiety, but gradually, as they talked about them, first in therapy and then at home with Kindred, all became able to share the deep grief for Katie which they had earlier kept contained in their separate and lonely inner worlds.

Over time, it became clear each person had had symptoms of emotional disturbance deriving from unresolved issues in the couple's marriage. Mother had become bitter and withdrawn, father avoided coming home, and Kindred acted out her own anger and grief by being a rebellious teenager. As marital issues resolved, the family was able to release the deep emotions felt from Katie's death.

If we pay attention, we can discover how our own family unit functions to maintain its members' balance and stability. Despite the ever-changing quality of family life, some patterns may have existed for generations. Our family is not just its current reality but all the family stories we have told, the secrets we have kept, and the archetypal motifs that have colored our personal experience. As the years go by, we continue to create those stories, building our family myth. Only partly personal, but influenced by The Family Archetype, this myth is an innate psychological pattern. Also, infinite motifs emanate from The Family Archetype: we speak of "the human family," "the Holy Family," and sometimes even of coworkers as a family. "Family" becomes a metaphor for almost any close connection or joint endeavor.[8]

Binding such family metaphors together, however, is the idea that the family serves to protect its members from the outside world. The Family Archetype not only connects to the Mother, Father, and Child Archetype, but also serves as a *temenos*, a Greek word meaning a sacred precinct or king's domain where a person might expect to be held in safety. The family as temenos is a safe haven, we hope, from harm arising from outside the family; nevertheless, it may generate suffering to those within. To take a fairly common example, Keith's family prided themselves on their strong New England background, particularly individuals' right to privacy that is part of that tradition. But a complex of strict Protestant values (including ethics held for many generations) kept his parents silent about their oldest son Eddie's death from AIDS.

One important thing in my family was presenting a united front to outsiders, living up to 'correct' social norms. If we deviated from my mom's standards of behavior, she would challenge us with, 'What will the neighbors think?' Another of her favorite sayings was, 'Don't air your dirty linen!' So we all kept the family secrets inside the house. In fact, a lot was so secret that we tried to keep it from each other. For instance, nobody talked about my mom's wine intake after Eddie's death. She just quietly sipped herself to sleep. And my dad was always wanting to be a big deal with guys he hung around with, so he certainly wasn't going to say anything about Eddie. He pretended I was the perfect son and talked about me.

Eddie's death was sort of shameful for my parents, the way he died and all. And, after the funeral, I followed what I had been taught and kept everything to myself. Soon Eddie was never mentioned in the house and it was as if people outside didn't even remember he had died. Everybody seemed to think that our family was just fine.

Unlike Keith's family, families accustomed to disclosing thoughts and expressing feelings are more likely to share their individual grief with one another. While allowing each member to mourn in her own way, such open families have no fear about telling the truth, and parents do not hide grief from their children. Communication, which we have already seen is the most important element in healthy grieving, is encouraged. Open family communication gives a greater chance not only that marriages survive but that siblings will be enabled to enter fully into life.

Grieving families also strengthen by appropriate rituals. Rituals like the Foy's home burial can enhance the family system and positively energize the Family Archetype. In Part Two, I'll suggest ways to celebrate the deceased child's birthday and acknowledge the anniversary day of his death. When all family members, including the youngest children, plan and help perform these ceremonies, the burden of loss gets shared and the load on each heart is lightened. One could say that such rituals become a specially heightened form of family communication, not only among its individual members but also with the larger culture and society from which we derive so much of our strength and meaning.

Adolescence and the Loss of Innocence

The time to say goodbye to childhood and ready oneself for the adult world is a crucial period of development. For the boy, adolescence is influenced by forces from The Hero/Warrior Archetype, urging him to compete courageously and use his talents to excel. In folklore and fairy tales, this is symbolized by dramatic episodes of heroes fighting dragons. The teenage boy's mission does not have to be a physical test. It can be any undertaking requiring toughness and tenacity: school grades, musical skill, or scientific exploration. The dragon symbolizes anything that hinders the boy's quest to satisfy his underlying aim: entering the adult world of love and work. For the adolescent girl the dragon represents the hindrances in her path to womanhood. Her task is training the dragon so it becomes useful to her. In fairy tales she is represented by the princess, who often holds a dragon on a leash.[9]

One confusing task of adolescence is moving away from the safety of parents and experiencing life independently. Getting the courage to make this transition can be difficult, and the prevailing adolescent attitude of invulnerability, unconsciously held by many teenagers, is one force that helps. But during a period when most of her peers feel invulnerable, an adolescent who loses a sibling is shocked into the reality of death. In fact, the death of a sibling often causes bereaved adolescents to believe that they will themselves die young, in some sudden and unexpected way, by accident perhaps. These adolescents frequently can't make long range plans or engage in goal-oriented behavior. Having lost their innocence, neither can bereaved adolescents fully enter into their schoolmates future-focused life: college, career, and marriage. Their school work may suffer because of their inability to concentrate. Constantly worried, they may have a general sense that things are always about to go wrong. And because of the natural adolescent tendency toward risk-taking, this dread can become a self-fulfilling prophecy. Abuse of alcohol and drugs, and reckless driving, are outlets for such strong contrary emotions, as ambition and anger, on the one hand and, on the other, guilt, self-loathing, and loneliness.

Adolescents are usually well aware of family dynamics and how the family has changed since their sibling's death. If they are given a safe place to express feelings, they will complain about incidents when they were not told the truth or when they felt left out of significant discussions or events. Being keen observers of parents' feelings and behavior, they may now feel unusually responsible for their well-being. They grieve not only for the deceased but for their parents' suffering.

Seventeen-year-old Mary Sue complained of severe headaches and nausea. After doctors found no physiological cause, her mother sent her to me for psychotherapy. Working with me weekly during her senior year in high school, she continued to be an excellent student, and received a scholarship to a local university.

Throughout the year, however, Mary Sue grieved over the loss of her nine-year-old brother, whose death in a boating accident two years before left her as sole surviving child. She composed poetry about her brother, wrote him letters, and imaginatively showed him photos. Greatly concerned about her parents' estranged marriage, particularly her father's violent outbursts and her mother's passivity, she worried what would happen to her parents' marriage when she left for college.

Mary started college in September. She had been encouraged to join her mother's sorority, where she was welcomed. She had every reason to succeed in college, but following an unconscious pattern of triangulation, she was driven home to avert her parents' divorce. By Christmas, she had flunked out.

One developmental task of adolescents is slowly moving away from the nuclear family and toward greater intimacy with peers. But in spite of their need for peer support and intimacy, most surviving siblings report that their classmates, having never been close to death, can't understand their deep suffering. Still bereaved, a surviving sibling thinks of the deceased every day, sometimes for years, but finds few people with whom to share her thoughts. When such a teenager does find friends capable of sharing her burden, she is tremendously helped.

In their normal struggle to form a new identity, adolescents also attempt to establish an individual world view: religious, moral, and political. Part of developing their individuality is coming to grips with life's biggest questions: "Who am I? What am I here for?" The death of a brother or sister, however, initiates them into an especially deep and difficult quest for meaning.

Some of the characteristics of an "initiation" have been explored in the preceding chapter, where I described *initiation into mourning*. Here we saw that initiation is something one must *go through*, involving periods of *chaos* and *isolation* and *letting go* of a part of oneself connected to a previous way of being. When the loss of a sibling catalyzes an initiation into such a special quest for meaning, a young person, after much struggle, may become wise beyond her years. Sometimes she recognizes this wisdom only in retrospect, long after she has completed the required steps of initiation. Now age twenty-six with a four-year-old son, Monique, who lost her brother to a genetically transmitted disease, was such an adolescent.

> For a long time, I didn't make a commitment to anything or anybody. I was so angry with God for letting my brother suffer so. Slowly, I realized that maybe God didn't have control of everything. I started to remember how brave he had been, and when I saw other disabled people in a wheel chair or something, I'd go talk to them. I think having lost a brother at such a young age has made me a lot more compassionate. And now that I have my own kid, I can understand what my mother went through and I'm not so mad at her. I'm glad they have the test to determine that I'm not a carrier.

Younger Children's Reaction to Death

Because children grieve differently from adults, they may appear not to be mourning at all. One adult client confessed her long held guilt that as a child, the day her sister died, she went to a neighbor's to play. This woman has been mourning her sister's death for thirty years. With help, she recalled how bad she felt about her sister's death, even though she chose to play. Children often resume play even while hurting inside. They need more physical activity to release their strong emotions. Having a shorter attention span, they also require frequent respite from their grief and will often alternate short periods of mourning with pursuing other interests.

Children's reactions to death are also influenced by their concept of its finality, an understanding that progresses as they pass through successive developmental stages. In the early years, supposing death reversible, children believe a brother or sister will return and are not likely to be devastated. They attribute the imagined return of life to the good effects of ambulances, hospitals, or doctors who will magically revive the deceased. In the middle years, most children recognize that death is permanent, but some, even at age nine or ten, still believe the deceased will return.

We can already see that there is no set age for each developmental stage of a child's understanding. When asked, "What will happen when you die?" one nine-year-old said that his mother, father, and grandfather would help him come back alive. Another eight-year-old replied, "You go to heaven and all that will be left of you will be a skeleton. My friend has some fossils of people. A fossil is just a skeleton." A ten-year-old responded, "I think I'm going to be reincarnated as a plant or animal, whatever they need at that particular time."[10]

Although children often provide concrete answers when asked what will happen at death, answers suggesting finality, they also manifest an intuitive sense that growth of some kind can continue after death—just as the drawings of dying children in Rhoda Kellog's work show a sense of life's wholeness. A child who hears the story of ""Little Red Riding Hood," for example, understands that when the little one was swallowed by the wolf, she really "died." Yet she also understands that Little Red Riding Hood comes to life again (springs from the belly of the wolf). The theme of life's transformations is the message of many fairy tales, and it also seems that children have an archetypal knowledge of the life cycle of death and rebirth, just like adults. Fairy tales portray transformation concretely—a frog actually turns into a prince, for example, only because children have not yet learned to think in abstract terms.

Children also know intuitively what they need in order to heal themselves after loss, but they cannot heal alone. First, they must be freed of carrying too much concern for their grieving parents. Children are so attuned to the unspoken moods and feelings of their parents' sadness that they may try to protect them by not showing their own. The most important aid in a child's grief process is a safe environment where she can express her thoughts and feelings. Paradoxically, by *not* hiding her own grief, a mother can begin to provide that safe environment.

If a child feels safe, she will begin to create a story about her relationship with her sibling and her own thoughts and feelings about the death. Mothers can help each child understand her personal experience by encouraging her to talk about what she misses most and what she would have liked to have been different. Here again, the story will not be told in one sitting. Though very difficult, it is important that a mother be available whenever her child is ready to talk. By sharing her own experiences then and asking open-ended questions, both at a time when a child is ready to share, a mother creates a continuation of the family story with her child.

To help a child comprehend what may happen when a person dies, we can also offer new dimensions in imagination through fairy tales, art work, and religious stories, thus lessening the fear of death and also giving more meaning to life. Children are particularly drawn to fairy tales because authentic folklore stories enhance imagination, alleviate anxieties, clarify emotions, and suggest solutions to problems. They enrich a child's life because they start where she really is in her psychological and emotional being. A child comes to grips with a problem in simple form: everything is either black or white, for that is how her mind works. Fairy tales echo this clarity, but present more than the sunny side of life. They accomplish their inclusiveness by taking seriously our need to be loved, our fear of being worthless, and our fear of death, and they teach the child that struggle against severe difficulties is an unavoidable part of human existence.

Like their mothers, children need to develop an imaginative life for the deceased to inhabit. The thought of her child's death is too horrific for a mother unless she is able to move into an imaginative realm where she can find a safe place for her child to be. There, she slowly develops and nurtures an inner relationship. A surviving child also carries the experience of her sibling's death throughout her life, and she too needs an inner image of continuation. By encouraging a child to draw pictures of her family, a little one may find a place in her drawing for her missing sibling. She may also find comfort in writing letters or poetry to the deceased. Six-year-old Maggie found great comfort, and relief from her fears, by painting pictures and writing poetry. She wrote the following poem on Halloween, honoring her three-year-old brother who drowned in a swimming pool.

About My Brother

About my brother, he was the best
I haven't any scissors
But I have a spare of love to give him another heart.
I haven't any glue either,
But for Halloween, I'm going to be a Cat Woman
I've already got my costume
I think he would like it.

When I call to him, it makes me want to scream
I LOVE YOU, CHIP!

You are on my TV screen in my heart
But my heart has a little feeling,
A sad one, it's true
I won't sell it for some money,
I won't sell it for love.

I won't sell it for anything
But you fly like a dove.

By encouraging drawing, questions, storytelling, and writing about the deceased, a mother can also identify some negative thoughts that may be plaguing her child. Children often believe in magical thinking, that just thinking something can make it happen. Because they sometimes harbored aggressive fantasies in the past, they may even think the sibling's death their fault. Simply hearing once and for all this is not the case will not convince them otherwise, but careful listening combined with thoughtful questions and comments about one's own concept of the cause of death may alleviate their sense of guilt.

Sometimes anxiety will cause a child to repeat the same questions over and over again. Nevertheless, mothers should answer all questions truthfully and succinctly, in language the child understands. A child needs encouragement to talk about the actual day of death even if she often repeats questions like, "Where was I that day?" "How did I hear about the death?" "What did I do next?" "What was it like at the funeral?" "Where is my sister now?"

Surviving children also need continued reassurance, even if they show little outward emotion. There is almost always a heightened fear of being separated from their parents. Because humans cannot survive without a nurturing other, our archetypal fear of abandonment is present from birth. After the death of a sibling, abandonment fear arises, not only from missing the deceased but also because parents are often emotionally unavailable. School phobias, nightmares, bed wetting, and psychosomatic ills are symptoms of this fear which is often called separation anxiety.

Because all children feel vulnerable, those who have been taught there is a loving and heavenly Father are more likely to feel protected even in times when parents fail them. Conversely, however, when a child dies, her siblings strive to answer the same questions as the parents about God's power and love. In the following chapters we will see that *how* a child dies introduces a variety of factors that complicate this existential struggle.

NOTES:

1.   William James, *Talks to Teachers on Psychology*, Mineola, New York, 1899, p. 77.
2.   Joseph Campbell, *The Hero With A Thousand Faces*, Princeton, 1968, p. 16.
3.   Edward C. Whitmont, *The Symbolic Quest*, Princeton, 1969, p. 182.
4.   Robert Bly, *Iron John*, New York, 1992, p. 67.
5.   George Michaelson Foy, "Burning Olivier," *Harpers*, July, 1999, p. 47.
6.   Robert Frost, "Home Burial," *The Norton Anthology of American Literature*, New York, 2003, pp. 1124–26.
7.   For an explanation of Robert Frost's poems, see Edward Garnett, "A New American Poet," *Critical Essays on Robert Frost*, Philip L. Gerber, New York, 1982.
8.   Terrill L. Gibson, "Incest and Imagination," *Psyche and Family*, Laura Dodson & Terrill Gibson, ed., Wilmette, Illinois, 1996, pp. 1–31.
9.   For a full analysis of adolescent development, see Sue Crommelin, "Archetypes in Adolescent Development and Psychopathology," *Psyche and Family*, Laura Dodson and Terrill Gibson, ed., Wilmette, Illinois, 1996, pp. 59–79.
10. DeSpelder and Strickland, *The Last Dance: Encountering Death and Dying*, New York, 2002, p. 354.

Chapter Five

THE UNLIVED LIFE: FETUSES AND INFANTS

*They shall hunger no more, neither thirst any more; neither shall the
sun light on them, nor any heat. For the lamb which is in the midst of
the throne shall feed them, and shall lead them unto living fountains
of water: and God shall wipe away all tears from their eyes.*
— "THE ORDER FOR THE BURIAL OF A CHILD"
A BOOK OF OFFICES (1914)

When No Life Has Been Lived: The Barren Woman

Women's desire to have children is documented throughout history, particularly in the Bible. The Old Testament tells the colorful
story of Jacob's love for Rachel. When the two first met at the well,
they felt an immediate attraction. Jacob asked her father Laban for her
hand in marriage, but he demanded servitude for seven years before
assenting. At the end of the seven years, Laban cheated Jacob on his
wedding night, substituting his elder daughter Leah for Rachel, and
Leah became Jacob's first wife.

Still in love with Rachel, Jacob contracted to serve another seven
years in order to make her his second wife. Even when it became certain
that Rachel was barren, Jacob loved her, while hating Leah. Though
he slept with Rachel often, he used Leah to get his children. Rachel
jealously watched her sister try to win Jacob's love by bearing one child
after another, until there were six sons and a daughter.

While working in Laban's wheat field, one of Leah's sons found some mandrakes, fragrant root plants used both to induce fertility and increase sexual desire. Leah offered the mandrakes to Rachel in exchange for a night with Jacob. But Leah again conceived, and Rachel remained barren. When Leah grew too old to give birth, she sent her slave handmaid for Jacob's use as a concubine. Because it was customary that an infertile wife present her handmaid to her husband, Rachel did the same.

Rachel's relentless sorrow for children *who were not* recurs as a heart-stirring metaphor in both the Bible and in more recent literature. Rachel envied her sister and told Jacob, "Give me children or I shall die!" When the prophet Jeremiah mourns for a scattered Israel, he likens his grief to Rachel's:

> Thus saith the Lord; A voice was heard in Ramah, lamentation and bitter weeping; Rachel, weeping for her children, refused to be comforted for her children *who were not.* (Jer. 31:15)

Centuries later when he feared Jesus' birth, Herod slew all the children in Bethlehem, and Rachel's grief is heard again:

> A voice was heard in Ramah
> wailing and loud lamentation
> Rachel weeping for her children
> she refused to be consoled
> because they were no more. (Matt. 2:18)

More recently, Melville's *Moby Dick* depicts Captain Ahab's refusing to stop and help *The Rachel*'s captain hunt for his son, swept overboard.

> But by her still halting course and winding, woeful way, you plainly saw that this ship that so wept with spray, still remained without comfort. She was Rachel, weeping for her children, "because they were not."

Modern feminists protest the Bible's seemingly representing important women like Sarah, Rachel and Hannah as valued only for their reproductive powers. We should note, however, that Hannah prayed from her own deep desire to conceive. Her husband Elkanh chided her for it: "Hannah why weepest thou and why eatest thou not and why is thy heart grieved? Am I not better to thee than ten sons?" But Hannah kept praying silently "in the spirit" for her own sake (Samuel 1:6–8).

In fact, women seem to have an archetypally driven desire to bear children. Submitting to this archetype today, however, comes at a high price, for Rachel's mandrake has been replaced by expensive fertility drugs and painful procedures, each in vitro fertilization costing between $8,000 and $10,000. When drugs and procedures fail to produce a child, the modern couple may pay thousands of dollars more to a surrogate mother, whose function is not far removed from that of the ancient Hebrew handmaids of Leah and Rachel.

Rachel's weeping for "children who are not" echoes today in Mary Sue's sadness. Though she has an adopted daughter, now successfully completing her first year of college, Mary Sue wants to be pregnant. Because she is approaching menopause, she knows that she must soon give up hope for the miracle she has long cherished. Still, she desires the experience of what she calls "a major event," carrying her own baby in her womb.

As through the years Mary Sue diligently tried to conceive, sex became a grim task between her and her husband Donald. She felt so much pressure to have intercourse exactly at her ovulation that sometimes she imagined her doctor in the bedroom, coaching her. Over many years, her fruitless experiences with gynecologists became traumatic, causing her to feel as if she had handed over her body to physicians, making them her rulers.

> When I first went to my regular gynecologist, he hooked up this antiquated equipment, like a torture device, to blow carbon dioxide through my tubes to see if they were open. One of them wasn't, and it hurt, really bad. The only thing the doctor said to me was, 'Well, you will never be pregnant.' I was still in awe of doctors in those days, and I totally lost my voice, like a lamb to the slaughter. Another time I remember coming out of anesthesia just as the doctor was telling my husband we would never have a child. I felt I really had taken something away from my beloved. I was a huge failure.
>
> And then going home I had so much pain that I had to crawl up the steps to our second floor apartment.
>
> But in spite of all this I still went along with anything a doctor suggested. Even after we adopted Katy, I tried in vitro fertilizations.

Jan's case is similar. Just turned forty-five last month, she is currently undergoing her third in vitro fertilization. She relentlessly fights against feeling a sense of doom about her advancing age.

> In terms of fertility, forty-four sounds better than forty-five, but there are still women who have babies at forty-five, forty-six, or forty-seven, and my health is good.

Many factors converged to put Jan in her desperate position. Years when she could have tried to have a child were devoted to graduate school and practicing law. Then, too, she couldn't find a compatible partner, and she didn't want to upset her conservative family by having a child without being married. Now, married for five years, she remains childless. In retrospect, she feels she should have tried for pregnancy much earlier, even if unmarried.

> Now, at last, having a child is much more important than worrying what people will think. I advise younger women not to wait for the perfect situation; even don't wait to get married because it may not happen. Do an in vitro, artificial insemination, sperm donation, or embryo donation. There are all kinds of choices for having a baby if you want one.

Following her second in vitro fertilization, in two weeks Jan will learn if she is at last pregnant. Trying to be more realistic this time, she still wants to remain hopeful and to keep a positive attitude.

> The first time I went through it, I had the expectation that it was going to work, even though statistics do not bear that out, and I allowed myself to get carried away and too excited and too hopeful. I sort of deluded myself. That time, I'd taken the drugs, and developed several eggs. They took the eggs out of me and fertilized them. The eggs developed into good embryos, and then they transplanted them back inside me. But I had problems with the last step of the process, and the implantation failed.

Currently, Jan's thighs are swollen and sore from egg-producing hormone injections she gives herself every day, a process she began at the onset of her last menstrual period. After the first injection, she was forced to lie in bed three days, suffering side effects of migraine headaches and mood swings.

Last time I became so angry with my husband that I manu-
factured a crisis and slammed my bathroom door so that the
wall mirror broke. I was screaming, crying, and out of control.
It was a terrible scene. This time, I have been calm, but the
headaches are terrible. They say every cycle is different. These
are serious drugs, unnatural to the body. Some say the effects
can be lasting, possibly cancer-causing because uterine cancer
is related to one's hormone levels.

Jan maintains a strict health regime, eating mostly fresh vegetables
and fish and supplementing her diet with vitamins and Chinese herbs.
Sharing information about her efforts with women on Internet chat
rooms helps relieve her anxiety and depression.

This is not a fun thing. It's serious business, but it's worth it
to have a child. I know women who have been through it seven
times, ten times, and they don't have good readings. They do it
anyway. They want to have a baby. It's so sad.

In order to enhance her chances for pregnancy, Jan has also called
on more feminine and spiritual sides of her personality. She stopped
practicing law, believing it requires too much aggression not conducive
to motherhood. Now she is cooking, gardening, and writing, trying to
remain calm and restful. To help achieve peace and tranquility, Jan has
built a fertility altar in her home. She burns special candles, and, on the
advice of a Voodoo priestess, she has a bowl of honey set beside ritual
fertility objects found in the Yucatan. As she longs for the experience
of what she calls "the indefinable," Jan practices meditation.

What I try to do is to visualize myself with a baby, to feel on
some level that it is real. This time it could happen. I'm like
"Hey, I believe it could happen this time!"

If Jan is unable to conceive, she is still determined to become a
mother. Although her age may prevent her from adopting an infant in
the United States, she has searched the internet for foreign adoptions
and even received a video of several Russian infants wanting homes.
Having consulted friends with adopted children from Guatemala and
China, she explains,

If you have to use a foreign adoption, it's another huge expense,
but I will do it nevertheless. Considering my age, I wouldn't

mind a three- or four- year-old, but I want to make sure the child is okay, at least a child that I can nurture, not one with fetal alcohol syndrome or some other other illness that would render me helpless.

While some childless mothers fulfill their maternal instincts by adopting, others find meaning through professional work, creating a full life for themselves. Those stricken with the Childbearing Archetype, however, often carry a persisting "shadow grief," similar to a bereaved mother's lingering sadness.[1]

The Miscarriage

Peggy Orenstein protests that there is little acknowledgment in either Judaism or Christianity of miscarriage, no ritual to cleanse the grief. Her own pregnancy ended at eight weeks, thousands of miles from home, in Tokyo, where ironically her reporter's assignment was studying Japan's declining birthrate.

When she had first learned she was pregnant, she had been ecstatic, at once beginning to fantasize about her baby. Though politically pro-choice and not believing an embryo a person, from the moment she became pregnant, Peggy sensed a living connection, which she visualized as a thin silvery thread uniting her with her unborn. She talked to her new companion every day: about her work, her husband, and her life back home; conversations that began the moment she awakened and ended with her last thoughts at night. But one morning in the subway she felt a snap. She intuitively knew the thread was broken. The gynecologist soon confirmed that she had suffered a miscarriage.

Peggy and her husband, who had accompanied her from the United States, grieved their loss as they faced the D and C procedure together. Even though the whole ordeal was very sad, Peggy decided to stay in Japan to finish her work while her husband returned home to his job. Though still able to function, she walked around for days in a morose haze, not knowing what to do with her sadness. "How can I mourn what I don't believe existed?" she thought. "I tell myself that this wasn't a person. It wasn't a child. At the same time, I can't deny that it was *something.*"

Remembering that she had seen many roadside shrines dedicated to the deity Jizo, guardian of the weak, commemorating miscarriages, abortions, stillbirths, and deaths of young children, Peggy decided to perform the mourning ritual called *mizuko kuyo*. *Kuyo* ceremonies commemorate the dead, and *mizuko kuyo* specifically children caught between the worlds of life and death. Though there is no English word for a miscarried or aborted fetus, in Japan any fetus is called *mizuko*, "water child," because an ancient Buddhist belief holds that existence flows into a being slowly, like liquid. Children solidify gradually over time until the age of seven, when they are then considered to be fully present in our world. Then at age sixty there is a celebration of a symbolic second birth as the older person slowly returns to the primordial waters. The *mizuko* lies somewhere along the continuum, in that liminal space between life and death, but belonging to neither. It is expected that Jizo will help the *mizuko* find its path to reincarnation.

There are various ways that a Japanese woman can perform *mizuko kuyo*. She might participate in a formal service officiated by a priest, make a simple informal gesture such as lighting a candle, or make a more or less elaborate personal offering of food, drink, flowers, incense or toys, a message handwritten on a wooden tablet, or her own Jizo statue. Hers can be a one-time offering or she may repeat the ritual monthly or annually. Some women do not begin the practice until later in life, claiming they were busy at home raising other children. As demands in their life diminish, they may go to the temple often, participating in services of chanting and drum beating. Sometimes husbands and children will participate. The communal service is often followed by a social hour in which the priest's wife serves refreshments. Though some regular participants become friends, their personal reasons for performing the ritual remain private, rarely discussed among themselves.

The Eastern mind is capable of holding ambiguities too foreign for most Westerners to grasp. Many women performing *mizuko kuyo* have undergone abortions, so they pray not only to remember but also to apologize. The Japanese tend to accept both the rightness of abortion and the idea that *mizuko* is a form of human life. This acceptance later became especially comforting to Peggy after her miscarriage.

When first seeking relief from sadness by making her own *mizuko kuyo* ritual, Peggy stopped to buy toys as offerings before proceeding to Zoz-ji, a complex of temple buildings dedicated to Jizo. But as she walked among rows of *mizuko* Jizos, baby-faced Gods wearing caps crocheted by mothers in mourning, she found the place dark and gloomy.

Peggy decided to leave the temple in search of some place more in tune with her needs. She knew that location is important to those practicing this ritual, and many Japanese women travel miles to worship in a temple that particularly moves them. She went to another Buddhist temple, where she had earlier met a friendly priest and presented her toys to Kannon, goddess of compassion, who also receives *mizuko* offerings. Placing her toys at the Kannon's feet where they joined two chubby stone babies, Peggy prayed, then clapped her hands three times and backed away. Next she gave $40 to the priest to chant a lotus sutra for her and her miscarried fetus.

As a journalist with a skeptical heart, Peggy calls herself "a cynic by nature." Yet at the moment of praying, she began to believe.

> Maybe learning to live with the question marks—recognizing that 'closure' does not always occur—is all I really needed to do. I hadn't expected, coming from a world that fights to see life's beginnings in black and white, to be so comforted by a shade of gray. Yet the notion of the water child made sense to me. What I'd experienced had not been a full life, nor was it a full death, but it was a real loss. Maybe my *mizuko* will come back to me more fully another time, or maybe it will find someone else. Surprisingly even that thought was solace.[2]

From one point of view, ritual itself can be thought of as an archetype. That is, the human mind has been conditioned by its experiences over hundreds of thousands of years to use rituals as a way of coping with the impact of common but significantly moving events. Viewed from another angle, we can also see rituals as a primary response to the great archetypes themselves, or rather to those experiences which we apprehend as especially powerful because we are preconditioned to do so. Death is such an archetype, so is marriage's union of man and woman, so too are birth, the coming of adolescence, the journeying beyond adolescence to maturity, and so forth.[3] Everywhere on earth we typically meet such events with rituals, which both help us shape these significant experiences and, in turn, we are shaped by them.

Though not exactly at peace when she left the temple, Peggy felt a little easier. By saying goodbye to the fetus, she had at least done something to commemorate a most significant and complex event in her life.

Sudden Infant Death Syndrome

SIDS—abrupt death of an infant under one year of age unexplained after thorough investigation, is the leading cause of death in children one month to one year old. Unfortunately, SIDS is a diagnosis of exclusion, and investigation's frustrating blind alleys often cause further trauma to a child's parents. Death scene investigation first involves interviewing them, as well as other caregivers and family members. After collecting photographs and clues from the death scene, police take the little body to be autopsied. Then a medical examiner reviews the child's clinical history with her parents and her pediatrician. Waiting for the diagnosis can be excruciatingly painful, but some parents are naturally relieved if examinations reveal no preventable cause of death.

Mothers whose infants die of SIDS feel particularly guilty, however, when told the death might have been caused by their behavior. They may learn with terrible force that the leading risk factor is cigarette smoking or the second is putting the baby to sleep in a prone position. Other risks include the fetus' low weight gain during pregnancy, illegal drug use, and sexually transmitted diseases. But even mothers unburdened by such factors feel guilt, admonishing themselves with "if only's."

Those who had premonitions about their child's death often feel guilt for failing to listen to their instincts or because they were unable to convince physicians of impending danger. They may always feel they could have saved their children.

According to a recent study conducted by Southwest SIDS Research Institute, premonitions of a baby's death are more common among parents who eventually lose babies to SIDS than among parents in control groups who don't. Sometimes fathers as well as mothers report several times sensing an impending loss and having strong increased anxiety as the death approached. Wendy's and similar stories prompted the study of premonitions researched.

> During the first trimester [of the pregnancy] I sensed that the happiness his birth would bring would not be long lasting. A few months before birth, I would, on occasions, find myself contemplating a nearby cemetery, where my son is now buried. The day he was born and I first held him in my arms I felt, for no apparent reason, he, my son, was not supposed to be with us. Probably two or three weeks before his death, I would be awakened from my sleep and think about SIDS. The day before he died, a voice sounding very similar to my own, would repeatedly say, "Take a good look. This is the last time you will see him." [4]

After her baby's death, Wendy experienced nearly unrelenting anger, confusion, guilt, and massive grief. Although receiving little support from others, she had discussed her premonitions before the child died. She felt she should have acted on them aggressively.

Other mothers met similar fates. After sensing that something was going to happen to her infant, Mary repeatedly sought the assistance of physicians but was sent home with only empty reassurance. The night before their baby died, both strongly believing something was wrong, Mary and her husband took her to an emergency room. They were told she was "fine," but Mary continued feeling uneasy and nervous. As she walked toward the baby's bedroom, the sleeping infant over her shoulder, she saw their reflections in a mirror and "knew" that her child would die that night.

Such stories of premonition may add support to the idea of a mother's lasting personal bond with her child, one beginning at conception and continuing beyond the grave. The bond is probably influenced by strong archetypal forces merging a way of knowing beyond mere reason. Rather than being denied, every attempt should be made to verify its message.

Many mothers reporting premonitions also described contacting their dead infants through dreams, visions, or close feelings. After these positive experiences, they held firm belief that their children were cared for and loved in another realm. Health-care professionals who validated these experiences as natural and normal events were helpful in the mothers' grieving process.

If we imagine, like Plato, that our child comes from a preexistent spiritual realm to choose her own parents on earth, we come to embrace the mystery of her short life, knowing that she returns to a celestial home. This understanding that the spirit never dies is universal, found not only in all great religions but in most ancient cultures as well.

Sioux Prayer of Passing

> Never the spirit is born
> The spirit will cease to be never
> Never the time when it was not.
> End and beginning are dreams
> Birthless and deathless and changeless
> Remains the spirit forever.
> Death has not touched it at all
> Dead though the house of it seems.[5]

In spite of humankind's belief in an undying spirit, many cultures, finding child death unfathomable, give unique significance to the death of a child. As Japan has Jizo, guardian of dead children, to appease a woman's sorrow, Hindu religion holds that infants not be cremated because they are shortly expected to return to a fuller, more joyful life. In Jewish and Christian thought, innocent children are believed to go immediately to heaven. Mothers everywhere are comforted by accepting the mystery of life eternal. As Samuel Taylor Coleridge expresses defiantly in his poem "On an Infant which died before Baptism," an innocent child breaks no laws and does no harm. The only imaginable place for such a spirit is in the hands of God.

> Be, rather than be called, a child of God,
> Death whispered! With assenting nod,
> Its head upon its mother's breast,
> The Baby bowed, without demur—
> Of the kingdom of the Blest
> Possessor, not Inheritor.[6]

The Mortally Ill Child

When Natasha came to my office to talk about her recently dead girl, she was wearing a locket with her daughter's picture and carrying a scrapbook which colorfully documented Sophia's short life from the moment of her conception, one evening exactly twelve years after her parents' first kiss. Natasha had photographed all the big events of this first pregnancy—hearing the fetus' heatbeat, attending Lamaze classes, touring the maternity ward, celebrating a pre-birth Mother's Day, and opening presents at the baby shower. A handsome print of the paired double eagle, the Russian symbol proclaiming a royal heir, announced Sophia's birth photo. The mother, completing her degree in Russian history during pregnancy, lovingly welcomed the baby into the world.

> I will never recapture the innocence of that first pregnancy and the joy I felt when I first held Sophia, but that happiness lasted only twenty-four hours. The next day the doctor told me she had a serious heart defect. I was alone in the room and terrified and all I heard was that Sophia might not live.

The nurses brought Natasha a pump so she could store milk for the baby. Though having had a painful caesarean incision, Natasha, not wanting her milk to be tainted, refused all medication. She spent the next weeks at the hospital, cradling her baby for hours a day.

> I'd also have to hold Sophia down while they would stick her ... for six weeks I did that. There was hope so I knew it was all right, but at the same time, I felt as if I were betraying my baby.

After Sophia was temporarily discharged from the hospital, knowing that her daughter awaited a serious operation, Natasha tried to make her life as normal as possible. Photos show each family member holding Sophia in her beautiful gown on the day of her Christening. When I remark that "she looks like an angel," Natasha quickly reminds me that nobody wanted to think of her that way. They wanted her to live.

Natasha goes on to tell how one of the most difficult acts of her life was handing her baby to the nurse for the operation. She and her husband passed anxious hours before being allowed to see their infant.

When, at last, they entered the operating room, the surgeon told them Sophia's heart had stopped.

> When I knew Sophia was dead, I only touched her head. I didn't dare to hold her because there was a trickle of blood coming from her nose, and I was afraid that something worse would happen.

When a nurse tried to console Natasha by telling her that while most people don't get to meet their guardian angel in this lifetime, Sophia now knew hers, Natasha became infuriated.

> I wanted to smack her because she was trying to be kind, but who in the hell cares about a guardian angel when they lose a baby.

Later Natasha learned this same nurse had rocked her baby after death, soothing her into the world beyond.

As we talked, I could tell part of Natasha was still numbed by her pain. So early in her deep grief, she wanted nothing to do with a cruel God who could allow her baby to suffer and die. Here was the whole heaviness of death, the stage when there is no longer anything to anticipate or imagine. I thought about "Sophia" and why her mother had chosen such an inspiring name, "Sophia" being the Greek name for the Divine Wisdom Archetype, a quality implying a feminine force to be part of the Godhead.

I knew Natasha was aware that Sophia is a great symbol in old Russia, one depicted in many treasured icons. For Russian orthodox Christianity, an icon, whether in a household, shrine, or church, is more than a representational image: it is an actualization of the Divinity itself. In one of the earliest icons of Sophia, the famous Icon of Novgorod, she appears as a female figure magestic with wings and a fiery countenance.

I wondered, however, whether Natasha knew that the tradition of Sophia as archetypal image is much older than any Russian icon. She can be traced from the earliest prehistoric worship of the Great Goddess, through Isis, and later into the wisdom books of the Old Testament.

I am wisdom, I bestow shrewdness
and show the way to knowledge and prudence ...

Those who love me, I love
those who search for me find me.
In my hands are riches and honor,
boundless wealth and the rewards of virtue ...

(Proverbs 8:12–21)

In the New Testament, her independent existence becoming muted, the qualities of "Sophia" were embodied in Jesus Christ and the Mother Mary. Nevertheless, The Divine Wisdom Archetype, one of the feminine faces of God, is forever present in human experience. It expressses itself in intuitive ways of knowing God, in that experiential knowledge which increases and complements what is learned from reason and the written word. Great Sophia's wisdom consists of love, kindness, compassion, bounty, and the life force itself—the earth-like power to nurture and create and also to cradle what is no longer alive.

While Natasha's grief was still so raw, I decided not to discuss any of my mind's wanderings about Sophia at this time. Natasha rightly acknowledged she would never recapture the innocence of her first pregnancy. But that day, coming to my own understanding about Natasha's loss and the losses of all women whose children have died, I had Sophia as my inner guide. Certainly it is through the divine feminine that we women find our hearts' knowledge and our identity with the earth, its great cycles of death and rebirth. We nurture and at the same time we are fed. We can come to see that though we are wounded, we are able to grow stronger. Though we are never able to answer the question *why* we were unable to conceive or had a miscarriage or had an infant die, we can move toward a larger understanding, one wherein the question *why* is no longer so important, even though the event itself forever changes our lives.

NOTES:

1. Found in parents whose children die, a form of chronic grief that reveals itself in emotional dullness (psychologist Ronald Knapp).
2. Peggy Orenstein, "Mourning My Miscarriage," *New York Times Magazine*, April 21, 2002.
3. For an archetypal study of miscarriage, see Judith A. Savage, *Mourning Unlived Lives: A Psychological Study of Childbearing Loss*, 1989, Wilmette, IL.
4. Patricia Christenson, Richard Hardoin, M.D., Judith Henslee, Frederick Mandell, M.D., Melvin Morse, M.D., and Carrie Griffin, *The Effect of Premonitions of SIDS on Grieving and Healing*, Southwest SIDS research project (in progress).
5. Elisabeth Kubler-Ross, *On Children and Death*, 1983, New York, p. 126.
6. Samuel Taylor Coleridge, "On an Infant Which Died Before Baptism," *The Oxford Book of Death*, D.J. Enright, ed., 1987, p. 285.

Chapter Six

The Long Illness and the Special Case of Aids

It requires an enormous act of faith on the part of parents to truly believe that their children, however brief their lives, were given to them as gifts from God, to deepen and enrich their own lives.

— Henri J. M. Nouwen

Anticipatory Grief: From Fatal Diagnosis to Death

When her child is first diagnosed with a terminal illness, a mother fills with shock and disbelief. Indeed, the moments when she receives the fatal news are often more traumatic than the child's death months or years later. By then she usually has learned to accept the final disaster a little at a time. Especially when the child has suffered greatly, though death is still unbearably sad, she may even welcome it.

The afflicting diagnosis first overwhelms her by shattering the normal world she lived in before, and the new one she inherits seems unbearably frightening. Frantic to find new safety, she rushes to medical books, the internet, or support groups in order to research the disease and make informed decisions. Studying her child's specific treatment needs, she may become an expert about the likely course of that illness.

Accompanying him to physicians' offices, laboratories, and hospitals, and spending days and nights feeding him, leads her into an archetypal transformation in which she becomes an initiate, one thrust into special realms of knowledge about a disease, a child's sufferings, her own torment, and that of others.

In the early months, a mother typically hopes for the discovery of a medical cure; later she may pray for miracles, but toward the end, she often asks only for a final modest remission, a few weeks without weakness and pain. As the illness has proceeded, the physical, emotional, and financial demands of long-term care have become increasingly debilitating to her and other loved ones. Forced to rearrange family schedules to accommodate the child's treatment, she is unable to give siblings their usual attention. They become easily neglected, because fathers pressured by high medical expenses devote hours to working, thankful their earnings make some tangible contribution to the almost helpless situation.

In this process, the family gradually mourns the slowly accumulating losses of their loved one. A mother grieves each new limitation: he can no longer attend school, becomes too weak to run, loses his hair from chemotherapy treatment, feels further debilitated by pneumonia, or is depressed by a new hospital confinement. She takes each setback into her heart. Her *anticipatory grief* prepares for the final loss, and by accepting its inevitability in small stages, to some degree, she has already faced the worst.

But before that moment, she has been slowly stripped of her mothering role. Health professionals have increasingly taken over the child's care. In her desire to cuddle her little one, she is rebuffed because he now feels too much pain to be touched. Later, the listless child who knows he is dying has lost interest in her storytelling, helping with toys, or her suggesting future plans. A dying child sometimes turns away from his mother or even becomes uncooperative, for now he has lost all hope. Even those parents who have maintained some pretense that their child will get better are at last forced to anticipate the end.

The Dalai Lama rightly calls us all to accept and to prepare ourselves for the archetypal suffering which is necessarily part of human existence.

By reflecting on the types of suffering that we are subject to, you can mentally prepare for those things ahead of time to some degree…but you should not forget the fact that this does not alleviate the situations in your life. It may help you mentally cope with it, reduce the fear and so on, but it does not alleviate the problem itself. For instance if a child with a birth defect is going to be born, no matter how strongly you thought about it ahead of time, you will still have to find a way to handle it. So this is still difficult.[1]

Dealing with the Mother and Nurse Archetype

For some women like Ella, whose daughter Jennifer was diagnosed at birth with cystic fibrosis, all the lifelong tasks of caring for a disabled daughter were preparation for the girl's death in early adulthood. Cystic fibrosis is a fatal genetic disease in which patients' glands secrete thick sticky mucus, clogging vital digestive and breathing ducts. Treatment, consisting of high doses of antibiotics, physical therapy, and inhalation therapy, is expensive and time-consuming. Research shows that most surviving siblings in families battling cystic fibrosis report that the mother bore the weight of care-taking, even in times of crisis.[2]

When Ella needed help caring for Jennifer, she called her sister, for Jennifer's father was uninvolved with his daughter's treatment. The couple had grown apart after Jennifer's younger brother was born. Ella stayed married because "it was too much trouble to get a divorce, and my kids wanted us together." She devoted her time to her daughter.

Throughout Jennifer's life, Ella administered one of the needed physical procedures, postural drainage therapy, which sometimes took as many as four hours a day. Regularly, she placed the girl on a tilting board and thumped her chest to loosen mucus. Ella also kept track of complex doses of pancreatic enzymes, antibiotics, bronchodilators, and vitamins which she gave Jennifer every day. This mother watched for danger signs of fatigue, guarded against colds and flu, and suffered extreme anxiety whenever Jennifer needed emergency hospitalizations beyond the month-long one each year after receiving high doses of antibiotics. Withstanding painful procedures, Jennifer survived to early adulthood by receiving an emergency lung transplant that kept her alive for nineteen more months.

> I remember the Christmas Eve Jennifer's beeper went off. She always wore a beeper so she would know when to go to the hospital for the transplant. 'Mom, my lungs are here!' she shouted. She was always upbeat, even to the end. And she did everything. The last year of her life we took cruises, and she even had roller blades.

When Jennifer came home to die, Ella passed days and nights on the sofa beside her bed, sharing the final weeks of life.

> I knew how to do everything she needed, all her therapies and medications. I was almost a nurse.

In many ways, a mother caring for her terminally ill child *is* a nurse.

The nurturing aspect of the Mother Archetype is related not only to feeding but to care-taking and healing. From the beginning of time, because they brought forth new life, mothers were recognized as healers. Mysteries surrounding pregnancy and birth were thought to give women magical powers akin to those manifested by the Mother Goddess.[3] Isis not only breathed new life into Osiris, she also dispensed helpful herbs to favorites, chanted incantations for their benefit, and brushed her cleansing wings across sick bodies. Today, mothers understand that their child's recovery depends on more than scientific medical procedures. They give soothing and loving nursing to enhance the child's medical treatment. Attending to the child's soul needs, matters of the heart, mothers reach back to those Great Mother's nurturing ways. By reconnecting feminine healing ways, they mend the split between mind and body posited by Rene Descartes during the Renaissance.

During their months of heartfelt care, mothers of a terminally ill child may have moments of bonding as intimate as the symbiosis between infant and mother, a state of psychological and biological oneness. Sometimes, however, such women may have difficulty distinguishing between their own wounded self and their suffering child. The result is unbearable pain, as Hillman explains.

> For the mothering attitude, it is always a matter of life and death; we are obsessed with how things will turn out; we ask

what happened and what will happen. The mother ... infuses the power of life and death into each detail, because the mother's relation to the child is personal ... *archetypally personal* in the sense that the child's fate is delivered through the personal matrix of her fate, becoming fate in general which she then is called.... The growth she furthers is all-out and passionate, the death overwhelming, *mater dolorosa....*[4]

Under normal conditions, by contrast, most mothers slowly let go of identifying themselves with The Mother Archetype, even though it is sometimes painful to do so. They continue to nurture, but they also watch as their well child grows up with help, not only from mother, but from older siblings, grandparents, teachers, social workers, clergy, doctors, and nurses. Gradually understanding that they cannot possibly meet all their child's needs, they particularly welcome the services of helping professionals.

The tradition of accepting help with child-raising and caring for the sick goes back to ancient times. Wealthy women employed wet-nurses for breast-feeding and care of the baby and sought advice from women healers working with botanical prescriptions and with the inner, unseen realm. At Aesclepieia, Greek sanctuaries for healing, pilgrims asked for help from three goddesses of health: Hygeia, for prevention, Epione, for alleviation of pain, and Panacea for cure. In the Christian era, mothers looked to nuns, almost all of whom were concerned with healing and caregiving. Today, when in great need for tender understanding and care, we imagine there is an ideal nurse like Florence Nightingale, the Lady with the Lamp, radiating goodness and compassion toward the sick.

Besides running risks from being overpowered by The Mother Archetype, a mother who is the sole caretaker of a terminally ill child may also unconsciously identify with the ideal nurse and be overwhelmed by forces from The Nurse Archetype. Closing the door to other interests, she may become alienated from family members, unable to see the needs of her other children. To the detriment of her child's care, she may refuse or limit the help of others, including people in helping professions. Then again, if she is too self-sacrificing to attend to her own physical health—her need for fresh air, exercise, and adult company, her intense feelings may lead to frustrations and outbursts that leave her filled with guilt. While nursing her dying child, she suffers the loss of her own future as well as the child's life.

Hoping to avoid such problems, the professional nurse may offer an alternative model to mothers, one enlisting the useful energies of the Nurse Archetype without being overwhelmed by it. Although multiple loss is her steadfast companion if she works with the terminally ill, the professional nurse knows to balance her own grief feelings with compassion and composure. Though frequently reminded by her patients' fates of her own and her loved ones' eventual deaths, and though she may feel guilty when her own healthy children greet her at home, the positive force of The Nurse Archetype helps her maneuver through these reactions. She feels support from the long tradition of persons caring for the sick and gathers strength from identifying with the noble profession she has chosen. Contemplating her example may help a mother avoid harmful excesses.

Though some mothers have no regrets about caring for their sick child, Ella, who spent twenty-four years as nurse-mother, often doesn't know how to occupy herself now. She sometimes works three jobs just to keep busy and to stay away from home. She visits Jennifer's friends who also suffer from cystic fibrosis, keeping informed about their progress, who has died and who is expecting a transplant, and enjoys sharing her friend's grandchildren. In addition, everyday after work she goes to the gym. Since Jennifer's death she has lost sixty pounds.

> My whole life revolved around being with Jennifer and talking care of her. It is hard to learn to take care of myself.

Though Ella has done well in many ways, other mothers who have plunged into nursing children with long fatal illnesses, afterward find themselves increasingly isolated, misfits among their peers whose healthy children still live.

Ways of Facing the End: Conflicting Tasks

As has already been partly implied, mothers of terminally ill children usually face many conflicting tasks: maintaining normal family projects while living for the moment, caring for the child while preparing for her death, allowing the child both separateness and dependence, holding on to her and letting go. Mothers must endure the tension of polarities until they are blessed with some resolution. Often the answer cannot be put into words, entailing an acceptance or act of grace that brings peace beyond one's rational understanding.

Many mothers, both before and after their child's death, try to keep the ways of the family as normal as possible for their healthy children; in fact, some siblings report that they were never aware of the seriousness of their brother or sister's illness until the end. Some mothers are able to use suppression as a defense against the emotional and psychological split arising from both having to care for their child and, at the same time, prepare for the coming death. When the illness is yet not manifest, these mothers try not to think about their child's short life span. Some even stop believing that their child will die. Friends and relatives unwittingly encourage denial of the imminence of death by trying to keep up a mother's spirits, urging her not to give up hope.

> I actually forgot about it sometimes, or I said to myself, "Don't think about it." Then a picture on TV about dating or college brought me this terrible anxious feeling and I thought, "He won't get to do that."
>
> Stella

When it is no longer possible to suppress or deny their child is dying, many mothers opt for making the best of every pain-free hour. Living for the moment is reasonable when hope for long-term survival is lost. Afterward, grieving mothers derive comfort from knowing that their child's last months were filled with good experiences. Overindulgence, a common parental response to a dying child, both at the time and later, seems to bring a feeling of satisfaction to a grieving mother.

> Randy had everything before he died because I worked to give him all the things he wanted. I bought a boat and he also played football and had a girlfriend. He lived a full life, even though he knew it wouldn't last. We didn't talk about it: we just always enjoyed each other, going to movies and dinner, doing all the happy activities in life, and he was always proud to be with me wherever we went.
>
> Stella

Knowing that time is short, moms naturally want to stay close, and a very ill child often requires close supervision. But most mothers also feel their child needs to complete the developmental tasks appropriate for their age. For example, when it is possible, the dying child seems happier if she is able to return to school and be with her classmates.

Toward the end, moms struggle with tough questions about their child's medical care, particularly the hard decision of terminating treatment, and the final choice whether the child will die at home or in the hospital. Afterward, some mothers suffer for months about their decision to stop chemotherapy or discontinue life support systems. Feeling so sad themselves, physicians are usually of little support. Dr. Arthur Ablin, Director Emeritus of Pediatric Clinical Oncology at the University of California, San Francisco, has words which may comfort women still tormented by their decision.

> All too often, the decision to abandon the goal for cure and, reluctantly, accept the reality of inevitable death of a child is too painful and, therefore, never made. This paralyzing pain occurs with equal frequency, perhaps, for the family and the doctor. We of the medical profession have no equal in our ability to prolong dying. We have a powerful array of mechanical, electronic, pharmaceutical, and biotechnical interventions at our command. We can keep people dying for months and even years. Applying or withholding this armamentarium is an awesome responsibility and it requires infinite wisdom to know how to manage it wisely and correctly. We can do good by applying these tools correctly but can also do incalculable harm through over-utilization. Physicians and families alike must work together to avoid the possible pitfalls.[5]

Mothers whose child had a terminal illness usually feel thankful that they had the opportunity to say goodbye to their beloved, and some think a child's sudden death by accident or violence would have been worse to bear. Being present at the child's death is usually regarded as a healing experience, and mothers speak of their anxiety when they feared their child might die alone. Sir Rabindranath Tagore, the Indian Nobel Laureate for poetry, captures the poignant night-time plea of a mother who wants her child to hold on to life through the night.

Do Not Go My Love

Do not go my love without asking my leave.
I have watched all night and now my eyes are heavy with sleep;
I fear lest I lose you when I am sleeping.
Do not go my love without asking my leave.

I start up and stretch my hands to touch you.
I ask myself, "Is it a dream?"
Could I but entangle your feet with my heart
And hold them fast to my breast?
Do not go my love without asking my leave.[6]

When all hope is truly lost, sensing that the child is protecting the family by holding on to life, some mothers give their child permission to pass on. Afterward, many say they learned about death by watching their children's attitudes toward dying, and most mothers agree that even four-year-olds knew they were going to die. Dying children who tried to pretend that everything was OK did so only to protect family members by masking their own grief.

After months of debilitating treatment, sweeping emotional swings of hope and despair, and depletion of all financial aid, Susan and her husband decided to stop treatment for their eight-year-old son suffering from leukemia. This decision meant there would be no more resuscitation using CPR and electric shocks to the heart. Their son then died in peace in a private room at the hospital. By the time the funeral was arranged, Susan was already exhausted from the months of fighting cancer and from the disappointments following each of her boy's setbacks. She showed me pictures drawn by her son titled "What Will Happen When I Die". Susan had talked openly with him about what it would be like to die, how he would be greeted by his grandfather and great grandparents. Her son's drawing of heaven, depicting that greeting, was comforting and reassuring. Fatally ill children often show adults that dying is a natural process.

Elisabeth Kubler Ross' studies of children's awareness of terminal illness convince us that children seem to accept the possibility of death more readily than their parents. Because they have an intuitive sense that life continues after death, they usually show no fear. Ross points to drawings and poems created by children who knew they were going to die, even before their physician's diagnosis. Mothers, who would gladly die in their children's place, become humbled and inspired by watching the suffering that leads dying children to acceptance, a transformation whose effects on those tending them is subtly evoked by Gerard Manly Hopkins in his poem "Felix Randal."

Felix Randal

Felix Randal the farrier, O is he dead then? my duty all ended,
Who have watched his mound of man, big-boned and hardy-handsome
Pining, pining, till time when reason rambled in it and some
Fatal four disorders, fleshed there, all contended?

Sickness broke him. Impatient, he cursed at first, but mended
Being anointed and all; though a heavenlier heart began some
Months earlier, since I had our sweet reprieve and ransom
Tendered to him. Ah well, God rest him all road ever he offended!
This seeing the sick endears them to us, us too it endears.
My tongue had taught thee comfort, touch had quenched thy tears,
Thy tears that touched my heart, child, Felix, poor Felix Randal.

How far from then forethought of, all thy more boisterous years,
When thou at the random grim forge, powerful amidst peers,
Did fettle for the great grey dreyhorse his bright and battering sandal![7]

In the poem, Hopkins, a Jesuit priest, watches over Felix Randal, a young blacksmith, who first cursed the sickness that weakened him but then softened his heart and accepted his fate, particularly after receiving the last sacrament. Remembering Felix in his prime, the priest's emotional response testifies to the blacksmith's uniqueness while he lived. He was a strong and "hardy-handsome" youth—seemingly invincible. Hopkins knows he has comforted Felix, tries to shrug and move on, but cannot help recognizing that he in turn has been touched and changed by sharing the intimate moments of the man's dying. "This seeing the sick endears them to us, us too it endears."

At this point the poem reverberates with even higher meanings. Its enduring final images of the old strong Felix evoke an eternal transformative force, one that can, for example, turn a plodding dray horse's shoe ("bright and battering sandal") into suggestions of enduring force, transcendent delicacy, and unquenchable light.

The Special Case of AIDS

First recognized in the United States in 1981, AIDS is the advanced form of HIV viral infection. As is well known, treatment for AIDS patients focuses on improving and lengthening the quality of life and preventing their weakened immune systems from causing infections or cancers. At present there is no cure.

Though AIDS can be transmitted by such entirely impersonal means as blood transfusions, in the United States and Europe the disease has spread primarily through homosexuals' intimate contact or through illegal drug users sharing hypodermic needles. Because many people disapprove of homosexuality and illegal drug activity, both AIDS victims and their mothers may be condemned and ostracized. Just as her adult child may have had to struggle against prejudice and hate, so may the mourning mother. Consequently she may have to face complex conflicts both with herself and others. She may be tormented by guilt and shame pulling her one way and pride in her child pulling another way. She may vacillate between resenting others and empathizing with their reasons for stigmatizing her and her child. Such conflicts arise from being subject to forces inherent in The Outcast Archetype and especially its powerful subtype, one fueled by society's fearing contagious disease, The Leper.

The Outcast Archetype: Leprosy and AIDS

The Outcast Archetype is an ancient psychological pattern that can seize upon anyone shunned by society. While many social circumstances (violating of tribal taboos or laws, for example) have activated The Outcast Archetype from earliest times, a primary one has been illness. Those with serious skin infections or festering sores, long associated with grave contagious diseases, have often become outcasts. Recoiling from people so afflicted, societies have subjected them to strict regulation.

In the past, "leprosy" (the term was often ignorantly used to cover many skin infections) forcefully evoked The Outcast Archetype, and mothers of AIDS victims must often contend, both inwardly and outwardly, with social reactions whose power is akin to those brought on by this dreaded, ancient, and formerly mysterious illness. The very word "leper" calls up ancient inchoate associations in our minds, making it a particularly frightening symbol of The Outcast Archetype. Even when we may never have seen a leper, we inwardly shrink at the word.

Over millennia, rudimentary notions of disease-contagion mechanisms, combined with ignorance of the actual nature, causes, and treatment of a host of skin diseases, created a mighty psychological complex in the collective mind. As early as the fifteenth century B.C. "lepers" in India became models for The Outcast. Mutilated by a chronic infectious disease causing skin discoloration and growths, victims were stigmatized as being "unclean," both in a superficially visual meaning and in a more powerful psychological sense.

The disease probably came to the Western world from Egypt, where its bacteria may have flowed in Nile waters. Returning crusaders carried it (and many other contagious illnesses) throughout Europe, and whenever it or diseases seeming the same appeared in the Middle Ages, lepers were compelled to wear special clothing and carry a wooden clapper to give warning of their approach. The Catholic Encyclopedia details these outcasts' nearly total isolation.

> They were forbidden to enter inns, churches, mills or bake houses, to touch healthy people or eat with them, to wash in the streams, or walk in narrow footpaths.

Added to the "leper's" burden as Outcast, moreover, was the ancient belief that his disease (and even such other less dangerous skin disorders as psoriasis) arose from Sin, particularly those sins listed in Proverbs 6:16 as hateful to God: a proud look, a lying tongue, hands that shed innocent blood, a wicked imagination, a false witness, and the creation of discord. When Job is smitten with boils from the soles of his feet to his crown, his friend Eliphaz attributes such suffering to God's need to correct and punish. A second friend, Bildad, warns Job that without repentance his skin will be devoured by leprosy, "the firstborn of death." Job is spared this disease but God punishes other Biblical figures with it—Miriam, Uzziah, and Gehazi.

The Homosexual as Special Outcast

The Outcast Archetype with which a mourning mother must contend is further fueled by a special fear and hatred that many Western people feel toward homosexuality. Such emotions derive authority from literal interpretations of certain Biblical texts. Though many liberal clergy preach tolerance and love for AIDS victims, other religious figures have used the disease to rally condemnation of homosexuals. Though these clerics disclaim any hurtful intention, their doctrines often encourage homophobic attitudes that foster exclusion of AIDS sufferers as special Outcasts.

In a moving essay, Rosetta Dubois-Gladson, ordained minister of the African Methodist Episcopal Church, depicts her son's struggle to reach out to his minister / mother, her realizing how certain church leaders punishingly fostered application of The Outcast Archetype to homosexual AIDS victims, and her eventual crusade against such church-sponsored Outcast stigmatization.

> It wasn't until July 5, 1994, that Craig took my hand and said that he had something he wanted to tell me himself because we had never kept anything from each other.... He told me he was HIV positive. He discovered it in 1990 when he applied for insurance, but he told no one. I grieved then and I grieve now for the isolation my son endured. I needed to know why, WHY he couldn't tell me? So I asked and he answered, "I knew that you, my mother, my best friend, Rosetta, would be there for me, but I didn't know if Reverend Rosetta DuBois-Gadson would be."...
>
> AIDS was, and still continues to be, so abhorrent to many church leaders and members that they turn their backs on it. And I just learned that my own son feared that this part of me would do the same. There came a revelation that I can only describe as divine. I was filled with righteous indignation and I could feel the strength building in me. My rage had to be transformed into action. All fear had to leave me because I was

being launched into a new ministry that I never would have imagined.[8]

Mothers who grieve the loss of a gay child carry in their memory the burdens of moral dilemmas which they had to face because of society's condemnation of homosexuality. A gay child's "coming out," often during the vulnerable period of adolescence, was likely to have been traumatic for both child and parent. Sometimes it creates a wedge between mother and father, while in other families both parents disavow their child. Such estrangements can complicate grieving and exacerbate the guilt and remorse mourners might feel.

Furthermore, after the traumatic experience of "coming out," many homosexuals migrate to urban areas to escape hometown prejudice. If they return home later because they have AIDS, their culture shock may combine with their parents' fear of stigma to cause serious friction between caretaker and patient. On the other hand, if they decide to stay in the gay community, the mother coming there to be caretaker feels thrown into a totally foreign world. In large urban areas, AIDS victims follow the Archetypal Outcast's pattern of separation and isolation. They constitute for themselves and those near them a special culture of suffering and mourning, for they have experienced multiple losses of lovers, friends, and neighbors. A mother, arriving at this unusual community, faces the challenge of how to successfully enter it. She may never have met her adult child's partner, but even if she and the partner are already friendly, she may not easily understand or appreciate the deep commitment between her son and his lover. Because marriages between gays are unlawful in many places, she probably has not participated in a social ceremony sanctioning their union. Coming now to take full charge of her dying son, she may be shocked to learn that he wants his lover to be primary caretaker. Later conflicts with the partner may arise over funeral arrangements or estate settlement. Some mothers may also be asked to participate in those rituals, such as candlelight marches and "celebrations of life" that reaffirm the legitimacy of being homosexual. Unable to find a place in their belief systems for their son's homosexual life, these grieving mothers struggle with ambivalence and anger.

In most cases, moreover, after nursing her dying AIDS child, a mother enters the mourning process already physically and mentally exhausted. In the final stages, she may have seen her son suffer grue-some symptoms like skin and oral cavity lesions from Kaposi's sarcoma, diarrhea, gastrointestinal bleeding, pulmonary problems, and AIDS dementia complex. If managing dementia has been difficult, as is often the case, mothers feel special remorse for any disharmonies that have marred their final hours together. Then, too, his death may leave her feeling so powerless that she fails to take comfort in available resources. In my own city, where there is a large and active Compassionate Friends support group that holds open monthly meetings, I have yet to see a single mother whose child has died of AIDS. Sometimes these women seek telephone counseling but feel shy attending groups, a situation we hope to change. Even on the phone, however, some mothers hide their complicated grief, not mentioning AIDS as the cause of death, saying only that their child died of pneumonia or leukemia.

Valerie: Mother, Nurse, and Mourner

Unusually vital women like Rosetta DyBois-Gadson are able to incorporate their Outcast's dying into an expanded belief system that gives them added strength. In her own less heroic way, Valerie has also integrated her losses into a new philosophical perspective, enabling her to act and help others.

After several miscarriages, while serving in the Peace Corps in Honduras, Valerie and her husband adopted a nine-month-old boy. Described as "a boy who never stopped," at age five, John was diag-nosed with Attention Deficit Disorder. Aggressive and totally fearless, he was an independent youngster, partly because he always felt differ-ent in his parents' white New Orleans neighborhood, where he was teased about his olive complexion.

After thirteen years of marriage, Valerie's husband fell in love with another woman and left his daughter and adopted son with their mother. Valerie married an authoritarian man who didn't get along with the children, so John moved out as soon as he finished high school. At nineteen, he told his mother he was gay. Her initial reaction was concern, but soon became reassuring, and loving.

I said, "I didn't know. I never suspected. You had so many girlfriends. I knew you were having difficulties, trying to work things out, but I didn't understand the problem. I think, however, we probably should talk about the fact that the lifestyle you have chosen is not going to be an easy one. The gay world is almost a community within itself. There isn't a problem with us, but it's outside us. I don't know what to tell you."

Valerie believes her son's downfall came because he never found a single partner. At twenty-five, he lost weight and suffered from diarrhea. Tests showed he had a full-fledged case of AIDS.

For a while Valerie was able to keep her job, just managing to fix John's meals and medicate his tortuous bone cancer. "There's not a day in my life that I don't hurt," he told her.

Soon Valerie quit her job, and when her second husband left because he couldn't cope with John's AIDS, she moved upstairs with her son. From Valerie's nutritious meals, John grew strong enough to vacation in Hawaii with her and his sister. There he found people with coarse black hair and dark skin, people who looked exactly like him. At thirty, he was experiencing the time of his life.

Coming back to New Orleans, he hoped to have another celebration at Mardi Gras, but in the middle of a parade he came home to bed for what proved to be the last time. Valerie began giving him morphine and when he went into a coma before dying, she took comfort that he was at peace. "Otherwise, you really feel that you would rather die yourself or be going through the pain yourself," she said.

Today Valerie volunteers for the AIDS Task Force, delivering meals to patients, just as her son had done until he was too ill to help. "A lot of people whose children have died with AIDS work with the Task Force," she says. "They are doing something useful for people who others will have nothing to do with." What is surprising, however, is that while her son was ill, Valerie didn't know any other mother whose child was dying of AIDS. "Even though New Orleans has a large gay community, there is little support for the family," she says. "Most of my friends I've met afterward, preparing meals in the kitchen."

Valerie tells her story with quiet acceptance, but not all women are able to arrive at such peace. Many women drug-injection users who are mothers of young HIV-infected children are likely to be infected themselves. They are at high risk for a bereavement, exacerbated by self blame, survivor guilt, and renewed or increased drug use. Overwhelmed by multiple losses, AIDS mourners can't satisfy their deep needs to grieve each one separately. Those whose death has been filled with interpersonal conflicts may suffer from ruminative thinking, guilt, and pessimism. In each situation, the mourner must realize that her child's AIDS death was beyond her control. Even though she may have failed the child at some point in her life, the twelve-step serenity prayer offers its useful key:

> God grant me the serenity to accept the things I cannot change, the courage to change the things I can, and the wisdom to know the difference.

NOTES:

1.   The Dalai Lama and Howard C. Cutler, *The Art of Happiness*, New York, 1998, pp. 138–40.
2.   Joanna H. Fanos, *Sibling Loss*, Mahwah, New Jersey, pp. 23–34.
3.   Barbara Ehrenreich and Deirdre English, *Witches, Midwives, and Nurses: A History of Women Healers*, New York, 1973, p. 37.
4.   James Hillman, *A Blue Fire*, New York, 1989, p. 244.
5.   Nancy Keene, ed., "Saying Goodbye," *Childhood Leukemia*, Sebastopol, CA, 2000, p. 422.
6.   From the Indian author and guru Sir Rabindranath Tagore: *Collected Poems and Plays*, and set to music by Richard Hageman (copyright 1917 by Shirmer, Inc.).
7.   Gerard Manly Hopkins, "Felix Randal," *The Norton Anthology of English Literature*, vol. 2, New York, p. 1550.
8.   B. Goldblum and Sarah Erickson, "True Story Three: A Story of Grief and Inspiration," *Working With Aids Bereavement*, San Francisco, 1999, p. 59.

Chapter Seven

SUDDEN AND VIOLENT DEATHS: ACCIDENTS, NEGLIGENT HOMICIDE, AND MILITARY CASUALTIES

La mort c'est grand, c'est plein de vie dedans.
(Death is big, it's full of life inside.)
— FELIX LECLERC, QUEBECOIS POET

ACCIDENTS

A high school graduation party ends in a fatal car crash.

Unaccountably a tree falls through the roof over a bedroom, killing a sleeping infant.

A son painting the side of a house slips off a tall ladder and breaks his neck.

A scuba-diving daughter is found drowned, ten minutes too late.

A popular athlete practicing basketball free throws in a playground falls down, shot in a sudden gun battle between two gangs he didn't even know.

Sudden deaths shock mothers in ways different from the child who suffered a long illness. By the end, the mother of a sick child knows she had done everything possible to save her child. Draining as long term care is, she finds comfort in having prepared for the death, perhaps even a sense of relief that the child suffers no more. In contrast, accidents often end life abruptly, without warning.

Caring mothers worry when their child is overdue coming home, or when late at night the telephone rings, possibly portending terrible news. In every case, however—whether knowledge of the tragic event comes from the police, a doctor, or a loved one—the moment a mother learns of her child's fatal accident forever stamps itself in her memory.

After the initial shock, mothers begin to search for the cause of the accident. But even when the case is clear and comprehensible, they find it almost impossible to accept that their child was hurt. Often they search on, even seeking ways to blame themselves for the death. Desperately, they replay events, believing that their child's life hung on one little decision: to go swimming rather than play ball, to take a certain airline, to be sitting in the front passenger seat of a car. If only they had intervened then! Mothers blame themselves even more when they have been at the scene of the accident. Surely, they think, they could have somehow prevented it by taking greater care.

Why Have Accidents?
Aristotle's View and the Myth of Balder

After the death, mothers continue to struggle now with the deeper questions excited by their child's unexpected fate: "Why did this have to happen?" Humans' need for an understanding of accidents goes back in time. Aristotle went so far as to divide all reality into either *essence* or *accident*. Essence is stable and orderly, designed by the "prime mover" of the universe. It resides in eternity. Accident typifies our normal imperfection, our lives, pendants to essence. Without accident, the world we know would not exist, because accident brings change. Mythologically, even the gods are not protected from accident.

Of course, any such rational explaining of the universe's workings brings little comfort to a mother whose child has accidentally died. But by contemplating certain principles—that there is an eternal design, that all life is subject to accident, and that change is necessary for life as we know it—she may free herself from unwarranted guilt, a guilt she may be holding, if only to provide some explanation for her child's death. Archetypal tales often help show us the limits of our power and, therefore, of our responsibility. The myth of the Norse oak tree god Balder (beautiful and good son of Goddess Frigg and great god Odin) tells of a mother trying to shield her son from all harm.

> Balder's heavy dreams seemed to forebode his death. Thereupon the gods held a council and resolved to make him secure against every danger. So the goddess Frigg exacted an oath from fire and water, iron and all metals, stones and earth, from trees, sickness, and poisons, and from four-footed beasts, birds, and creeping things, that they would not hurt Balder. When that was done, Balder was deemed invulnerable; the gods amused themselves by setting him in their midst; while some shot at him, others hewed on him, and others threw stones at him. But whatever they did, nothing could hurt him; and at this they were glad. Only Loki, the mischief-maker was displeased, and in the guise of an old woman he went to Frigg, who told him that the weapons of the gods would not wound Balder, since she had made them all swear not to hurt him. Then Loki asked, "Have all things sworn to spare Balder?" She answered, "East of Walhalla grows a plant called mistletoe; it seemed to me too young to swear." So Loki went and pulled the mistletoe and took it to the assembly of gods. There he found the blind god Hother standing at the outside of the circle. Loki asked him, "Why do you not shoot at Balder?" Hother answered, "Because I do not see where he stands; besides I have no weapons." Then said Loki, "Do like the rest and show Balder honor, as they all do. I will show you where he stands, give you a bow, and do you shoot at him with this twig." Hother took the mistletoe and shot it at Balder, as Loki directed him. The mistletoe struck Balder and pierced him through and through, and he fell down dead. And that was the greatest misfortune that ever befell gods and men.[1]

Frigg's compulsive thoroughness attempting to protect her son ends by showing that no amount of precaution can completely shield a child. Paradoxically, however, she still finds hope in the mistletoe.

Other legends tell how mistletoe, imperishable because it grows without ground and remains green throughout the year, houses the soul of Balder. Though the parasite mistletoe is the instrument of his death, it also implies some sort of everlasting life.

Creating Meaning After Accidental Deaths

To many of us, asking a mother to find meaning in her child's accident often seems unreasonable. We may feel women who can do so must be "true believers"—narrow, blinded souls. In fact, whether for believers or seekers, the process is usually dynamic, involving a personal struggle. Kate, for instance, an active church member, has followed the same religious teachings throughout her life and through them has practiced a close relationship with her God. Sally, on the other hand, abandoned her childhood religion and searched for God in new philosophies. But both women have slowly and painstakingly created some significant meaning out of otherwise devastating losses.

Kate's letters to friends and to her son after his death embody her struggle. Her first letters describe details of Andrew's accident and its immediate aftermath.

Dear Friends,

On Friday, October 13, our beloved nine-year-old son Andrew was struck by a car and killed. We believe he was killed instantly, although Gary immediately tried to administer CPR and was relieved soon by professionals who tried to revive him. Andrew was also taken to a nearby hospital where other life-saving measures were taken, but to no avail.

There are so many things I want to tell you. It was a Friday night, and Andrew, Gary, Geoffrey, Elizabeth, and two of her friends and I were going to Nick's football game. As we drove closer to the school, we began following an ambulance. Sitting in the front seat between Gary and me, Andrew wanted to know why the ambulance didn't have its lights on. We explained that it was not taking anyone to the hospital; it was just going to be at the game in case any football players became injured. We tried to park in the lot by the school, but there were no places. Suddenly Andrew told me a story from his summer camp. He said, "Mom, the first girl I ever asked to dance screamed and ran away." He and I laughed at his funny story.

We ended up parking alongside the two-lane highway across from the school. The next few minutes are a blur. I got out on the passenger side, and Andrew bounded out behind me. Then I asked Gary to pop the trunk so I could get the stadium seats out. The girls all crossed the street safely. Geoffrey started to cross, but Gary grabbed him by his shoulder, because a car was coming from the left. As soon as it passed, Andrew darted across and was struck by a car coming from the right. Neither Gary nor I saw Andrew get hit, but we heard it. It was such an awful sound, that I dropped to my knees and screamed, and Gary ran to Andrew, who had been thrown thirty feet by the impact.

Within a half-hour of our arrival at the hospital, the doctors came to give Gary and me the sad news that Andrew could not be saved. It was so terrible and so shocking. Geoff (age eleven) and I took a walk around the hospital corridors later and he expressed his worry that Andrew had died without being forgiven of his sins. He said, "Mom do you think it is okay if I ask God to forgive Andrew of his sins, because you know Andrew sinned at least once a day?" I assured Geoff that that would be okay with God. Nicholas was pulled out of the game at half-time, and told that his brother had been in an accident. Gary took the kids in to tell Andrew goodbye, and then Gary and I went in. Our baby looked as if he were asleep, except for the abrasions on his face, and the bump on his head. Gary and I kissed him goodbye. A doctor who entered after we left said that he knew he was in the presence of an angel because there was a light shining around Andrew's head. He said other nurses and doctors noticed it, too, and were all talking about it.

Some of Kate's letters show how she is open to receiving God's messages by symbolically giving meaning to outside events.

Dear Friends,
    That Sunday after Andrew died, Gary and I woke early. Andrew's obituary was in the paper. We drank our coffee, so desolate. We had a bouquet of green and white helium-filled

balloons. We decided to walk over to the church parking lot and release the balloons. Andrew had spent so much time there—bicycling, skate-boarding, roller blading. When we let the balloons go, the white ones all rose straight up into the sky—to heaven it seemed. The green ones seemed to bobble and bounce across the street toward Jimmy and Johnny's house and our house. It was so astonishing. Andrew seemed to be saying, "I'm in heaven, but I'm also here."

In later letters, Kate pours out her grief, but begins to find an inner relationship with Andrew.

Dear Andrew,

I miss you! Today is October 31, Halloween. You should be in Mrs. Bloom's classroom right now, anticipating a Halloween party. Andrew, there is no peace in grief. In the first few days after your accident, I went over the details of that night, a part of me hoping that I could change the outcome. I cannot change the outcome! It frustrates me so! I wish I could go back and take your hand! And make you hold my hand while we cross that treacherous highway! But I cannot. God has many wonderful laws, but one of them is that you cannot go back and change things.

Dear Andrew,

Dad read *Embraced By the Light*, and one part made him cry. The author talks about part of our purpose being to use our imagination to the fullest. Andrew, you once said, 'I have a great imagination, and sometimes I let it go wild.' Andrew, this is what makes your leaving so hard. Your life was filled with happiness and promise. How could it have been cut short?

My faith is tested by losing you. I love you so. I enjoyed you so! I want to ask you about the mansions you talked about in your paper. Andrew, I want you back! I cry and I cry, but it doesn't bring you back.

Andrew, grief is a foreign country and I don't like it. I want to go home. Home is my family of seven. I want you back, and I can't have you. My heart is broken.

Dear Andrew,

A couple of nights after you died, I dreamed that I was crying and praying to God. In my dream, God answered me and
said, "It was in my plan; I took his hand." And suddenly, I
could see you, running across the street, but instead of being
hit by the car, God reaches down, and taking you by the hand,
lifts you up into heaven. I want to believe that you are with our
Heavenly Father, and that you are truly okay. But I miss you
so, and I wanted you to experience so many things that you
never will. Life on earth has always been such a gift to me, and
I wanted you to have that gift, too. But now, even for me, life
has lost its luster. There is no joy. The light in my life has been
extinguished.

In the last letter, Kate describes her growth after almost three years
of grieving.

Dear Friends,

Now over two years have past since Andrew's death, and I
pray I again begin to embrace the joys of life. My new knowledge is a gift borne of pain, and a gift which came at a great
price, but I feel an empathy for other suffering people I did
not have before. I have taken the bite of the apple and have
been thrown out of paradise and that is true to the marrow of
my bone. But, I say this almost guiltily, because I do feel I am
blessed with my children and my husband, but I now have the
knowledge, you know … I still think I, like Eve, have a good
place to live, but it isn't paradise anymore. Before I lost Andrew,
it was paradise.

Even though Sally still cries a lot when thoughts of her three-year-
old son Chip's accident spontaneously arise, like Kate, she has found
blessings in the life she now has. Chip was playing in the swimming
pool at his cousin's house when he drowned. His aunt tried to revive
him before the police and paramedics arrived. Chip was dead before he
reached the hospital.

Sally had already faced many difficulties before this unthinkable
tragedy. Now, in reviewing these difficulties and trying to make some
sense of her experiences, Sally philosophically describes them as lessons that she somehow had to learn.

I just have to learn and take the good out of it and work with that well.... I would say this, there has been good coming from the death, but I would trade it in a second to have my son back. I'd live in ignorance for the rest of my life to have my son back.

But I do feel there's been good in it. I feel I've grown to be a better person. I try to be more compassionate. Before I was very much interested in just taking care of my little family, just being self-centered. Now I'm more aware of the world around me ... but I don't want to sound like I'm this great person. You have to be careful not to be self-serving, to be so full of yourself.

Sally and her husband were married for ten years before their first child was born. Those ten years of infertility were very painful for Sally, who comes from a large Roman Catholic family.

All my family were popping out babies left and right and everybody wants to know when you're having a baby ... I just wanted to be a mother and have a family.

The couple went through the difficult processes routinely suggested by fertility doctors, office consultations, taking body temperature before intercourse, and surgeries—nothing that would contribute very much to a loving relationship. In spite of these challenges, however, Sally has been happily married in what she calls a "close and stable union."

After waiting ten years, Sally first felt blessed with her beautiful baby girl, until she learned that Maggie was born with a degenerative heart defect.

I felt like after ten years, how dare I be given such a sick baby! I have not really gotten over that, though I have buried a lot of pain. It still continues to be a big part of my life. I need to work on that, but there's been so many other things that I have to push it away.

Sally watched as her baby seemed to die, getting sicker and sicker each day, having to be fed every two hours around the clock, being under the care of a doctor Sally didn't trust. Finally, at five months, Maggie underwent an operation that saved her life.

Because she thought she could never endure what she had been through with Maggie, Sally didn't want to become pregnant again. So Chip came as a total surprise, and when she knew she had a healthy baby boy, Sally felt thrilled. Now their happy family was complete. Financial obligations resulting from Maggie's surgery were settled. Life was the best it had ever been, until the day after his third birthday when Chip drowned.

At the Waldorf Education Association where Chip attended nursery school, Sally tends a garden in memory of her son. For over ten years, she has been a student of anthroposophy, a system of ideas about spiritual life developed by Rudolf Steiner. The preschool utilizes Steiner's educational theories. Studying Steiner's works has helped Sally give meaning to her loss.

> I was raised Catholic, and it got thrown out the window after Chip's death ... you know, you lead a good life, then you die and go to heaven. The death really changed me, and what changed the most is my coming to believe reincarnation is possible. You don't have to have a catastrophe to be presented with lessons in life ... it's not what you're dealt, but how you deal with them.

Facing Fate

As mothers losing children to accidents make conscious efforts to determine *how and why* these cards have been dealt them, most encounter the useful idea of "fate." Ever since humans became thinking beings they have been concerned with fate: what is in store for them, how life will be then, and its meaning. Our English word comes from the Latin, *fatum,* meaning something spoken, such as a decree from God. When a catastrophic accident overcomes her child, a great part of a mother's grieving process involves struggling with fate, for the tragedy seems incomprehensible.

Incomprehensible it may be, but sooner or later one may gain comfort by submitting to the key aspect of the notion of fate: inevitability. Whatever else we believe of it, this is its core.

In Greek cosmology, Zeus loved the goddess of Necessity, Themis, who brought forth three lovely daughters, The Fates. All living things must eventually submit to these divinities, individually named Clotho, Lachesis, and Atropos. Life's thread is woven by Clotho, measured out by Lachesis, and finally cut by Atropos. They laugh at our feeble attempts to cheat them because their work is absolutely unalterable by either gods or humans.

In Scandinavian and Germanic mythology, the Norns sit at the foot of the tree of life, the Yggdrasill, and water its roots. Their names are Urd (past), Verdandi (present), and Skuld (future). Buddhists and Hindus explain the disparities in human fate with Karma, the impact of an individual's past actions on his future, but though we may know our actions in this life, they derive from past lives we can neither know nor change. In Judaism, Christianity, and Islam, fate is in the hands of a monotheistic god. All is the will of Yahweh or Allah. Christians, attempting to explain how an all-loving God can bring such harm, argue about what is predestined and what is free will. But most people—of all religions or none—seem to have an easier time explaining the unfairness of life if their world view includes some concept of fate as a ruling force in the universe, beyond our control.

NEGLIGENT HOMICIDE

Medical Malpractice: Wanda's Fate

Though acceptance of fate, no matter how we conceive it, is an essential part of the grieving process, and though the wisdom of the ages tells us that being stuck in self-pity or angry defiance doesn't change things for the better, when death results from gross negligence, as in Kim's case, a mother's anger and need for reparation scorch her soul, leaving little room for renewal.

Kim had completed her studies four months before graduation. Returning home to await the results of her engineering licensing exam, she went for a routine allergy shot. The injection put her in a coma. Because Kim had been slightly sick with flu, she should not have been given the shot. But nobody warned her. A physician, who still practices medicine despite being proven negligent, refused to insert a tube into Kim's larynx so the girl could breathe, "because no x-ray machine is available." The doctor also failed to perform a simpler procedure, tracheotomy, that could have saved Kim's life.

Kim's parents sought justice through the courts. At the deposition, Kim's mother Wanda was beside herself. Thinking that Kim's mother might retaliate with some sort of physical assault, the physician worried about her own child's safety.

Looking at me with astonishment at being so misperceived, Wanda asked:

> Can you believe she thought I could take a child's life? I was furiously angry, yes, but it was the doctor's cool, unemotional attitude that most enraged me. She sat straight faced and answered 'no comment' to all questions.

Because the negligence was so obvious, the case was settled in only ten months, but Wanda found little comfort in her victory. On the first anniversary of Kim's death, Wanda was still furious so she called the doctor's office.

> I reminded her that it was a year since my girl had died. "You Goddamn killed my baby," I said. "Why didn't you intubate?"

A Plane Crash: Carmen's Fate

Another mother, Carmen feels the same intense rage when she thinks about how the negligence of Value Jet Airline employees caused a deadly crash, killing her daughter Anna. Flight 592 was carrying volatile oxygen canisters, and many lacked required safety caps. Federal investigators found that no electrical spark ignited the fire: the canisters themselves started it, killing 110 people. After the crash, the Department of Transportation imposed an emergency ban on the shipment of oxygen canisters. Too late for Anna. Carmen remembers her hysteria when she was notified of the crash.

> I kept hitting my head against the glass door so hard my family thought it would break. The worst part was knowing I would never kiss or hug her again. And then they found no remains. There were 4000 body pieces, and the government said it would be too expensive to identify bodies.

Carmen received generous monetary reparation for her daughter's death, but she wasn't satisfied.

> Getting some money wasn't important. The reason I sued was to *punish* them. I was glad to see that in Dave County, where the crash occurred, the people responsible for loading the canisters were indicted on criminal charges. I don't hate because hate destroys. But I hope those people who have 110 lives on their conscience go to jail.

A mother's primitive, unrestrained anger rages up from the depths of her soul when her child is needlessly, negligently killed. In times of war feelings are often more complicated.

DEATH IN THE MILITARY

Sacrifice of the Hero

Hero Archetype myths begin with a person's deciding to undertake a special journey or with his being unintentionally thrown into an important adventure. In either case, the archetypal Hero is always up to the challenge, having such required traits as temperance, courage, and loyalty. Heroes shoulder the moral objectives of saving an individual or a people, or supporting a particular idea. When a son or daughter first puts on a military uniform, he symbolizes his hero initiation, dying to an old life and being resurrected into a new one in which he discovers qualities in his nature he didn't know he possessed.

Because there is no military draft today, our armed services consist of individuals who, knowing the risks involved, choose to fight. They feel pride and honor in serving their country: highly trained to kill, they also must be willing to die. Like mythological heroes, they learn to submit themselves to perilous duties, undertaking such hazardous tasks as operating heavy equipment, negotiating mine fields, contending with poisonous gas, or just acclimating themselves to severe foreign climates. Despite these hardships, most grow in desiring action.

Small units also develop a sustaining camaraderie no outsider can appreciate, shared connectedness and high-spirit emotions further motivating them. Such feelings can bring courage and comfort to a soldier while he lives, and though thrusting himself into danger, he may feel more alive than most of us left behind. Many mourners are comforted when they realize he died serving the cause or group he loved and doing the expert and meaningful job he trained for.

Very often in the volunteer army, a soldier has chosen his specific job. It was only after her son's helicopter crashed that Dorothy began to realize how much flying meant to him. She learned that he had often said, "I can't believe they pay us to do what I love most!"

Eric had been her "prize child," the first boy in a family with three girls. As a youngster he enjoyed hunting with his dad in the Vermont countryside. But that relationship became strained when his father, depressed because of business failures, zealously threw himself into the World Wide Church of God. No longer allowed to participate in traditional holidays now, Eric endured long drives to solemn hours of Saturday church services. Because Dad became steadily more oppressive, coming to believe in the sacred rightness of physically punishing his children, Dorothy finally divorced him.

Perhaps Eric's opposition to Dad's stern rigidity helped make him want to fly. While still in high school, he obtained his pilot license, and after graduating from college, joined the army to become a helicopter pilot, serving in Korea, Bosnia, and Iraq. Though he tried other army work, no job except flying interested him. When he died, he had been promoted to the highest level of Chief Warrant Officer.

Regretting she didn't participate more, Dorothy advises mothers to learn all they can about their children's lives. She believes she missed too many cues from Eric, a quiet man who wanted his mom to know how much army life meant to him. She now realizes he had found his own family, so to speak, in the camaraderie among men in his unit and that he died doing what he most loved.

Joseph Campbell clarifies our frequent misunderstanding of sacrificial acts:

> The old idea of being sacrificed is not what we think at all. The Mayan Indians had a kind of basketball game in which, at the end, the captain of the winning team was sacrificed on the field by the captain of the losing team. His head was cut off. Going

to your sacrifice as the winning stroke of your life is the essence of the early sacrificial idea.[2]

The story of five Sullivan brothers, young men who lost their lives in 1942 when the cruiser *Juneau* was torpedoed in the Pacific, became a collective rallying point for the war effort. After all her boys died together that single day, Mrs. Sullivan received stirring personal condolences from the President of the United States.

> The knowledge that your five gallant sons are missing in action, against the enemy, inspired me to write you this personal message. I realize full well there is little I can say to assuage your grief.
>
> As the Commander in Chief of the Army and the Navy, I want you to know that the entire nation shares your sorrow. I offer you the condolence and gratitude of our country. We, who remain to carry on the fight, must maintain the spirit in the knowledge that such sacrifice is not in vain. The Navy Department has informed me of the expressed desire of your sons: George Thomas, Francis Henry, Joseph Eugene, Madison Abel, and Albert Leo, to serve on the same ship. I am sure that we all take pride in the knowledge that they fought side by side. As one of your sons wrote, "We will make a team together that can't be beat." It is this spirit which in the end must triumph....
>
> Franklin D. Roosevelt

After the boys died, their parents and sister Genevieve found meaningful roles. Themselves elevated by participating in The Hero's service and sacrifice, they visited war production plants, urging employees to produce more weapons to end the war sooner. Their war bond drives and other patriotic campaigns culminated in the 1944 movie, *The Sullivans*, bringing the family consoling and uplifting public support.

Complicated Mourning in the Military

But other mothers must face more ambiguous and difficult grief. Steven Spielberg's *Saving Private Ryan*, for example, tells of a rescue squad sent to save the surviving son of a mother who has already lost three boys in World War II. When a preacher and an army officer drive up to her Iowa farmhouse to give news of her last son's death, the mother, watching from the front porch, falls to her knees. Then the screen image fades away, as if acknowledging that our witnessing so much grief would be unbearable.

Like all mourning mothers, those whose sons died in war remember exactly how they heard the news. Caroline lost two sons to action in France during World War II and another to disease contracted in the South Pacific. Her daughter Jenny, who still holds a monthly mass for her brothers, remembers with abiding resentment how coldly the bad news was delivered and the shock her mother suffered from these loses.

> They send you a telegram or write you a letter, and the words come so cold. The bad news always comes to the mothers, and that's when the crying starts. The mothers always get it.... My mother never let the rosary beads out of her hands. She was constantly praying for the boys.

During the 2003 Iraq war, Staff Sergeant Terry Hemingway's mother had already seen military officers arriving to tell the bad news at other mothers' homes. Nothing, however, prepared her for a later revelation about another event she had witnessed. Having watched live television coverage of a car bomb exploding beside a Bradley Fighting Vehicle, only later did she learn that her son had been inside.

> While I watched television, I hoped it wasn't Terry. Of course I knew it was somebody's son ... and I worried for that person. I felt for that family. I just didn't think it would be Terry.

In the military, unfortunately, death is often a normal event. Sometimes, however, just because it is more expected, family members may have less support when their loved one dies. Those with families not related to soldiers watch wars repeatedly unfold on their TV screens and can become immune to an individual's tragedy. They see a soldier's death honored with a gun salute, and forget how grief is a long, individual affair.

Often when the death occurs on foreign soil, wrong decisions can be made about where to transport the soldier's belongings and body. Mothers are frequently unable to render support to grandchildren and spouses living far away. A spouse's grief may be further complicated when she must make suddden arrangements to move out of government housing.

Mothers also report how gaps in communications and even conflict-ing reports about their soldier's death added more pain and confusion to their grief. Sometimes, officers simply do not know details about a death occurring thousands of miles away. In other cases, the cause of death may have been contained in classified investigative reports and not released. Those who have to wait until death is definitely declared live in particular agony.

> I don't know why they told us he was missing when someone must have known that they had all vanished in a huge explo-sion. We were torn up with tension thinking he was out there somewhere. If they had at least given us something, said what they expected, we wouldn't have spent twenty days hoping.
>
> Pam

Particularly because she knows her son to have been capable and responsible, Dorothy, another mother, wants to learn the details sur-rounding his death. But she is still waiting to receive official notice that will rid her of conflicting rumors about "mechanical difficulties" or "friendly fire." She hopes to exchange more information from families she met at the TAPS Memorial Day Service.

Out of personal tragedy, her husband's death in an army aircraft crash, Bonnie Carrol founded TAPS, the Tragedy Assistant Program for Survivors, in 1994. Because she gained strength from other fami-lies who had lost loved ones, she recognized the power of peer suport. Today this volunteer organization offers counseling and a national net-work of trained Peer Mentors who have lost a loved one in the armed forces.

Dorothy feels she herself has received a lot of support from TAPS and also from a Casualty Assistance Officer assigned to help recover Eric's belongings, arrange funeral services, and offer financial aid. The government flew her to Georgia to meet the other grieving families and then paid for her Memorial Day trip to Washington, D.C. Dorothy explains her complex reactions.

> Their help has been enormous. It's even somewhat embarrass-ing, when I think of the millions of mothers whose sons died in

two World Wars or in Korea and Vietnam, I feel their reaction to my loss is out of proportion.

In this struggle, most American service families believe our war in Iraq will help stop terrorism. At the Memorial Day service in Washington, I found few families who didn't agree with Bush policy, so I kept my opinions to myself. There was much sadness there. It was too emotional to bear for long periods so I took an afternoon off and went to the Smithsonian. Our sorrow was too great, but for those who really believe in the war there was more comfort.

Wars Without Support

Mothers who doubted the war effort in Iraq had a difficult time when their sons were killed in action. One mom remarked:

> I hope the chemical and biological weapons the administration officials said Saddam Hussein had are found in Iraq. It would help me make sense of my son's death.

Others had argued with their sons about the uselessness of the war. "This is not what God created man to do," Lillian said, and meeting some of her son's fellow service members at a memorial service, she realized how different she felt from them.

> They thought his death was an honor. I didn't see it that way and they were upset about that. To me, as a mother, you know, it is not an honor. But they feel it's an honor, and I must respect that.

In the end, most military mothers who opposed the war were able to find solace in their son's bravery and responsible actions. Ruth's son, Tristen, died while fighting for control of the Baghdad airport.

> He was doing his job. He had no choice, and I'm proud of who he was. But it makes me mad that this whole war was sold to the American public and to the soldiers as something it wasn't. Our forces have been convinced that Iraqis were responsible for September 11, and that's not true. I told Tristen he should not go for that. All he would come back to was, "Mom, I have to do my job."

Deaths in Vietnam

A son's dying in the service of his country complicates and pro-
longs his mother's grief when war efforts are actively opposed by large
numbers of citizens. Though the Vietnam war ended in 1975, some
mothers' continued mistrust of government and sense of betrayal keep
grief unresolved. With an average age of only nineteen, Vietnam soldiers were the youngest to fight our country's wars, some never having
spent a night away from home. Their youthful deaths were expectedly
hard for mothers to bear. Furthermore, widespread American shame at
our war efforts caused many mothers to hide their grief from others,
protecting their sons' memory by not talking about where or how they
died. When so many Americans still depersonalized and dehumanized
those who fought there, many mothers grieved in silence. Later on, particularly with the completion of the Vietnam Memorial in 1982, however, thousands of families finally found a way to mourn and remember
their loved one.

As is well known, beginning with its dedication on November
12, 1982, people visiting the Vietnam Memorial left behind archetypally charged symbols of aching grief, continued remembrance,
thanks, and honor for those beyond the grave: dog tags, photographs,
letters, medals, clothing, teddy bears, Bibles, wedding rings—an
unimaginable array of personal items are still deposited today and
the Park Service staff continue to categorize and store them. People
who stifled their grief for years now bring objects that had special
meaning to an individual soldier. Some mothers return each year
for their child's birthday or anniversary, always leaving something
special behind.

Though Ben McDermott was a strong athletic guy who loved
motorcycles and fast cars, his parents left his teddy bear at the base of
Panel 18 West on their first visit to the Memorial. Taking the bear to
Washington was a spur-of-the-moment decision.

> My dearest Ben,
> I miss you and think of you so much. Every day in my
> prayers, I thank God and Jesus for caring for you and pray that
> will continue. I'm bringing "Teddy Bear" and a picture of your
> loved race car. I realize they can't stay there long, but they are

yours and I want them to be with you. In time I hope we can all be together.

> Love to you my dear Ben.
> Much love,
> Mama
> Dad[3]

World War I and World War II: Blue Stars Turn to Gold

Unlike Vietnam-era soldiers, grieving mothers whose soldier sons died in World War I and World War II were supported by receiving full honors for their sons' sacrifices. During World War I, President Wilson asked American women to wear a Blue Star representing each family member in service and a black band with a gilt star for those who had died in war. The purpose was to support devotion and pride rather than a sense of loss. For the more than 60,000 mothers whose children died serving in World War I, the Gold Star represented Heroes on behalf of freedom, and it became the rallying point for grieving mothers. Gold Star membership opened in 1941 to mothers of soldiers fallen during World War II, in 1950 for the Korean War, and in the 1960s for Vietnam. Unfortunately, because of strong anti-war sentiment during the Vietnam era, many mothers feared displaying their stars.

Those like Oxidine, however, wore it proudly. Living today at Gold Star Manor, a facility built to house mothers whose sons died in combat, she feels ambivalent about the future of the Gold Star mothers' organization.

> Since peace has prevailed in recent decades, Gold Star membership is dwindling. All the World War II mothers have died off and most of the Korean ones. I regret the thinning of our ranks. We always said we never wanted another mother to become eligible, and here is the war in Iraq, increasing our potential membership pool. So many are getting killed or injured, though! I hate to watch it on TV. It brings tears to my eyes.

Honoring All Heroes

Though mourning a son lost in combat is complicated, patriotic traditions like the Gold Stars help mothers to be proud of their brave sons who died defending our country. Deceased soldiers can be buried with full honors, including the playing of TAPS and the folding and presenting of the United States burial flag. Memorials such as the Tomb of the Unknowns at Arlington National Cemetery remind us of the sacrifices many have made.

Mothers may want to be strong and brave in the face of their Hero's death, but they should remember they, too, are heroes. When we stop thinking about ourselves and our own self-preservation so are we all. Then we undergo what Joseph Campbell calls a heroic transformation of consciousness.

> For the Aztecs, who had a number of heavens to which people's souls would be assigned according to the conditions of their death, the heaven for warriors killed in battle was the same for mothers who died in childbirth. Giving birth is definitely a heroic deed, in that it is the giving over of oneself to the life of another....[4]

NOTES:

1. James George Frazer, *The Golden Bough*, New York, 1963, p. 704.
2. Joseph Campbell, *The Power of Myth*, New York, 1988, p. 108.
3. Laura Palmer, *Shrapnel in the Heart*, New York, 1988, p. 21.
4. Joseph Campbell, *The Power of Myth*, New York, 1988, p. 125.

Chapter Eight

SUDDEN AND VIOLENT DEATH: MURDER

Revenge is a kind of wild justice, which the more man's nature
runs to, the more ought law to weed it out.

— SIR FRANCIS BACON

Cain's Murder of Abel

"Murder!" The word itself so frightens mothers that at first they can't bring it to clear consciousness. Inwardly, they hear instead, "gunned down by a robber," "killed in a crime of passion," or "a body found at the side of the road." Only slowly can a mother come to her more primal realization of what has happened, because her child died from the act most proscribed in our culture, since before God's commandments were handed down to Moses. As she finally allows herself to grasp what has happened, her inner world is shaken in particularly deep ways.

The Old Testament God responds to the first murderer declaring that he be banned from the spot on earth on which he killed; and that further, the earth as a whole will no longer give him nourishment or strength. His alienation from earth is an archetypal punishment: for him the basic underpinnings of human life are removed.

The mother of a murdered child also suffers this archetypal experience of the earth being pulled from under herself, fundamentally sullied by intimate association with the archetypal evil deed. Christina

Rosetti's poem, "Eve's Lament," further develops symbols of the uniquely shocking quality of murder: it is not only that Eve weeps, the beasts of the field forget nourishing themselves, and the consequences of metaphor for murder is an archetypal separation from nature supporting us and all other sentient life.

> Thus she sat weeping
> Thus Eve our mother
> Where one lay sleeping
> Slain by his brother.
> Greatest and least
> Each piteous beast
> To hear her voice
> Forgot his joys
> And set aside his feast.[1]

At the beginning of our culture, Cain's murder of Abel figures as a second Fall of Man, one we understand more immediately than eating fruit of a mysterious Tree of Knowledge. Indeed, the murder dramatically shows us that "knowledge of Evil" which we humans must face, and murder becomes more in archetypal meaning, The Worst Event. When the concept "murder" fully enters her consciousness, a mother faces deepest evil, a knowledge so personally felt even more paralyzingly by its forever fusing her with humankind's archetypal potential for cruelty and violence, and with the equally archetypal alienation following it.

Shock and Post Traumatic Stress

Exactly how news of her child's murder is delivered can be important to a mother's eventual healing. If she is told in person, with empathy and concern, she may later cherish the kindness of the messenger, who stood with her during the most horrible moment of her life. If she receives only unvarnished facts by telephone, or worse, if she learns of the death through the media, she will probably feel still more isolated from humanity. As with accidents, no matter how gruesome the event, however, she will probably want to know its exact details. Denied access to photographs or bloody possessions, she may further suffer by imagining the very worst. Often, she becomes even more determined to know the whole truth.

Her grief-fueled, passionate emotions can be frightening, not only to loved ones and criminal justice officials but also to herself, for she fears for her own safety and the safety of her surviving children. Worse, however, are the horrible moments she imagines her child may have suffered. Pictures of the crime constantly intrude on her thoughts and nighttime dreams. Stunned with perplexity, she cannot fathom how one would kill intentionally, particularly how one would deliberately murder her cherished child. Enraged, she may plot revenge in cruel and sadistic fantasies, planning how to make the murderer most suffer, becoming in her thoughts the perpetrator's own torturer and murderer. Unfamiliar with such poisonous ideas, she must struggle with her shadow, the unconscious part of her personality, an aspect of herself she may never before have consciously experienced. Haunted by such recurrent thoughts and nightmares, she may even begin to question her own sanity.

Though these disturbing experiences feel unique and nearly unbearable to each mother, they are common to persons suffering from posttraumatic stress syndrome (PTSS), characteristic symptoms of people exposed to extreme trauma. The original event combines with succeeding stressful tasks after the murder—dealing with media, police, and prosecutors—to make mothers suffer PTSS for years. In addition to intrusive disturbing thoughts, she typically becomes hypervigilant. Fraught with vague evil expectations, breathing becomes shallow, she sweats, her eyes dart suspiciously, and she startles at common events, apprehending them as threats to her safety. A government official's missing a routine appointment, a bus driver's rudeness, an open window's falling suddenly shut—all these can send her nerves and muscles into painfully useless spasms. Then too, as pretrial court proceedings drag on, a mother may funnel her thoughts and energy into them, thereby delaying grieving. Filled with edgy outrage, she tries to put sadness on hold, a maneuver further robbing her of psychic energy.

Once the trial begins, she may wrap her entire life in its inevitable ups-and-downs, all of her emotions becoming dependent on decisions or delays in the unfolding technicalities of judicial proceedings.

Mothers are naturally disappointed when the prosecutor, judge, or jury lessens the charge, calling the death "manslaughter," or "negligent homicide," or "accident." They usually find plea bargaining an outrage and become additionally infuriated when hearing dates drag onward for months or years or when they themselves are not informed of trial dates or when, in some states, they find themselves barred from the courtroom. Mothers who can attend the trial may witness their son or daughter being maligned and devalued by the defense attorneys, attempting to minimize the crime. But unless called as witness, mothers must submit to silence until the sentence hearing. Only then will they be allowed to speak (or to submit a written victim's statement), describing the impact of their loss.

Linda's story, which follows, exemplifies much of the stress mothers of murdered children feel encountering the criminal justice system. We also see the struggle to find a way out by making a contribution to the well-being of others.

Confessed Murderers in a Senseless Robbery:
Struggles with Criminal Justice

On a hot humid evening in July 1998, Linda's son Kevin and his partner Doug walked their dog in front of their home in New Orleans' French Quarter. Two African-American men approached them, asking for a cigarette and then demanding money. Learning that their victims' wallets were at home, the robbers drew guns and forced Kevin and Doug to lead the way into their house. Once inside, however, the owners slammed the front door, catching the robbers' arms. Then they crouched against the door to keep the robbers out, but the intruders fired five shots through it, two striking Kevin's neck and two hitting Doug's arm. Kevin died almost instantly. The robbers fled.

A week later, a tip to Crimestoppers led police to the robbers, both quickly confessing and being indicted. Two months later, Kevin's mother Linda came face to face with the murderers at their first hearing, a truly shocking experience. Because judges give first degree murder charges priority, the District Attorney announced the trial would begin in six to twelve months. But now, five years after the killing, Linda still waits. Meanwhile she has attended many hearings before an insensitive local judge who frequently attempted to be funny. The defense appealed to the State Supreme Court, arguing the unconstitutionality of the grand jury's racial composition. The Supreme Court eventually seated seven African-Americans and five whites, designating an African-American female foreperson. The case was sent back to the Fourth Circuit Court of Appeals, where the applicability of that ruling was contested by the prosecutor. Currently, Linda is waiting for the Supreme Court to review the latest appeals.

> I've always been a take charge person, but now I feel helpless. I'm sorry that I trusted the system from the beginning rather than contacting politicians who could have influenced the procedures. Now I have no idea if anyone is doing anything. The case may just fall through the cracks or get dumped into someone's drawer and forgotten. I read about a Tulane student who was murdered twelve years ago. Her family still returns to New Orleans, trying to settle their child's unsolved murder, trips that are a terrible financial and emotional burden. When I read that article, I never dreamed that we, too, would have such long delays: our murderers had confessed!
>
> I finally realized after the argument before the Supreme Court that I had to refocus, to try to put my energies into new activities. It worked for a while, but always new legal events demand my attention. Right now I have to deal with changes resulting from a new District Attorney's taking office.
>
> A couple of times during this ordeal, I've thought of becoming a court advocate for other victims' families, to be there to explain what happens. The system forgets that we didn't all go to law school. I know that advocates are in place in some cities, and I think there's great need for them.

Unfortunately, no matter what happens in the eventual trial, Linda will always carry the pain of Kevin's violent death. Moreover, in nearly every case involving child murder, a court's decision fails to bring the complete emotional satisfaction the mother had expected. Even when a "guilty" verdict eventuates, most mothers lack the sense of relief they hoped for. When the offender is found "guilty" without having so pleaded, mothers face the prospect of his endless appeals. If a just prison sentence is imposed, they worry about the possibility of early paroles. And when the sentence imposed is too light or the offender is found "not guilty," the injustice poisons her grieving process with unending resentment.

Archetypal Justice: Orestes and The Furies

Moreover, strong complex emotions the mother of a murdered child harbors press against the grain of all legal systems. She yearns for quick justice, decisive punishment, and vengeance. To a large extent, she psychologically identifies with such symbols of Archetypal Just Vengeance as the mythical Furies of ancient Greece. These three daughters of the night mercilessly persecuted murderers and other serious wrongdoers. The mother of a murdered child brims with natural human emotions these Furies represent: Alecto, the unremitting, Megaira, the envious, and Tisiphne, avenger of murder.

Unfortunately for such a mother, her strong and natural desires run straight into the robust edifice of the legal system—with its procedures, courts, trials, advocates, deliberations, and so forth—which the evolution of society, from small and simple to large and complex, has erected. Imperfect as it may be, we all acknowledge that the formal apparatus of justice mainly represents a forward step in human social development, one which Aeschylus portrays as the culmination of his famous trilogy, *The Orestia.* In the last play of that work, Aeschylus creates what amounts to an etiological myth—a symbolic explanation of how the city state of Athens came to erect its justice system.

The social problem depicted in this new myth is how to create an institution which can stop a cycle of violent vengeance: father killing daughter, mother killing father, son killing mother, son being tortured. As Aeschylus' myth goes, seeking vengeance for the theft of his brother's wife, King Agamemnon sacrificially murders his daughter, Iphigenia, so that his army can sack the city which unjustly protects the thief. Agamemnon's wife, Queen Clytemnestra, mother of Orestes and the murdered girl, in turn, murders King Agamemnon. Her son, following the same path of vengeful justice murders his murderer mother. Pursuing the path themselves, The Furies torment Orestes for years, while exiled he roams the world, trying to make his own penance. At last, claiming his penance complete, Orestes seeks refuge at Athena's shrine (Goddess of Athens, where the play is being performed, and also The Goddess of Wisdom.)

The Furies appear as plaintiffs, in the interest of justice, claiming the right to continue torturing Orestes. Representing defendant Orestes, Apollo argues the man has already atoned for his sin. The Furies retort that if the judgment goes against them, humans will no longer fear their wrath, and violence will go unchecked. Despite this forecast, Athena casts her final decisive vote against the Furies, and Apollo, Zeus' interpreter, wins the suit. From this time forward, according to the new myth, the right of punishment in Athens is reserved to its courts of law.

Cookie's Story: Murder and Mediatrix

The Greek god Apollo, who wins Orestes case against the vengeful female furies, symbolizes objectivity, law, scientific clarity, and logic. Our justice system is built upon these Apollonian ideals, which in their positive aspect create harmony and order. In his negative aspect, however, Apollo is remote and lacking in sympathy. As the Furies claim, he "loves not grief, nor lends an ear to it."

Women, having strongly felt connectedness to others, often have their own emotional sense of justice, one better attuned to the Greek Furies. Some women also have intuitive knowings of what is true or just, ways that encompass more than merely weighing a logical argument or fact against another of equal force. One so gifted in this intuitive thinking has the burden of being a *Mediatrix*, a woman who mediates between the conscious and the unconscious world, and who insists on the valuing of our personal responses and experiences. Because Cookie is such a woman, her reactions surrounding her daughter's murder and the murderer's trial were particularly complicated and meaningful, as the following summary of her experiences will reveal.

She always slept lightly until she knew her three girls were safely home. One night she woke up about 1:45 am, walked to the front door and looked outside to watch the moonlit sky. Returning to bed, she began praying to the Blessed Mother, but fell asleep during her prayers. In her dreams she heard a crash and her daughter Shelly screaming for help. She saw her Shelly drowning, being held down and fighting for her life. Cookie woke up and started to dress;

she was going to the Bayou. "What are you doing? You only had a bad dream," her husband argued, finally convincing her to go back to sleep. Two hours later, the phone rang. Shelly had been in an accident; the car was in the Bayou, and her body at the morgue. In spite of the telltale dream, Cookie first thought the call a prank.

At the morgue they gave her Shelly's purse. Still, hoping against hope, Cookie thought the purse might have been stolen. When she finally accepted the terrible reality, she told her husband to get a gun, go to the hospital, and kill the man that had murdered her daughter. She knew that Shelly couldn't drown unless held down. She had won many ribbons and medals as a competitive swimmer, participated in water ballet and synchronized swimming, and could hold her breath for minutes without panic. Most important, Cookie now saw that her dream also confirmed her daughter had been murdered.

> My dream was so real that I could feel her pain, and I knew she was fighting him off. I heard her screams. If I had listened to the dream, I would have searched the Bayou at once. But in the dream, the drowning place was further up the Bayou than where it actually happened. I am not a good swimmer, and I may not have found her. If only I had prayed more to the Blessed Mother, perhaps I could have saved her.

A Louisiana State University medical student had driven his car into Bayou St. John after a night of heavy drinking. As the car sank, he climbed out the sun roof, making no attempt to help Shelly escape. Witnesses said he was more concerned about his car insurance than whoever might be in his vehicle. "I didn't know the bitch's name. I just picked her up in a bar," he said. At Charity Hospital medical friends tried to cover up the amount of alcohol found in his blood.

Though Cookie knew what really happened to her daughter, she couldn't prove it in court. On the pretense of giving her a ride home, the medical student, a new acquaintance, had driven Shelly to City Park and tried to rape her. Cookie knows her daughter would never willingly have gone to a park with a stranger. She also would never get in the car of a man who simply picked her up in a bar. Before the trial, Cookie would sit in the park, where she believes her daughter had struggled. Investigating this place on their own, Shelly's friends had discovered the tire marks of the murderer's car. By meditating and listening in this place, Cookie learned intuitively that her daughter had been beaten, thrown in the car, and held underwater until the murderer could escape.

But in the legal matter of her daughter's murder, Cookie had to face a court system and particularly a District Attorney's office reflecting Apollonian values which ignored her inner personal knowing. Consequently, walking up the steps of the courthouse each day was a terrible challenge. She always came with her family and took Shelly's ashes with her. In the end, though what she knew in her heart could not be proven in court, she was able still to put the murderer behind bars. By also using her more practical and rational side, she gathered evidence and obtained over 5,000 signed petitions. Many witnesses appeared to attest to the perpetrator's drunken behavior and lack of remorse. In the end, he was given fifteen years in prison, the maximum sentence for vehicular homicide. Cookie and her husband are now working to have him permanently barred from practicing medicine. They have also written to every state medical board, alerting them to the murderer's history of careless, lethal irresponsibility.

With sad irony, Cookie remembers giving her daughter "a half-joking pep talk," the evening of the murder.

> I had stopped saying this sort of thing years ago, because Shelly had shown herself to be so responsible and cautious. But as she was leaving the house, I said, jokingly, "Be careful, don't pick up any strangers." Instead of joining in the joke, though, she sounded annoyed: "Don't treat me like a baby! You've been telling me things like that since I was three years old!" I remember the incident because it was so unlike her to snap back like that or ever be sharp with anybody.

We can ask: Why was Cookie joking in the first place? We all know how often jokes tell the truth. Was this Mediatrix unconsciously aware of some danger that would befall her daughter? Cookie's intuition and her not acting on it throws light on deeper meanings of the Bluebeard fairy tale.

Bluebeard and the Dark That Won't Be Seen

In the story, a certain lady of rank has two beautiful daughters, and Bluebeard asks that one become his wife. He leaves it to the women to choose who it should be. Both daughters repeatedly insist they will never marry a man with a blue beard. Besides, they remark the man's having already had several wives who mysteriously disappeared. The girls do agree, however, to accept Bluebeard's invitations to parties, music, dancing, and feasts.

After a time, the younger sister begins to think the beard not so blue and the gentleman who owns it a very civil and obliging person. Soon she agrees to marry him. About six months after the wedding, Bluebeard, telling his wife he has business in the country, gives her his keys, with specific instructions that she not open the closet at the end of the long gallery on the ground floor. When the wife's curiosity gets the best of her, she opens the closet and finds the heads of her blue-bearded husband's former wives. Fortunately, in the story, her brothers save her from the same fate.

The fairy tale shows how danger can await innocent maidens lacking life experiences needed for self-protection. In the final moments they spent together, perhaps Cookie was intuitively aware of her daughter's vulnerable innocence. Like other mothers, she may have found herself torn between her vague sense that some harm may be lurking and her desire not to interfere with her daughter's well-established autonomy.

Murder in the Family: Jennifer, Nelson, and Colleen

A real life Bluebeard tragedy occurred when Colleen's daughter Jennifer was murdered by her husband Nelson. Even before their daughter's marriage, Colleen semiconsciously began to see the elements of a murderer's profile in Nelson. He didn't seem the kind of man her daughter would instinctively have chosen: eleven years older, with a big pot belly, Colleen sometimes joked that "he looked foreign and menacing, resembling Sadam Hussein." He also loved guns, which Jennifer feared.

Thinking afterward about causes of the murder, Colleen recalled Nelson's obvious need to control Jennifer. After the baby was born and she wanted to go back to work, he insisted on her remaining home. The couple also began having troubles with his ex-wife. Jennifer became fed up, but in order to keep her happy, Nelson bought them a house next to her parents. When she finally started working again at the jewelry store, however, he snapped, becoming extremely jealous. Late one afternoon, he barged into the store, shot her, and then a fellow worker. The next night, in an empty shopping center parking lot, he also shot and killed himself.

Colleen recalls:

> It wasn't always bad. Many times we really liked being around him. He was funny; we would play cards together and be in tears from laughter. With our ten grandchildren, we were always partying, and Nelson was often the one to bring the food.

She realizes now how she also noticed a darker side. Yet, like other mothers, she couldn't bear to look at it squarely, much less confront the problems which would arise from doing so. She knew that he was hardened to pain and that he even believed he owned his woman.

Thinking back, Colleen remembers when Nelson took her daughter to his native country in South America.

> I thought about white slavery. I sensed there was a problem in the marriage. If he guessed that she might leave him, I thought that there would be trouble.

The Archetype of Maternal Suffering

Like Colleen, other mothers torture themselves with ways they might have prevented their child's murder. But even if they are able to identify a missed act or opportunity, they must rationally come to understand that their self-punishment far exceeds their fault.

Until such time of liberation, these mothers are in the grip of a maternal archetype well symbolized by Niobe, Queen of Thebes. She represents the primordial mother in her aspect of Maternal Suffering, not from the travail of birth-giving, but rather as soul-sorrowing parent. Once very proud of seven sons and seven daughters, Niobe bragged about her many children, unwittingly offending the goddess Leto, who had only two, Artemis and Apollo. In revenge for Niobe's offending their mother, Apollo and Artemis slew her children with their poisonous arrows. The bodies lay in their own blood for nine days, because anyone seeing the horror was turned to stone. Niobe fasted and wept these nine days, but her ghastly suffering so disturbed the gods that they turned her into stone as well. Today, so legend says, her form remains visible in a massive rock formation in her Grecian homeland, petrified in mourning, though streams of water continuously fall from her apparently weeping eyes soaking the stone beneath.

Revenge or Forgiveness

After the murder of a child, mothers often have overpowering desires for vengeance, but they also ask themselves how much they should work toward forgiveness or whether it is even right to try to forgive. For those raised in the Christian-Judaic tradition, blood revenge retains much appeal. An outgrowth of tribal times is the law of like, "as a boy for a boy, a man for a man, an eye for an eye and a tooth for a tooth." (Exodus 21: 23–25). In later Hebrew writings and in the New Testament, however, adherents were instructed to foster a spirit of pity and forgiveness in their hearts. To forgive, according to Jesus, is to be Godlike. These colliding archetypal messages of reparation or forgiveness can painfully divide a mother's emotional response to a child's murderer.

It is important to understand, however, that forgiveness implies neither forgetting the trauma nor remembering it with the original intensity. Our closely clutched grudges hold us yoked to hostility and inner turmoil. Consequently, as forgiving proceeds, one's emotions can become less tied up in the crime and one has more energy to give elsewhere. In fact, to live our lives fully, we must forgive others again and again. *The Merchant of Venice* describes how forgiveness delivers liberation.

> The quality of mercy is not strained
> It droppeth as the gentle rain from heaven
> Upon the place beneath. It is twice blessed;
> It blesseth him that gives and him that takes.

But in actual practice, whether a mother's forgiving a murderer enables her to let go and move on with her life is a complex issue. For one thing, prisons are filled with eager forgiveness-seekers, but these same people often don't know themselves well, nor what deeds they may be moved to do in the future. Have they fully plumbed the roots of their old desires to hurt others? Other criminals remain so hardened they won't even seek forgiveness.

Mothers must also be aware that their conceding premature forgiveness can be pathological, a way of avoiding essential knowledge about our naturally human darker impulses. At a minimum, mothers must first feel their hurt and anger, and then they must become aware of their own vengeful fantasies, before they can conjure up enough real love to forgive. Emanating from their unconscious shadow, their own murderous feelings must be made conscious if they are to act with inner freedom. In the end, mothers may come to understand that a little revenge was good for the soul, allowing her to move to an active state, free from overwhelming feelings of powerlessness.

Some mothers, however, decide they will never forgive the murderer. In *The Brothers Karamazov*, Doestoevsky makes a poignant argument for this position in Ivan's speech to his brother Alyosha. Unable to accept church doctrine justifying our suffering as atonement for the sins of our forefathers, Ivan argues that nothing explains why little children sometimes suffer.

> I meant to speak of the suffering of mankind generally, but we had better confine ourselves to the sufferings of the children ... in the first place, children can be loved even at close quarters, even when they are dirty, even when they are ugly.... The second reason why I won't speak of grown-up people is that besides being disgusting and unworthy of love, they have a compensation—they've eaten the apple and know good and evil, and they become "like god." They go on eating it still. But the children haven't eaten anything, and are so far innocent.... If they, too, suffer horribly on earth, they must suffer for their fathers' sins, they must be punished for their fathers, who have eaten the apple; but that reasoning is of the other world and is incomprehensible for the heart of man here on earth.[2]

Like Ivan, a mother may feel the crime of child murder is beyond her human capacities to forgive, not merely the murderer but God himself, or life in general. Some argue that mothers don't even have the *right* to forgive their child's killer, believing that only the murdered child and God have it. Others talk of forgiving a little at a time, but perhaps what they really mean is that the intense emotions of hate and revenge diminish as the years go on. Debates about forgiveness dominate the Internet chat rooms at the Parents of Murdered Children web-site. Here are some of their different views:

> Forgiving was the most healing thing I did in my life. It's a choice, not something you have to do. I struggled for years healing my heart. I decided to let go of the anger a little at a time. As the anger was leaving, I began feeling a light heart when I thought of him. I didn't know what forgiveness was going to FEEL like. I felt a warmth in my heart for him. My husband went to the prison, too, and he said it was like a truck load of pain that left his heart.
>
> Betty

> Maybe it's the antidepressants I'm on but the intense hate is gone. Still, I don't feel as if I've forgiven the murderer. I just don't want to pass on hate.
>
> CE

> When I went to tell the killer that I was no longer mad at him, he was shocked. He doesn't understand forgiveness.
>
> Betty

> Doesn't there have to be some sort of remorse before there can be forgiveness? Can't you tell the difference between INMATE MANIPULATION and remorse?
>
> June

> The murderer of my daughter is in prison for life without parole. If he had been given the death penalty, I could have thrown the switch without one feeling of remorse. We need to forgive ourselves, not the murderer.
>
> Connie

> All my children have learned to forgive and I was their teacher. My youngest daughter has been to see the murderer; she had questions to ask him. We have all learned to open our hearts to everyone.
>
> Betty

There are so many better things you could do than talk to kill-ers. Go visit sick children in a hospital. Your preaching about how you love the killer just turns me off.

Joy

Isn't what you are doing more like "pearls before swine" than forgiveness?

June

FORGIVENESS is a long word. Some people may not be able to get past the letter V. Others may get to that last S and not get past it. Some may get all the way through the word and be able to forgive. But no matter how far you get, it is OK NOT TO FORGIVE.

Carol

These mothers' reflections suggest the hard complexities entangling issues of revenge and forgiveness. Even if we believe with Rheba that it is okay not to forgive, we should probably still understand that it is better to slowly let go of vengeful hate, releasing ourselves from nega-tive bonds that hinder our living fruitfully.

NOTES:

1. R. W. Crump, ed., *The Complete Poems of Christina Rossetti,* Baton Rouge, 1987, vol. I, pp. 156–57.
2. Fydor Dostoyevsky, *The Brothers Karamazov,* Random House, New York, 1950, pp. 282–83.

Chapter Nine

SUICIDE AND MENTAL ILLNESS

SUICIDE

(Perhaps because he
did not know his
geometry)

At ten one morning
the youth forgot.

His heart was growing full
of broken wings and artifical flowers.

He noted in his mouth
but one small word was left.

When he removed his gloves, a fine
thin ash fell from his hands ...

— FEDERICO GARCIA LORCA

Shock and Never Knowing Why

Marilyn returned home from a school meeting to find her son lying on the den floor, covered in blood, his pistol beside him. Sobbing, she threw herself down to rock him in her arms and repeatedly screamed, "Roger, Roger! What happened? Oh my God,

Roger. No! NO! WHAT HAPPENED?" Still in a state of shock a few minutes later, she managed to pick herself up and dial 911. After the police arrived, they photographed the scene, then questioned and fingerprinted her (a routine procedure inevitably enraging a mother suffering the extraordinary misfortune of finding her child dead). Then the coroner's "technicians" came and put the boy in a black plastic container, looking to Marilyn like a long zippered garbage-bag. She became hysterical at the way they were treating his body. Given no further word by the police until after the autopsy, she then stiffly received their bureaucratic judgment that Roger's death was suicide.

A sixteen-year-old sophomore, Roger served on the student council, played both varsity football and basketball, and had always been an idealist, wanting "to rid the world of poverty, pollution, and war." Marilyn describes his suicide as "the classic 16-year-old perfectionist from a divorced family who broke up with his girlfriend and killed himself in a moment of insanity." But this explanation doesn't prevent her being haunted by the questions: "Why didn't he leave a note? Why didn't he die in bed like most suicides? Why had he only one bullet and that in the least lethal gun of his collection?" Just inside her, a doubt that his death might have been an accident still lingers. And even in those moments when she acknowledges his death to be a suicide, she still torments herself with the question: "Why did he take his own life?"

Like other suicides' mothers, Marilyn has poured over the past, looking for missed signs, weighing each clue that could possibly have saved Roger's life. His parents had recently divorced and Roger took his girlfriend's rejection hard, but he hadn't appeared chronically depressed. Nor was he an aggressive youngster prone to violent outbreaks; he didn't use drugs or alcohol, had lots of friends at school, and seemed no more impulsive than many teenage boys. Marilyn still finds it impossible to understand his dark, hopeless outlook the night he died. Fully six years after the suicide, she feels a familiar surge of rage whenever she thinks of his unlived life, while in the same moments guilt nags just above the edge of consciousness, plaguing her because she is still so angry with him.

Archetypal Underpinnings:
From Participation Mystique to The First Suicides

What mother would ever dream, as she rocked her newborn baby, that the infant she loved and nurtured would one day kill himself? As we have seen, in their earliest months, babies bond so infinitely with their mothers that two become one. Their *participation mystique* resembles earliest humans' feeling at one with nature and the mother goddess, lacking understanding of separateness. Surrendering themselves to the great cycles of sun, moon, and seasons, the vegetable death and rebirth around them, the universal round, they embraced the Great Mother's power, though doomed to die, hoping that, like nature, they would be reborn. Only gradually developing greater self-awareness could our ancestors act independently of the Great Mother and nature. Eventually their increasing independence gave them many gifts, including the fearful ability to choose between life and dying.

Writing nearly five thousand years ago, Enheduanna, a Sumerian moon priestess and the first woman poet in history whose name has been preserved, protests her misfortune and despair to Nanna, the Sumerian moon god, and considers suicide her destiny. In her poem which has been titled "Condemning the Moongod Nanna," she is still not free in our modern sense, however, for she attributes her will to die to Nanna, not herself.

> As for me, Nanna ignores me.
> He has taken me to destruction,
> to the alleys of murder.
> Ashimbabbar has not judged me wrong.
> If he had, what do I care?
> If he had, what do I care!
> I am Enheduanna.
> I was triumphant, glorious,
> but he drove me from my sanctuary.
> He made me escape like a swallow
> from the window.
> My life is in flames.
> He made me walk through the brambles
> on the mountain.
> He stripped me of the crown correct

for a high priestess.
He gave me a dagger and a sword,
and said:
"Turn them against your own body.
They are made for you."[1]

Attitudes about Suicide

We can not know when a prehistoric human first felt the need
to die by her own hands and what circumstances could have caused
her to do so. Though attitudes have varied through time and cultures, suicide has always held an important place in philosophy, law,
and religion. In ancient Greece, Socrates drank hemlock rather than
renounce his teachings and beliefs. Ancient Hebrews justified suicide
as a defense against the greater sins of idolatry and murder. But a
contrary view has also existed, one fed by an impulse to punish the
suicide for a seemingly inexplicable act. For example, in his *Inferno*,
Dante condemned suicide sinners to the seventh lowest circle of hell.
He transformed those who took their own life into bleeding trees,
their souls eternally eaten by Harpies, mythological figures with con-
torted female faces and necks and the feet and breasts of rapacious
birds. For many hundreds of years, Jews forbade funeral orations for
those who died by their own hand, and the Catholic church excom-
municated them. Martin Luther, also refusing them burial in holy
ground, thought suicide a sin; and Puritans were known to desecrate
the bodies of suicides. Only recently have attitudes toward suicide
again become more tolerant, placing emphasis on prevention rather
than condemnation.

But in his controversial book *Suicide and the Soul,* James Hillman goes
farther toward a positive view, bringing even suicide prevention into
question. Like Ecclesiastics, Hillman recognizes that "there is a time
to die," but he asks whether we need always wait for an outside force
to effect death. Should we not also listen to the Soul, our God within,
and follow its own dictate? Hillman believes that the act of suicide
often arises from an individual soul's evolution.

The effect of the death experience is to bring home at a critical
moment a radical transformation.[2]

He is only the last of many writers to defend a person's right to take his own life. In the early 17th century, the metaphysical poet John Donne, questioned the sinfulness of suicide by recalling that Christ gave himself voluntarily to death: "No man taketh it from me, but I lay it down myself." (John 10:18). In the eighteenth century, David Hume suggested that, under certain circumstances, suicide could be a duty toward ourselves. And in 1946, Jung wrote Eleanor Bertine that suicide can be in harmony with the unconscious of the person committing it, a step in a person's authentic psychological unfolding. At such a point, to prevent it would be wrong.

Illness or Senseless Choice

Mothers who have watched their adolescent children's first struggle too long with drugs, alcohol, or severe mental illness may sometimes agree. Less haunted by the unanswerable question *why* the child died, they seldom feel the suicide was directed against them. Often these mothers have tried desperately to make a meaningful connection with a mentally ill child, one suffering from a brain disorder such as manic-depressive (bipolar) illness or schizophrenia. In the process, they learned to look beyond obviously damaged personalities and to intuitively know aspects of their children that transcended sickness. Being aware that their children's essential humanity and spirit was trapped in seemingly inescapable illness, these mothers have reconciled themselves to suicide as a legitimate escape from suffering by those with little chance for a healthy, fulfilled life.

On the other hand, to those mothers whose children took their lives in impulsive moments of distress, any notion that suicide saves the soul and should not be prevented seems obscene. According to the Surgeon General, an adolescent American completes suicide every two hours.[3] Many of these adolescents could have probably led long, productive lives, if only someone had caught the danger signs in time and acted effectively, providing love, understanding, and therapy. Drugs or alcohol abusers may have been self-medicating wounds that might eventually have spontaneously healed on their own. Those who felt agonizing social isolation may have only needed help developing skills to make friends and become involved with life. Those suffering the death of a loved one, a family divorce, or a breakup with a girlfriend, were crying for help to overcome their grief. Most teenagers' reasons for killing themselves derive from commonplace pains of adolescent life, that probably would have lessened with time. In certain instances, one even wonders if a sort of melodramatic play-acting was involved, a gesture arising from their suspending awareness of death's finality. Research discovers that more than half of suicide attempts (including adults) are preceded by fewer than five minutes of premeditation. Even when suicides have formulated a plan beforehand, their ultimate decision to act is often a momentary impulse.

Kimberly, for example, was a spunky, attractive youngster who usually appeared smilingly happy, had supportive parents, good grades, many friends, and even a new beau. In short, she seemed to have every reason to live. Her mother May has rehearsed their final conversation "a million times," searching for clues as to why Kimberly would take her life: "Why didn't I see this coming? What kind of mother am I? What could I have done? I thought she had the whole world in store for her." But in the end, May proved unable to reassemble her suicidal child's psychological world. After many years, she gave up her somber questioning, accepting that she would never know precisely *why* her child died.

Because suicide is almost always an irrational choice, we cannot make *sense* of it. Then too, most adolescents, being naturally self-involved, are unlikely to think about the effect suicide will have on their family. Instead, they leave banally reassuring notes, only saying, "I love you, Mom," "Merry Christmas," or "Don't worry about me, Mom." Although a mother struggles with her anger—"Why did she do this to *me?*"—her teenager probably hadn't thought to hurt *her*. When killing themselves, older children often think their chaotic existence causes painful problems to many others so they are no good to anyone. Feeling themselves to be in such a dark situation, they also believe no amount of family love could help.

Guilt, Blame, and Shame from Suicide

Yet many surviving parents insist that more love and concern could have helped their child, and each feels personal guilt and also blames the other. Seven years after her son Tom's suicide, Ruth still struggles with her continuing guilt and blame.

> Even though my husband is now dead, I am still angry with him over our son's suicide. Before he died, we never spoke of it, but my husband knew I blamed him. He was too strict and sometimes physically and verbally abusive. We had a typical Fifties marriage, and I just never said anything. That's why I feel so guilty even today.

Besides carrying guilt and blame, mothers whose children take their own life must also contend with the shame and stigma attached to suicide. Like mothers of AIDS victims, those whose children completed suicide often endure silences from others too embarrassed or horrified even to write a note of condolence. Moreover, ashamed mothers may not seek the help they need, or they may incorrectly feel themselves to be shunned when they unsuccessfully seek support.

Eventually, May became capable of fighting shame and stigma. After shooting herself, May's daughter survived for ten hours at the hospital, even though doctors had pronounced her brain-dead upon arrival.

> There's a big stigma against suicide though people don't talk about it. Even at the hospital, the way the nurses and doctors treated us wasn't compassionate. It seemed like they thought this person wanted to die, where other people fought for their life. Afterward, even though I had friends, church, and family to help me, I always thought they were holding something back. So I ran an announcement in the newspaper and started a suicide victim group. I needed, we needed, a grief group designed solely for families of suicides.

Struggling with Mental Illness

Mothers whose children have completed suicide[3] after suffering mental illness frequently need enormous support, particularly if family members have refused to acknowledge the illness before their child's death. For example, even in early childhood, Will had an extreme personality. Being a difficult child to rear, he frequently became depressed, though at other times he was intensely gay and energetic. Whatever his mood, he had trouble with his girlfriend and lots of gambling debts.

Mary believed her son had a manic-depressive illness, but her husband would not even entertain the thought.

Since her son's suicide two years ago, Mary fights to keep her marriage together. Her husband gets angry, even threatens to kill himself, and twice he has left the house to live elsewhere for brief periods. Mary's other two children are upset about their father's excessive emotionality. And Mary is angry, too. She has to work to keep self-control, even as she ponders whether her son could have been saved.

The day Will died, Mary's husband had finally taken him to see a psychiatrist, but the doctor was late, and her husband became disturbed about "all the crazies in the waiting room." So the two left the office without seeing the doctor. That night, in his apartment near his university, Will hanged himself. His sister found him there dead, but she had to wait until her parents arrived: she was afraid to let him down.

Because psychopathology is the most common element found in suicide, parents must be aware of danger signs indicating childhood mental illness. Just as parents look for physical symptoms (colds, fever, and so forth), they need to check on the mental health of their child. Serious mental illnesses such as manic-depression and schizophrenia characteristically strike in the late teens or early twenties. Patients suffer hopelessness, agitation, paranoia, and shame. In remission, they dread their psychosis will return. When becoming aware of the damage, they often see no other way out.

> The awareness of the damage done by severe mental illness—to the individual himself and to others—and fears that it may return again play a decisive role in many suicides. Those patients with schizophrenia who are more intelligent and better educated, for example, who perform better on measures of abstract reasoning, and who demonstrate greater insight into the nature of their illness, are more likely to kill themselves. Patients who do well socially and academically when young and who then are hit by devastating illnesses such as schizophrenia or manic-depression seem particularly vulnerable to the specter of their own mental disintegration and the terror of becoming a chronic patient. For them and many others there is a terrible loss of dreams and inescapable damage to friends, family, and self.[4]

Studies of schizophrenia and manic-depressive illness consistently show they run in families, and researchers hope to locate the specific genes predisposing individuals for these disorders. When suicide runs in a family, mothers fear their children and grandchildren are at risk. Sometimes a mother will endure more family suicides than one.

When Polly was a young woman with three small children, her husband, a successful physician and creative painter, was diagnosed with manic-depression. Under medication, he lived a productive life, although he was troubled by severe mood swings, being sometimes slightly manic, but more often deeply depressed. One long depression eventually led him to put a gun to his head. Ten years later, Polly's 16-year-old son killed himself on his father's birthday. Polly now worries about her two surviving daughters and her grandchildren. The mood swings of her daughter, Marci, a talented writer who graduated from a prestigious Ivy League college, alienated friends, causing her to lose most of her support system. Periodically isolating herself, she then refuses to speak to her mother. On the other hand, Polly enjoys a close relationship with her second daughter Del and her two grandsons. The tragedies created by severe family mental illness have deepened Polly's insight and compassion not only in her life but in her clinical social work practice. In addition, she is an active member of the National Association for the Mentally Ill and participates in its "Journey of Hope" program for families having a loved one with mental illness.

Polly shared a particularly touching story in *NAMI Advocate,* written by a mother who lost two children to manic-depression.

> Love conquers all. Naively, I believed this for many years, but it is simply not so. I am a mother. I raised four children, two of whom did not live long enough to make sense of their world. These two children both developed bipolar disorder, and, try as I might, I could not help them through the clouds that descended.
>
> My daughter first showed signs of illness at fourteen. My son had finished college and was working when he descended into depression. His illness only seemed lighter because before becoming ill he had, for a time, functioned longer. He had also tried to protect me from his troubles, realizing I had his sister to worry about.

If ever there were a clear example of powerlessness, it would be trying to fix the mental illness of a loved one. What sustained me throughout nineteen years of illness with one child, and ten with the other, was simple hope: hope in God's help, hope that somehow things would turn around, hope that research would find answers to grant a measure of peace to these wonderful young people. Many times I pleaded with God to give this illness to me and take it away from my children. I would take all the pain, if only he would release them.[5]

Some mothers fight with their mentally ill child's problems for years, bearing the brunt of his sadness, anger, paranoia, and occasional violence. The rest of us need to acknowledge the normality of some mothers feeling relief, both for themselves and the child, when suicide occurs.

As I have already sketched, my own struggles as the grieving mother of a mentally ill child led me in many directions, some of which I have indicated. I kept very busy, moved abroad, discovered the power of Jungian insights, began training in Jungian psychoanalysis, and organized a doctoral research program on mother grief. I joined with many other mothers, and I examined the usefulness of many psychological approaches and techniques. What follows in the Chapters of Part Two is my distillation of all such experiences: Aids to the Mourning Process.

NOTES:

1. Aliki Barnstone & Willis Barnstone, *Book of Women Poets: From Antiquity to Now*, New York, 1992.
2. James Hillman, *Suicide and the Soul*, Dallas, 1965, p. 76.
3. Mental health professionals prefer "completed suicide" to "committed," because the latter usage implies a criminal act.
4. Kay Redfield Jamison, *Night Falls Fast: Understanding Suicide*, New York, 1999, p. 84.
5. Patricia Forbes, "Survival: A Mother's Story," *NAMI Advocate*, Arlington, VA, fall 2002, pp. 42–43.

PART TWO:
AIDS TO THE
MOURNING PROCESS

Chapter Ten

CLEANSING SHADOW ELEMENTS

In a dark time, the eye begins to see,
I meet my shadow in the deepening shade.
— THEODORE ROETHKE

THREE YEARS AFTER my son died, I still felt miserable. When a Jungian analyst first suggested, "Your difficulties might be due to your acting from the shadow side of your personality," I rejected the idea as completely false. Throughout these years of turmoil, had I not lived by my secret motto of uprightness: "act responsibly"? Not only had I worked long hours in my psychotherapy practice, I had also become an advocate for the mentally ill. But no matter how much I tried to give, the words "no good" daily intruded in my thoughts. Intense feelings of anger and shame filled the emptiness of my shattered belief system. Gradually, however, I began to acknowledge that even selfless and charitable behavior alone would not heal me. In time, I came to agree with my analyst: I was experiencing "loss of soul," and I needed to probe my most shadowy places in order to find it.

Within the collective unconscious shared by all humans C. G. Jung discovered The Shadow, manifesting itself individually in elements of our personality each of us doesn't recognize, The Shadow develops naturally in childhood. As we identify our conscious being with personality characteristics our parents believe "good" or "ideal," we unconsciously bury those other aspects of ourselves that fail to meet our positive self-images. Consequently, our very ego, the bright sun we depend on for encountering the outside world, casts an unconscious shadow, behind us, onto other parts of our personality. This fundamental polarity of light and dark, or consciousness and shadow, derives ancient authority from Taoism's Yin and Yang, representations of the two basic forces in creation. Neither value is absolute or superior. Moreover, just as we have seen that other archetypes have positive and negative poles, so even our shadow, filled though it seems with only unpleasant and immoral aspects of ourselves also contains useful energies and understandings. To take an opposite example, if being responsible has merit, then, at certain moments, being irresponsible does also. In Eric Neumann's words, a person willing to meet his shadow, "must find the moral courage not to want to be worse or better than one actually is."[1]

Through work with my Jungian analyst, I slowly learned how unbalanced my personality had become. By overvaluing my work ethic, I unconsciously contributed to the rage I felt inside. In addition, my motive to help others was not all good: part of its roots lay in feeling inadequate for not being able to help my son. To take another example, my righteous outrage at the lack of proper services for the mentally ill was partly inflamed by intense anger toward my family that had not helped my brother nor given needed support. I realized I had to separate out these motives if I were to find even a small inner peace.

Examining our conflicting emotions about a child's death points us to genuine moral tasks: discovering self-deceptions, untangling rationalizations of destructive behaviors, and making corrective change. But shadow work also entails learning to love ourselves by accepting our inferior parts, striving for wholeness rather than perfection. As in all other aspects of life, the path to healing lies in love and compassion, in this case love and compassion for oneself.

TYPICAL SHADOW FEELINGS:
ANGER, GUILT, SHAME, ENTITLEMENT

Anger and Coming to Spirituality

Grieving mothers struggle with anger on many fronts. For example, we may be angry at God for having taken our child. By admitting that we have such anger, we take first steps toward a new relationship with a Higher Power. Eventually, we can learn to find God in places we have had the most reluctance to explore. Descent into our personal underworld is part of soul work. It can begin spontaneously after our loss of innocence, but we discover later that it is essential before we become authentically spiritual. Mothers attempting spirituality without having worked out their negativities can indeed jump from one peak experience to another, but eventually they will fly too high like Icarus, who reaches the hot sun itself, thereby melting his waxen wings and falling into the cold sea.

After her daughter was murdered, Lucinda wanted to help other parents whose children died violently. She asked the local newspaper to feature an article about her daughter's life and to publicize her newly formed Parents of Murdered Children's Support Group. Although many couples attended the group at first, few of them continued. Lucinda presented herself as one who had found all the answers. Through her work with a minister, she had completely forgiven her daughter's murderer, and now she was ready to lead others to the same level of goodness. Her hostility was evident to others but not to herself, and her group failed.

As we have noticed earlier, anger is a natural and healthy response to loss. When her child dies, a mother feels desperate to find some reason for the tragedy. Not only does she cry out to her God, she may also rage against doctors, hospital staff, or police. She becomes caught in the anger of hopelessness. During early weeks of acute grief, she can easily displace her wrath onto anyone who crosses her path. However noxious to others, this aspect of grief reaction needs to be understood as a perennial expression of the human spirit.

In the beginning when grief and shock are raw, feel free to express your anger in any ways not destructive to yourself or others. Squelching feelings is more dangerous than ventilating, but prolonging catharsis serves little purpose. Negative patterns of blame and rage against unfair treatment can become self-perpetuating cycles of misery. As long as a woman identifies herself as someone wronged and helpless, she will be the victim of her own wrath. Natasha was still angry with God even after her second son Ben was born and tried to console herself by vowing never to forget Sophia, yet she also senses that sooner or later her attitude toward God has to change.

> I remain very confused about religion. I am furious when people want to explain Sophia's death by saying it was "God's plan." I know I should feel a sense of gratitude toward God, but I feel he still owes me. Having my son Ben doesn't make up for what we went through.

Unlike Natasha, who is aware of her anger, some women do not recognize it in themselves. They suffer from a common social prohibition against having or showing it. Unfortunately stifled rage can become veiled in all the addictions: alcohol, drugs, overeating, overspending, gambling, and sex. Intense anger can also hide behind stringent work ethics, busyness, or pride in being strong, and silently enduring a noble martyrdom. Such denials curtail our spontaneity, even destroying enthusiasm for life. Wrath denied can also move through the body in headaches, anxiety attacks, colitis, and fibromialga. Suppressing our immune systems, pent up rage may lead to even more serious diseases.

A woman who has difficulty recognizing her anger may dispel it by preaching, advice-giving, sarcasm, blaming, bitterness, or other unpleasantness. Another may turn her anger inward, feeling "hurt." Suffering in silence and feeling powerless, she becomes tearful and "hurt" at real or imagined slights. Though she may be someone genuinely slow to anger—patient, generous, and selfless—she must learn to show authentic anger when it is due.

Mary typifies the person not yet able to move from stifled darkness toward acknowledging and expressing her shadow anger. Though two years have passed since her son's death, she focuses on keeping her marriage together. Her husband's outbursts of rage sometimes reach the point of his threatening to put a gun to his head. Because of his intensely expressed emotions and erratic behaviors, Mary works particularly hard at keeping control.

You have to be in control of yourself and not let the situation control you. I feel like I have done this. It doesn't take away the pain, but there is a difference. You control what you can control.

In addition to saving her marriage, Mary feels she has to remain strong in order to help her aging mother, calm her daughter's rage at her father, and save her marriage. But her need to be in control has taken its toll on her body. Though she keeps up an attractive appearance, exercising to maintain a youthful shape, she suffers from a variety of physical ills: lower back pain, cold sores, diarrhea, and heart palpitations.

Fear of one's own anger can also create emotional distancing. Rather than disturbing a friendship, one mother moves into silent submission; another is so frightened by the enormity of her rage that she severs a relationship. Unhappily, such tactics lead to further disconnection as well as loss of self esteem. Mary says:

There are incidents that occurred because of my son's death. A couple of real close friends are no longer friends. It is because they weren't patient enough to see us through this bad time. It would never have happened if they had tried to understand what we were going through. I am just too angry to tell them all that I feel about those times. So we just don't see them anymore.

Unfortunately, these "cut offs" also occur with close family members: almost every mourning mother has felt betrayed by someone, often a family member. When a parent or sibling is unsupportive, anger arising from betrayal is sometimes too great to be contained, and mothers must decide about keeping that relationship or letting it go.

Pat said her family "blamed me for everything regarding my son's death," and continued to maintain that she "had probably been the reason he became a homosexual in the first place." To make things worse, her sister became furious when Pat would not conceal the cause of his death. "Why do I need to be around people like that?" Pat asked herself, and cut off all family ties for two years. But when her father became terminally ill, she and her sister were forced to renew their relationship while they cared for their aging parents. Now Pat has been practicing how to be with all her family and at the same time how to protect herself from their criticism. "I just tell them who I am, without getting into the drama," she says. "They can take it or leave it." Even so, Pat admits that having some family ties is better than being without them. "I'll never trust them as once I did," she admits, " but I wouldn't want my father to die without our reconciling."

It is important to warn those who have run away from anger that correcting the situation through sudden confrontations seldom succeeds, for it leaves others baffled and defensive. If you are also carrying a lot of residual rage from childhood events, expressing it may plunge you back into the whole complex of your enduring family drama. Too often therapists make the mistake of encouraging confrontation without warning of possible consequences. Danielle says:

> Rageful feelings had emerged after Johnny died. My therapist told me to let my father know just how angry I was with him for so many old hurts. So I wrote him a letter and let him have it, told him how I had felt all those years when he was drinking. Now neither of my parents want much to do with me. I feel as if I've lost my mother. She's loyal to us both and can't understand why I would sound off like that to my father.

The therapist could have suggested more constructive ways for Danielle to work through anger toward her father. As we will see in following chapters, energy generated by rage can be funneled into useful projects and creative acts. But, more importantly, Danielle could have also worked through her anger by attending to her inner life, the way another mother, Hanna, did.

> My son Buddy was killed working on an oil rig in the Gulf. I felt as if I'd never learn the true story of how he died. I was so angry, more angry I guess because his father was so passive about it. But slowly with the help of my therapist I began to realize that life has lots of tragedies and I can't rail against an unfair world for the rest of my life. I began to accept Buddy's death. Nobody escapes pain and mine just happened to be worse than most. But not worse than what some mothers across the world endure with their children. Or mothers in the Ghettos. I know now that life is hard, but I'm not angry about it. Once you're not so self-involved, you can't be angry about it.

A bereaved mother who previously expressed anger freely and vociferously, may need to differentiate among present rageful feelings, examining how childhood issues have shaped and continue to shape her reactions. After my son's death, I recognized how this undifferentiated anger from the past amplified my grief anger, putting unfair stress on my spouse. When I began studying my own anger patterns, I realized how much derived from my stepbrother's death and my perception that he had been mistreated and coldly forgotten. Then I began to see how this anger, repressed when I was a child, had regularly exploded into my everyday life, even intruding into my marriage to a man who himself is slow to anger.

When rage escalates between husband and wife, it is often a defense against the sadness both feel.

> My husband and I separated two years after Amelia's death. He said I was only interested in keeping the house clean. When we came home from work, all I talked about was laundry, when he would cut the grass, and when he would pay the bills. He said I sat in front of the TV until too late at night, that I should have come to bed with him at a reasonable hour.
>
> Lilly

> As long as we are fighting with each other these ways we don't cry. I know I pick on him for little things.
>
> Rheba

Directing his advice to men who have lost their capacity to feel, psychologist and poet Robert Bly warns, "If we don't weep, we make war."

In my own life, I have repeatedly experienced the wisdom in Bly's observation. As I became able to feel the deep sadness protected beneath my armoring rage, I gradually let go of anger. Acceptance of things as they are replaced outrage. I learned to hold sadness: in fact, I feel grounded when this true emotion is experienced. Being in touch with my sadness enabled me to be compassionate toward others. Now it also gives me freedom to feel joy, an emotion my anger had blocked. Now I can be spontaneous, laugh a lot, and I don't have to worry about outbursts.

Guilt

Most mothers feel guilt about their child's death, both from acts or failures to act. But mothers may not accurately evaluate their degree of responsibility. Once again, to get at the truth, grieving mothers need to examine and then differentiate their feelings. They may be lumping together all their negative emotions—childhood anxiety, for instance—and calling them all guilt.

Lucy's obsessions of culpability are a good example. She repeatedly told me she "did a lot of wrong things" in rearing her son and "failed to do other things" she should have. But when we started sorting out the supposed commissions and omissions, Lucy began to understand that much of her feeling guilty derived from not having pleased her own mother, either as child or adult. Rather than follow the strict narrow ways of her parents, Lucy had created a more relaxed style in her home. Examining the facts, we saw that freedoms she allowed her son had nothing to do with his dying, but they did violate mother's old rules. By differentiating among her feelings, Lucy gained clearer understanding of her own adult values but shed the false sense of guilt unconsciously created from childhood experiences.

Like Lucy, we can learn to distinguish neurotic guilt from the real guilt resulting from our doing moral wrongs. Such genuine guilt exists. It arises from authentic moral wrong as neglect, abuse, deliberate malice, irresponsibility, and so on. We may not have intended to do a wrong, but just as in our legal system, ignorance of the law is no excuse, our "not knowing" erases none of the sins we may have committed against a child.

If we have really done wrong, accepting our misdeeds is a crucial step in healing. Becoming genuinely contrite, we should also confess our legitimate guilt to a clergyman, therapist or loved one. Keeping secrets constitutes not "privacy," rather alienation from our own and society's humanity. Although the past cannot be undone, a new attitude, a greater awareness, and an active service to others can serve as recompense. In the end, such acts of contrition, repentance, and restitution relieve us from the debilitating burden of genuine guilt.

Though ambivalent feelings did not cause their child's death, mothers who remember a relationship filled with discord and antagonism have the hardest time with guilty feelings. They may be angry with the deceased child long after the funeral, particularly if death resulted from the child's gross negligence or suicide. Because they feel guilty about being angry, a self-perpetuating cycle of anger and guilt may block any possible progress through the grieving process.

Struggling with such ambivalent feelings eight years after her daughter Emily's death, Nancy still feels angry and guilty. Though Emily invited her to live next door after her parents' divorce, mother and daughter were frequently at odds, partly because years of dysfunction and alcoholism had poisoned their broken family. Constant arguments about Emily's health ensued. She complained of "low energy," but her mother called it "laziness," and "emotional." Emily refused to go to a doctor, using the excuse that she had no medical insurance. Finally, when her daughter seemed weaker than usual, Nancy arranged Emily's medical appointments, took vacation days, and accompanied her daughter to examinations. A week after she was diagnosed, Emily died of a tumor on her heart.

> If only I had gotten her to a doctor sooner, she may have been saved. I know it was my own anger with Emily that kept me from finding a way to convince her. She just looked so beautiful, as that. [Nancy points to a large portrait of Emily hanging over the mantle.] I said terrible things—that she only wanted attention and when she refused to help with the laundry, I called her lazy. I guess I feel guilty and angry about my whole life with her, so different from what my parents gave to me.

Such a mother's task is to make peace with her dead child, a job which may take years to complete. By developing a dialogue wherein she works through conflicts in the relationship, she can deal with many of the same issues that would have challenged her if her child were living. Matilda dialogues about her son's suicide through writing letters she can never send.

> Dear Reed,
> I am so angry with you because of the pain I feel. There is nothing I can compare it with. I miss you so much. I can not believe it has been almost six years. I baby-sat tonight, and I remembered how many times I rocked you. What happened to that innocence? I cry out angrily, "Why did you do this to me?"

Then I wonder if it really was suicide, and I feel guilty about my anger. I know I am one of millions of people who have lost a child, and yet I still sometimes feel that no one knows my pain. I am having a hard time tonight separating whether your death was an accident or on purpose.

Mom

The tone of this letter clearly suggests Matilda's relationship with Reed remains conflicted. She needs to examine past occurrences, one by one: what occurred, why, and what can be done about it now. Confusedly wondering why Reed still causes her so much pain, she forgets her son's anguish when he died, yet feels guilty about her anger toward him. She doesn't mention, much less question, her part in the relationship. Because she is still angry, knowing she is not alone in her suffering brings more guilty feelings than comfort. When she finds out what the tragedy requires of *her* and how she may actually be culpable, questions about suicide or accidental death will lose their importance, enabling her to make peace with herself and her son.

Though grieving, most mothers experience Matilda's shocked loss of innocence about our human existence. But they can condition themselves to look back at their younger days and acknowledge former failings. Perhaps they were not as attentive or as appreciative of their children as they now believe they should have been. Ann Landers quotes a mother's letter to her living daughter confessing missed opportunities.

I suddenly realized how much of your babyhood I had wished away. Being a mother is demanding. It robs you of so many freedoms, and I resented the fact that I had so many added responsibilities. And then I looked down at your soft curls and your trusting eyes. Suddenly I felt so ashamed. My heart almost broke. I hope and pray that when your first child is born you will be wiser and more mature than I was. I hope you will enjoy every phase of your child's growing up and not wish they would hurry and pass so you could be free of the "burdens" of motherhood. Life rushes by all too rapidly, my darling daughter, especially the lovely days and the beautiful times. Be smarter than your mother was. Don't let a single moment slip away unsavored or unappreciated. These days are priceless and afford you the greatest opportunities for fulfillment. Never again will your heart be so full.

Dianne, who lost her son drowning, brought me this column because it expressed some of her own regrets. She recalled how Tad had arrived soon after her marriage. At first she found it difficult to believe she had a baby.

> It was almost too easy. It wasn't planned; it just happened spontaneous. Not that we were sorry.

> My own mother was thirty-four when I was born, and she had much more sense of responsibility to her baby than I did. To coin a phrase, I have "under parented." You see, my husband and I were only children and we had felt overprotected growing up. So we wanted our children to have more freedom, but now I feel so guilty for all I didn't do for Randy—guidance, especially. I hate feeling this guilt.

> You asked *how* do I feel guilty. In many, many ways. I can't ever remembering experiencing the emotion of guilt before Randy's death. *Never. I never remember guilt before the death.* Oh, maybe, when I was little I was guilty about taking a piece of candy. But my parents never made me feel guilty. Nor my teachers. It was a foreign emotion to me, and when Randy died that's all I felt was guilt. Guilt about everything....

> I've been reading Depok Chopra's *Seven Ways to Spiritual Fulfillment,* and he describes *karma* as resulting from choices you've made. So now I'm thinking, what did I do to have all this bad karma? You know truthfully, I can't remember making so many bad choices in my life or doing lots of destructive things to people or anything wicked enough to cause me this "bad karma." And yet I feel guilt. Do you think I did something terrible when I under-parented?

I don't answer her question, but over time Dianne and I examine her past to see what guilt she may rightly bear and what she invents. People invent guilts for many reasons, but Kierkegaard certainly illuminates a common one when he asserts that humans would often rather feel responsible and guilty about a given occurrence than attribute it to Fate. Feeling guilt, he says, implies that we have the possibility of doing something about our condition. Those who fear they have little control of their world may disguise that fear by saying they are "guilty." Mothers who have lost children naturally worry they have no control of their world, inclining toward guilt feelings as a psychological defense against more frightening feelings of helplessness. Reluctant to give Fate her due, these mothers feel guilt over natural phenomena no one can change. Sally's apology to her dead three-year-old is an example.

> The main thing that I told Chip was that I was very sorry because even though I didn't cause his death through negligence, I felt guilt because I didn't give him good genes. I know that doesn't make any sense, since I had no control over it. I never talked to anyone about this.

The myth of Oedipus, familiar from Sophocles' plays, can help a mother determine the degree of responsibility and guilt she may hold regarding her child's death. Though a dense story to summarize, we can all benefit by periodically reviewing its outline. King Laius of Thebes and Queen Jocasta have a baby son, Oedipus. However, the Delphic oracle had once warned Laius that his son would kill his own father and marry his mother. So, after Oedipus' birth Laius has him left to die on Mount Cithaeron. Found by Corinthian shepherds and reared by the King and Queen of Corinth as their own, Oedipus grows up and consults the Delphic oracle, receiving the same prophecy as his father. Blindly supposing that the oracle refers to his foster parents and not wanting to do them harm, Oedipus doesn't return home. Later he encounters a stranger (Laius) on the road, argues with him, and utterly unwittingly kills his natural father. Journeying to Thebes, his solving the riddle of the Sphinx leads to his marrying its widowed Queen Jocasta, his mother. They enjoy a long period of prosperity, but when a plague breaks out, the Delphic oracle declares it will only be lifted by the banishment of Laius' murderer. Oedipus begins a vigorous inquiry. The dreadful truth finally coming to light, Jocasta hangs herself and Oedipus puts out his eyes. Now, accompanied only by his daughter Antigone, he roams the earth finally finding refuge in the Grove of Colonus, sacred to the Furies, those spirits of retribution whom we met earlier torturing Orestes.

But by the time Oedipus arrives, the Furies have reconciled themselves to the superior rule of Athenian law and are more gentle. Taking notice of how Oedipus has punished himself and probed his conscience during the years after his crime, they endorse the peace he has eventually made with himself. Though innocent of any willful murder or incest, he has rightly made expiation for his share of responsibility in those acts by self-blinding and self-exile. Not penitent, for he understood that Fate had dictated his life path, by differentiating guilt from responsibility, he could find peace in his old age and die with dignity.

Though people rarely meet Oedipus' dire fate, when we have courage to search inwardly, we can all recognize the blindness with which we have lived certain events. Then, facing those turns of Fate which forever remain beyond our understanding, we, like Oedipus, can at last find redemption and release. With wiser eyes, for example, Dianne now appreciates the precious gifts of life she once took for granted as a young mother. Sally can regret her genes or other personal imperfections, but she need not feel *guilt* over what she could not control.

Shame

When experiencing shame, we suddenly feel outside of ourselves becoming paralyzed by self-consciousness. Because shame is accompanied by powerful emotions that activate the endocrine system, most of us avoid any person or situation that might shame us, often resulting in our becoming more isolated. If we spend too much time alone, we may be overwhelmed by negative or even paranoid thoughts and, as with anger or guilt, alienate ourselves from caring people.

While guilt feelings usually claim grieving individuals, shame may affect many others around them, even an entire community. As we have seen, it particularly infects others when AIDS, drug overdose, suicide or murder cause death. Along with their collective outrage at the Columbine High School shootings, for example, local citizens felt shame that such violence could happen in their Colorado suburb, though discomfort could not be attributed to any particular acts by those who felt it.

Unfortunately, today's society offers few rituals or other customs to alleviate shame about our healthy and appropriate grief. In Jewish tradition, on the other hand, a person who had contact with a corpse and thereby became *tamai*, impure, could undergo elaborate cleansing rituals. Today some Jews carry on this tradition by washing their hands after leaving a burial. As we saw earlier, because death seems to be a taboo in Western society, no matter what the cause, even a few weeks after a funeral, the mourner can be an embarrassment to others who are eager to deny death's reality. Subsequently, she herself feels embarrassed and ashamed.

Though one may experience shameful feelings alone, they always involve implied perception of some "other," either another person, a group, an inner voice, or God—someone who is judging you. Because shame can interfere with mourning, we should deal with it. Borrowing from Jewish tradition, for example, we can wash it away. Begin such a cleansing process by identifying incidents that embarrass you or secrets you have been unable to share with anyone else. Look especially at any feelings of shame arising since your child's death. Try preparing a bath, which you fill with ritual power by adding herbs and oils.

Because others who you may feel are blaming you, are often evading their own shameful feelings by projecting them onto you, try educating them. Rather than embracing their negative view, teach them about the grieving process itself or about the cause of your child's death. As I've said, when my half-brother committed suicide from mental illness, my family felt so shamed that no one ever discussed him or his death. To the contrary, when my son, inheritor of the same genes, fell victim to schizophrenia, I alleviated my own shameful feelings by informing people about the disease.

When a child dies, a mother may also feel that God has singled her out for humbling. She stands helpless and defenseless before His eyes, inscrutably chosen to endure great suffering. Burdened with archetypal shame, she feels disgraced by God Himself, like Adam and Eve in the creation story, naked without any place to hide.

> And the eyes of them were both opened, and they knew that they were naked:
>
> And they heard the voice of the Lord God walking in the garden in the cool of the day: and Adam and his wife hid themselves from the presence of the Lord God amongst the trees of the garden.
>
> And the Lord God called unto Adam, and said unto him, Where art thou?
>
> And he said, I heard thy voice…and I was afraid because I was naked; and I hid myself. (Genesis 3: 7–11)

The story reminds us that though we pridefully try to conceal ourselves, we cannot escape being vulnerable. Archetypal shame can have redemptive effects, for it arises not only from our fears but also from a deeper understanding of what it means to be human. Having eaten from the Tree of Knowledge and lost innocence, we are keenly aware of our limitations. For some mothers, this realization begins a profound healing process.

Entitlement

Recall your child at eighteen months, happily believing herself the center of the universe.

Continuing to undergird our subconscious sense of self-worth at an archetypal level, such infantile grandiosity is essential to normal human development. Though children must gradually forsake conscious thoughts of invincibility and unrealistic self-importance, becoming aware of their real place in the world, some remnant of the early confidence remains. When too large, however, it can make them become self-absorbed arrogant adults, believing they *deserve* a life free of all discomfort, and thinking themselves entitled to whatever they desire. When events don't go their way, they fill up with rage.

Normally retaining some residual feelings of omnipotence and entitlement, we often want more than our share of life's good things, particularly in our times of loss. When Natasha, for example, decided to have another child immediately after her first baby died, she tried to allay her anxiety during pregnancy by convincing herself she had suffered enough.

> I feel God owes me one and will give me a healthy baby. But whatever God does, He won't have made up for taking Sophia. We didn't deserve that.

Such reactions can bring others to discomfort. In the first year's after Tad's death, Dianne now believes that her sense of entitlement interfered with friendships.

> My feelings weren't tempered. Everything else in my life had to run smoothly because I'd had enough. If anyone was late or canceled our tennis game, I'd blow up.

Looking back, she forgives and laughs at herself, "I guess everyone is entitled to a little entitlement."

In her poem "Black," Kay, too, cuts a little slack. She describes herself dressed in mourning clothes after her son's motorcycle accident, too depressed to follow the parking rules.

Black

Looking back into my black dress years
one morning I am driving to work in the rain
the wiper handle falls off in my hand.
It is black too. We can assume
the sky is, and my jacket, bought
for $5 soon after my son's death
and my stodgy shoes, which, before this,
I wouldn't be caught dead in.
I pull in at a coffee shop;
the only empty space is a blue one,
and I do, for the first time in my life,
I pull in, park, pop up my black umbrella.
The woman walking ahead of me turns:
"You don't look handicapped."
Then I have to stand behind her in line

The stranger adds:

"I'm sorry. But my husband is
handicapped, and I'm touchy about it."
"I don't blame you." I said.
But I was dark and full of evil thoughts.
My son's leg was torn off
when he was killed in his motorcycle.
I should be able to park in a blue space,
Who says the handicap has to be obvious?
Wearing a black dress on a sweltering day
ought to be enough. I'm not trying to look
like a poet, or like I'm from New York.
I'm black on the inside too.
When I slide back
into my car, the black lace from the lingerie
borrowed from a friend slips into view.
Nothing else is mine either.[2]

Though depicting her blackness and evil thoughts in "Black," Kay clearly implies that exaggerated entitlement can separate us from humankind and cause unnecessary pain. A devout Buddhist, she prays for all who suffer and recalls a story of mother grief that can still help move us out of crippling self-involvement and isolation.

> In the time of Buddha, a woman named Kisagotami suffered the death of her only child. Unable to accept it, she ran from person to person, seeking a medicine to restore the girl to life. The Buddha was said to have such a medicine, so Kisagotami went to him, paid homage, and asked, "Can you make a medicine that will restore my child?"
>
> "I know of such a medicine," the Buddha replied. "But in order to make it, I must have certain ingredients."
>
> Relieved, the woman asked, "What ingredients do you require?"
>
> "Bring me a handful of mustard seed," said the Buddha.
>
> The woman promised to procure it for him, but as she was leaving, he added, "I require the mustard seed be taken from a household where no child, spouse, parent, or servant has died."
>
> The woman agreed and began going from house to house in search of the mustard seed. At each house the people agreed to give her the seed, but when she asked them if anyone had died in that household, she could find no home where death had not visited—in one house a daughter, in another a servant, in others a husband or parent had died. Kisagotami was not able to find a home free from the suffering of death. Seeing she was not alone in her grief, the mother let go of her child's lifeless body and returned to the Buddha, who said with great compassion, "You thought that you alone had lost a son; the law of death is that among all living creatures there is no permanence."[3]

Going Beyond Entitlement: The Path of Necessary Suffering

In Western tradition, the story of Jacob's wrestling with the angel can offer perspective on our trials, helping disengage us from the punishing shadow of entitlement. One night when Jacob was alone, a stranger came, and the two wrestled until daybreak. Even when the stranger's touch disjointed his thigh, Jacob prevailed. Then the stranger commanded, "Let me go, for the day breaketh." But Jacob wanted to know the stranger's name, and would not let him go until the stranger blessed him. The stranger withheld his own identify, but he blessed Jacob: "Thy name shall be called no more Jacob but Israel." Jacob, wounded but awestruck, called the place Penial and exclaimed, "I have seen God face to face and my life is preserved." (Genesis 32: 24–31).

The name Jacob, "one who walks crooked," changes to Israel, "God is reliable." The new name confirms Jacob's profound transformation, one he memorializes by renaming the place where it occurred, Penial, "appearance of God."

Jacob's wrestling and travail symbolize the "dark night of the soul," suffering preceding an individual seeker's coming to divine light. Our own wrestling with God often requires dialogue and prayer: working through suffering without succumbing, practically speaking, to either hostility or despair, trusting that our complex personal experience will gradually lead us to some redemptive knowledge of the Divine. After great loss, the unbeliever and the devout can both find help in prayer, for it changes *us* more often than it changes outer circumstances. Also, by asking questions about our plight in prayer, we are more likely to make meaning out of our suffering.

Like Jacob, Job endures a dark night of his soul when so much giving his life meaning is snatched away: riches, family, and health. His anguish is the more profound because he believes he doesn't deserve such misfortune. When three friends come to comfort him, they argue he is being punished for his sins, but Job holds firm to an inner conviction that he is not responsible for his affliction. God restores Job's sense of proportion, reminding him of the difference between our human condition and his.

> Then the Lord answered Job out of the whirlwind, and said,
> Who is this that darkeneth counsel by words without
> knowledge?
> Gird up now thy loins like a man; for I will demand of
> thee, and answer thou me.
> Where wast thou when I laid the foundations of the earth?
> Declare, if thou hast understanding.

Who hath laid the measures thereof, if thou knowest, or who
hath stretched the line upon it?

Whereupon are the foundations thereof fastened or who laid
the cornerstone thereof

When the morning stars sang together, and all the sons of
God shouted for joy?

Or who shut up the sea with doors, when it brake forth, as if
it had issued out of the womb?

When I made the cloud the garment thereof, and thick
darkness, a swaddling band for it,

And brake up for it my decreed place, and set bars and doors,

And said, "Hitherto shalt thou come but no further, and here
shall thy proud waves be stayed."

Hast thou commanded the morning since thy days and
caused the day-spring to know his place

That it might take hold of the ends of the earth, that the
wicked might be shaken out of it?

It is turned as clay to the seal; and they stand as a garment.

And from the wicked their light is withholden, and the high
arm shall be broken. (Job 38: 1–15)

Awed by the questions and convinced of his own ignorance, Job
recognizes God's inscrutable power, and responding to his new understanding, God restores all Job has lost.

As we have already seen, we mourning mothers also interrogate:
"Why did my child have to die? Why did this happen to me?" The easy
consolations of comforting clergymen and well meaning friends are at
best inadequate. Their explanations often elicit indignation, pushing a
mother into deeper despair.

The sad truth remains that painful experiences do not necessarily make sufferers more mature, either morally or intellectually: some
people remain stuck in self-pity; others become selfish, paranoid, bitter,
and cruel.

"Why did this happen to me?" is essentially a personal religious
question. It can only be answered by finding our own meaning in suffering. The woman who instead stays stuck in entitlement, the victim
role, may be unwilling or unable to engage the archetypal quest for
understanding her life purpose.

We must grant again that human suffering necessarily troubles believers in monotheistic religions that view God as omnipotent, omniscient, and all good. If a benevolent God has complete control, then why indeed do suffering and evil exist? Rational explanations either see God's power as limited, or suppose the existence of evil to be only the absence of good, or hold that evil exists to allow humans free choice. Hinduism says that "evil" results from faulty perception, our low level of consciousness making us unable to see everything as a manifestation of God. The Buddhists, on the other hand, maintain that suffering results from attachment and desire.

In his book *When Bad Things Happen to Good People*, Harold Kushner says, "God can't do everything." By thus limiting God's power, we will understand He is not responsible for life's tragedies. Monotheistic critics see this concept as contrary to traditional doctrine: they cannot conceive God hasn't complete control. Accordingly, some believe our sinfulness brings about pain and suffering. Others maintain that if all went well in life, having no need for God, we would not seek Him. Others say that God suffers with us, for He sent His son to a human death.

In the stories of Jacob and Job, however, we find another answer. By undergoing the struggle of wrestling with the angel, Jacob came to see God face to face. Through his travail and questioning, Job, too, was finally able to see God. Both stories show that finding God is an individual and experiential quest, one that changes our psyches in ways beyond rational explanation. To advance the search, we must all shine the bright light of fact upon our feelings of entitlement. None of us is immune to the darker powers erupting from within and without. Each night on our television screen we see how they inflict suffering on others. War, disease, natural disaster, hunger, and violence are massive killers of the world's children. Why did we ever feel we would go through life unharmed? A mother in mourning for her dead child is one sufferer in the human family.

CLEANSING THE BODY

Traumatic experiences of child death and its consequent emotions affect the body. Many grieving mothers develop physical illnesses reflecting uncleansed shadow elements in their psyches. Preparing to cleanse such physically-entailed shadow elements, we should first become aware of the rich body/soul connection characterizing ancient traditions.

Archetypal Motifs in Soul/Body Healing

Jung took to using the word "soul" as the proper equivalent of the Greek word *psyche*. For Jungian analysts soul describes the vast range of human phenomena that one can call psychic. The "psyche" is then, the totality of nonphysical life. Thus soul is more than an individual; it includes the world soul, one's sense of humanness shared with others, and also soul in the spiritual and religious sense. Health requires attention to both body and soul. Human beings have always had some understanding of this connection. *Shamanism*, for example, the most widespread system of soul/body healing known, is at least twenty or thirty thousand years old.

Because he has encountered his own shadow, during an arduous initiation involving torture and symbolic dismemberment, a shaman is equipped to battle others' diseases. Shamans of all cultures healed their patients by motivating them to transcend ordinary definitions of illness. Two common elements are a shaman's ecstatic "travel" and his ability to enlist the help of powerful animals or guiding spirits. Protected by his guides, a shaman enters a trance enabling his soul access to the upperworld and the underworld. There he learns how to restore a patient's personal power.

The archetypal sense that body and soul work as a single entity dates from earliest times when healing arts developed from observing mothers giving birth, nurturing and soothing their children and witnessing nature's own recuperative powers. Understanding the connection of bodily sickness and soul, most healers invoked help from such healing goddesses as Inanna and Isis, using a combination of spiritual practice and medicinal herbs. Sumerian priest and priestess physicians combined spiritual practice, like incantation, with biological prescriptions. Their methods later influenced Egyptian and Greek healers. In ancient Greece, the afflicted flocked to Ascelpius' temples where they slept in a large room awaiting the god's entering their dreams. In dreams, they learned aspects of their diagnosis and treatment and on waking sometimes had a miraculous cure. Asclepian physicians also prescribed herbs, baths, exercise, purges and bleedings, like shamans relying on soul/body healing.

In various worldwide religions, later healing systems also developed, elaborately connecting body and soul. The Christian gnostic gospels, speak of infinite latent potential in everyone. Hindus call this *Kundalini*, often pictured as a sleeping coiled serpent lying at the base of the spine. When awakened, Kundalini rises through the body's chakras or spiritual centers, first purifying the lower ones and then activating the heart, to excite healing powers. Chinese Taoism holds that physical disease can be caused by excess of the seven human emotions—joy, anger, melancholy, brooding, sorrow, fear, and shock. Inborn *chi* constitutes the major energy. We can balance *chi* by practicing Tai Chi Chuan, an ancient Chinese exercise program still popular with millions of people today. We can borrow further from Eastern wisdom by awakening the chakras to achieve our potential in emotional and physical health. Many yoga and meditation centers offer this practice today.

From Cartesian Dualism to A New Mind/Body Connection

Modern Western medicine at first rejected the archetypal mind/body connection. The French philosopher Rene Descartes, who fathered scientific thought, pronounced the mind and body as separate entities. The body should be analyzed like a machine into its component parts. All else—what could not be proved logically and scientifically—belonged to religion. For three hundred years Descartes' dualism profoundly influenced how we understand and fight disease, gradually resulting in marvelous discoveries, including our present hopes for conquering many illnesses through genetic research.

Nevertheless, recent years have seen the rise of psychneuroimmunology, a new field within scientific medicine exploring mind/body interaction. We have learned, for example, that receptors for neurotransmitters lie on the surface of cells in the immune system, allowing the brain (mind) to signal the immune system (body) in times of stress. When emotionally stressed, our adrenaline rises, and so does the number of killer cells that fight disease. Normal grief feelings of sadness or anger tend to increase our physical immunity, but prolonged depression, feeling we can't control our world, or simple loneliness, can all diminish it.

In a study using actors, Dr. Ann Fulterman has shown that even very brief emotions positively affect our immune system. She asked actors to improvise a monologue based on a situation that would elicit sad or happy feelings. She found that both intense happy feelings and intense sad feelings increased the number of natural killer cells, those cells needed to fight disease. Other studies show that a tendency to suppress feeling is physiologically detrimental.[4] Perhaps one reason why women live longer than men is because women are more likely to freely express their emotions.

Holistic Health for Grieving Mothers

To stay physically healthy, we must deal with excessive feelings. When emotional trauma grips the body, we need to cleanse shadow elements arising from shock, despair, and helplessness.

To help put our existence in balance, we can search out metaphoric messages possibly concealed in physical symptoms. A diminished immune system, for example, may derive from feeling we live in an unpredictable world. Unusual aches and pains may be bodily expressions of our needs to be held and loved. By the same token, back aches may tell us we now carry excessive emotional burden, perhaps made intolerable by our lack of social support. Likewise anemia may point to a lack of joy in our lives, and weight gain from needing to sedate ourselves.

Even when we don't have physical symptoms, we may enrich our grief work by attending to our unified body/soul. For example, we may see wisdom in taking long nature walks to soothe our body rather than further shocking it in a power-walking program When we practice hatha yoga, rather than pushing the body to achieve difficult postures, we may choose to concentrate on centering ourselves. We may also begin meditation practices, whether to lower our blood pressure or to seek union with God. We may decide to lose our taste for fast food and instead savor what is natural and wholesome, or take time in the day for a cup of tea. And, of course, we can also choose to take advantage of all that modern medicine offers.

In the past fifteen years new medications, particularly antidepressants, have worked wonders for millions, including some of my own clients whose depression lifted enough for them to engage in successful psychotherapeutic work. Chemical changes in the brain accompany depression and can be helped pharmacologically. But when using drugs, we should clearly understand that no medication can cure grief. When the illness of depression impedes grief work, it should be treated with both medicine (body) and psychotherapy (mind).

NOTES:

1. Eric Neumann, *Depth Psychology and a New Ethic*, London, 1969, p. 111.
2. Kay Murphy, ed., "Black," *Women Poets: Workshop into Print*, New Orleans, 2003, p. 112.
3. The Dalai Lama and Howard C. Cutler, *The Art of Happiness*, New York, 1998, pp. 133–34.
4. Margaret Kemeny, "Emotions and the Immune System," *Bill Moyers Healing and the Mind*, New York, 1993, p. 196.

Chapter Eleven

Journaling, Dreams and Writing Your Life Story

But don't be satisfied with stories,
how things have gone with others.
Unfold your own myth without
complicated explanation
so everyone will understand the passage....
— Rumi

Grieving Mothers' Writing Samples

Many mourning mothers have written novels, poems, and nonfiction works, attempting to give form and meaning to their experiences.

• In *Paula*, Isabel Allende chronicles her personal and family history as she watches her comatose daughter slowly wither away. In her agony over her daughter's death, the author finds the capacity to love and live unselfishly.

• In *The Andrew Poems* Shelly Wagner mourns the drowning death of her five year old son. "What did I do with his shoes?" she asks. "I saved them in the Andrew Poems."

• Author Anne Rice had a premonitory dream of her daughter's turning blue and collapsing because of fluid in her veins. Later her beautiful little girl developed leukemia, dying two years after diagnosis. Her mother closed the door to religion and began to destroy herself with alcohol. Using images of supernatural beings who suck blood out of the living in order to survive, she began writing *Interview with the Vampire.* Metaphorically, Ann expressed there her anguish over leukemia's ravaging the girl. Grief brought Ann closer to her own darkness, but her imagination provided a saving grace.

• *Women Poets: Workshop into Print* features poems from Kay Murphy's *Black Cycle of Lyrics,* a work chronicling events following her son's death. Kay sent me commentary describing her labor to give symmetry to her writing, a reflection of our own search for order and wholeness.

On Thursday, 13 April, 2000, the universe provided me with the opportunity to write urgently, without architecture or embedding, quickly, desperately. My son, Scott was killed on his motorcycle....

The poems that responded to my son's death are pure in language, permeable as the veil between my dream and waking life. The syntax is straightforward. The one new thing in these poems is my need for symmetry, a kind of visual order beyond metre, suggesting visually a deliberate placement and measurement. When you are trying to save your life—and feeling guilty because you didn't save your child's life—there is no possibility for ideas to bear the unbearable.

Kay goes on to recount her successful struggles to legitimize her writing.

However, I feel guilty for writing poems about my son's death, as if I were using it to generate poems. I was already familiar with Margaret Atwood's lines, "Why don't you die / so I can write about it?" and been told that it is not the poet that feeds off the dead for a poem but the dead who feed off the poet ... Did writing mean I was not mourning my son properly....

I lost something that I had helped create out of my flesh—his disappearance was without warning, and it was complete: no negotiation or sacrifice has yet been accepted. Whatever it is that is in me that survives by creating, however, came furiously into power—an instinctual survival response. I cannot recreate my son and no number of poems will replace him. But I don't know what it will take to dissuade the mother in me that some day I will have made enough poems to bargain for his life.

Mourning mothers also design research projects about the impact of child death and self-help books for grieving parents. Ann Finkbiener suggests that her book *After the Death of a Child* is a trajectory.

> I think parents insert the (dead) children into their lives and continue living, one person now, parent-and-child ... This trajectory is neither the child's original path nor the parent's; it's somewhere between.[1]

Before he died, Ann's son was wildly excited and intensely focused on his creative art. His mother believes that by writing her book she incorporated the passion of his unlived life.

> This book, too, was nearly an obsession; working on it. I felt the same hell-for-leather intensity. And finishing it, I didn't feel relieved but frightened. What would I do next? What will I ever care about so much again?[2]

Like the authors mentioned, many other mourning mothers find an outlet for newly awakened creativity through writing. Though usually lacking intention of publishing their work, they begin writing prayers, poems or letters to the deceased. For myself, although I didn't recognize it at the time, such personal writing contained in my journal was the beginning of this book. Writing became something I *had* to do, an endeavor to create something new from what had died inside me.

Starting a Journal

Like the best modern women's diaries in history, our journals can explore our deepest beliefs, thoughts, and feelings. Generally more detailed than a diary, a journal can include biographical work, dreams, letters writing, stories, myths, and unique healing creations, such as poetry or drawings. Though you may begin by reporting events before and after your child's death, you can move deeper into the mourning process by expanding how you use your journal.

By putting words to your inner experiences, for example, you can tease apart intense emotions and confusing thoughts. Too often the griever feels beset by an enveloping gray psychological cloud. Naming emotions and describing them by actually writing words on paper moves them from your unconscious to a conscious realm, where you can examine them. What remains unconscious we often repeat, adding more pain to our lives but *conscious* suffering can bring us new meaning.

We have seen how catharsis (emotional release) moves us forward, particularly in the early stages of grieving. Writing assists catharsis, helping us shed cleansing tears to boot. A journal also serves as a safe container for anger, a place for our most murderous thoughts. By titling their anthology *The Assassin's Cloak*, Irene and Alan Taylor reaffirm how their authors' "evil thoughts," (to use author Kay Murphy's words) can be freely expressed and remain hidden.

From an archetypal standpoint—take the Isis and Osiris myth for example—journaling manifests our need to be broken before being formed anew. When we have been broken, we need time and a place for reconciliation. Recording reactions to events, examining conflicted relationships, and reforming values requires our dialoguing with self. Further, journaling gives an opportunity to express our changing relationships with others—our spouse, our living children, and the child who died, as well as God and the outer community.

Therapeutic Writing Techniques

Though valuable, writing only for emotional release, can become self-serving and unproductive. To progress, we need reflection and challenging self-evaluation. Ira Progoff's *Intensive Journal* includes daily ways to develop inner wisdom, and workshops teaching his complex method are available today. In addition, by reading Tristine Rainer's *The New Diary* or Deena Metzger's *Writing for Your Life*, you can further study and personally apply such techniques as these:

I. Practice stream of consciousness writing, bringing unconscious thoughts to consciousness by writing down every word that spontaneously comes into your mind. Though your words may first seem disconnected, as you contemplate them and play with their images and metaphors, you may find a valuable association.

> I'm tired don't want to write because my neck aches rather get cookie my rings on long fingers need to play piano again never play, never play games either too serious went to the old gate in the old house no a fence backed up to cemetery where he played

and now lies dead and playing is what I need but the lamps still
lit and sitting hungry wanting sleep wishing for daffodils.

Annie

Contemplating such a passage, a writer may find significant associations to "rings," "piano playing," or "the old gate"; she may muse
about motifs of feeding, sleeping, and communing with nature. What
are the symbols and metaphors behind these words? What relevance
may they have right now or in the near future?

2. Create dialogues with your physical body, different parts of your
personality, persons you know, or important events in your life. By
writing a dialogue, you can gain useful information about "the other,"
whether part of yourself or an actual person. But don't dialogue with *the
worst event*, the death of your child, until you are far along in the grieving
process. Waiting until she felt ready, Helene found that the dialogue
opened unexpected horizons.

> HELENE: Well, Event, you about ruined my life. You will never
> go away and I will never understand you.
>
> EVENT: You're not supposed to ask why I came.
>
> HELENE: Oh, I've heard that cliché so many times. I've asked
> why a lot but I never get an answer.
>
> EVENT: So things happen. Look at what's going on in Iraq.
>
> HELENE: I don't live in Iraq. I live in a civilized country where
> children don't die before their parents.
>
> EVENT: You know that's not always true. You can't see the sig-
> nificance of me so soon after I've come. You're just beginning
> to find some significance, aren't you?
>
> HELENE: Well, I'm trying to make some significance, I mean,
> you are so senseless, so cruel, so unexpected, so evil. How can I
> find any significance in you?
>
> Event: I sure have changed you, haven't I.
>
> HELENE: Well, I'm determined now not to let you ruin me.

EVENT: It's hard for you to admit, isn't it, that some good may have come out of me.

HELENE: Good? What's good about you?

EVENT: Nothing is good about me but some good has come from me.

HELENE: What are you talking about?

EVENT: How you've changed. Sad, but wiser and able to love.

HELENE: I still have a lot of anger, too.

EVENT: Maybe so, but you have more love than you did before I came, and you know a lot more too: how life really is and learning to appreciate it again.

HELENE: Perhaps that's true. I'm thankful for something but I don't know what.

EVENT: Thankful?

HELENE: Yes, I guess for surviving and wanting to live again.

3. To better understand relationships, write letters you will never mail to your parents, spouse, surviving children or deceased child. For example, wanting to show her sixteen-year-old son why openly grieving his sister's death is important, Mindy describes her birth family's habit of denying loss.

> Dear Tom,
>   I am trying so hard to reach you. I know you are hurting and I want us to talk about it. Can't we be sad together? In looking back at what it was like for me growing up, I can see now that we kids were never allowed to feel any loss. The myth was that all is good, that we are a good Christian family so that nothing should harm us. We weren't supposed to see anything bad. I remember one night after my father had a temper fit, my mother in her quiet, loving manner managed to have him calmed down and all of us going to buy a new car. Just like

that! My aunt died when I was sixteen, and I didn't go to the funeral and I still don't know much about her disease. All that was kept from me. She died young, too. It must have been hard on my mom, but she never showed it. I want it to be different with us.

Trisha, is still journaling many years after her son's death. Though many entries don't relate to her son, she occasionally writes him a letter.

Dear Steve,

Last night, two days before the tenth anniversary of your death, I dreamed that you were grown up, twenty-two, just the age you would now be if you were alive. You were dressed in a pin-stripped suit and talking about your tickets for the Saints' game. I couldn't understand why you had on a suit to go to a football game, but you looked real handsome. I wondered if you were married or had children. You were glad to see me. I often think what life you would be living now if you hadn't died. Sometimes I still ask myself if I should have allowed them to turn off the life support. But you were already dead, Steve. They said you were brain dead. That was the saddest day of my life. I still rethink about that and I think of you every day.

Love,
Mom

4. Make lists: your virtues and transgressions, courageous acts and fears. When you are able, make the most important lists of all, your joys and gratitudes. Trisha notes her Thanksgiving journal entry, written four years after her child's dying.

Gratitudes

For having inner peace more often
For the hurricane not coming
For Mike's new job
For wanting to live again
For not being afraid to die
For Susie finding a puppy she liked
For making love and feeling young

For the view outside my window
For staying healthy all year
For friends who love me
For living in America
For having my son, if only a little while.

5. Record your memories. Select photographs and write down the events they depict. The word *mourning* stems from the same root as memory. *Mnemosyne*, the Greek incarnation of memory, was mother to the nine muses who in turn gave birth to all culture. You can follow your memories with drawings, songs, or poetry. Recalling her son, Rheba writes a poem in her journal that raises biography to a mythic level.

Carter, my mythical bird
I see you hovering over us
Brushing us still with your wings
Letting us know you're here

I see you flying into the hunt
Armed with your bow
Girded with the spirit
To know that sport comes from
The true love of the chase.

Remembering and Recording Dreams

When you begin recording your dreams, you join thousands of other devoted dreamers in antiquity. The earliest records from the Assyrians, Babylonians, and Egyptians show they believed dreams to be messages from God. They interpreted most dreams as warnings demanding penance and sacrifices to the Gods. The Egyptians built temples in honor of Serapis, the god of dreams.

When seeking self-understanding from dreams, you may need to develop your own ritual. First try reserving a particular section of your journal for recording dreams. Keep the journal, a pen, and an accessible light by your bedside. Treat the first moments of awakening as very important, for becoming conscious in that short period between sleeping and full waking helps you to remember images. Perhaps only a shred of the dream is first available, but by immediately writing down exactly what you remember, more images emerge.

After recording as much dream detail as possible, remain awake and write down associations that come to mind. You may try to interpret a dream as you would a short story. Where is the setting? What is the plot? What can you say about the characters? What animals, objects or colors may have symbolic meaning? Which part of the dream generates the most emotion? From these elements you may reach some understanding of your dream. Giving the dream a title may help you identify its theme. Even an apparently trivial dream can be informative. Gradually, your conscious attention to any one dream will enhance awareness of other dreams.

Carefully recording of dreams during the grieving process can help to psychologically integrate the experience of loss and begin an intrapsychic relationship with the deceased. Dreams can tell us where we have been in our journey through grief. Two and a half years into the mourning process, Kate dreamed she was confused and fearful about possibly drowning, but the dream ends with her touching bottom and beginning her ascent.

> I am floating downward in a pool. I am surprised that I am floating downward. Why didn't I spring back up when I jumped in? I feel chagrin. Why didn't I look before I jumped? Then maybe I would have jumped into the shallow end. I have knowledge. I know somehow I have to keep floating until my feet touch bottom. Then I will be able to push myself back up the other way. Then I have doubt. But what if that doesn't work? How long until someone notices that I'm gone and rescues me? But then my feet touch the bottom and I do spring up on the balls of my feet. I begin my ascent.

Awakening, Kate felt encouraged. Sally also received encouragement during a difficult time after her son Chip's death. Her psyche created a mythical figure who serves as protector.

> In the dream, a woman is sitting with me. She is ... like a protector. I don't want to call her an angel, but she is somebody who obviously knows me and I am in her care. I feel that she is, for lack of a better word, a Guardian Angel, but not really because she doesn't have wings. We sit together in a very small

room and she strokes my arm or hair, in a very loving way. She is telling me, "You are okay. You are doing what you are supposed to be doing. I know it's hard, but you are learning your lessons." I am unable to remember what she is showing me, but they are aspects of my life.

We gain deeper self-understanding from a dream where a loved one gives advice. At first the advice may be mute and symbolic as when our child appears distant or uninterested, indicating that the life beyond has its own validity, and the separation of parent and child needs no further lament. Mary learned more directly that her son Will was moving on in his afterlife and that she should go forward with her own life as well.

I saw Will walking in a line of people with briefcases, seemingly going to work, looking straight ahead and walking briskly. He was on the near end, and he stayed back a little so I could see him and he said, "Look at me, Mom, I'm all filled out. I couldn't use those old clothes anyway." He resumed his place in line and the dream ended.

Rheba found a dream message from her son that related to her whole family. Carter had acted as leader in a family business that demanded hard work and long hours from all the sons. Their father was rightfully proud he had built the business, and he wanted to pass this legacy on to his children. Rheba explains her recurring dream.

I had many dreams that Carter would come back to me and say, "I had to die because I was burnt out from work and I thought maybe if I went away Daddy would understand." It was as if Carter were a savior for everybody else, kind of a Christ figure of sacrifice.

Rheba knew that her husband and her other boys needed to see how unbalanced they were becoming by putting too much energy into work. If business pressures continued to drain the men in her family, none of them would live much longer.

In another dream, Rheba found her will to live by absorbing strength from her son Carter, a champion swimmer.

Carter and I and two others are on a freestyle relay swim team. There is a course laid out with four pools roped off to eight

100-meter lanes. One swimmer from each team dives in, the next swimmer following. The event has all swimmers waiting until their team of four finishes a lap. Then they all carry a boat to the next pool, put it down on the grass, and then race again.

I'm our second swimmer, following Carter in sequence. I swim my first two laps slowly. Of course, Carter is very fast as he is a swim champion, and I wonder if my team is disappointed that I can't swim fast like him. After finishing his laps, he stands at the end, cheering me to go fast and telling me that I can do it. He is very encouraging. As the race progresses from pool to pool, I begin to swim faster, as though I'm gaining energy through the team's wanting so badly to win. At first I feel uncompetitive, but I seem to gain a strong will to win as we get to the third pool.

By the time we dive into the fourth and last pool, I'm right behind Carter, and as he kicks, my hands are touching his feet as I stroke ahead. He sometimes kicks my hands back, as if to keep the distance needed for his powerful kick, not to hurt me. He finishes, and he pulls me up at the end of the pool to wait for our two teammates to finish. He is hugging me and we are laughing. He is teasing me about how I was almost passing him at the end. He is very proud of me and the team. Of course, we win the race.

Rheba awoke from this dream elated and energized. The dream showed Carter's encouragement, helping his mother gain the will to win even though she had been feeling uncompetitive. Mothers often report that their child in their dream points to a new way of living or leads them to an important solution. Informed by the world beyond, the dreamed-child acts as a "psychopomp," a figure who guides the soul at times of initiation and transition.

In the beginning, mothers may have nightmares about their child's death, especially in cases of accident, murder, or suicide. Dreams may repeat an actual event of the child's death, thereby manifesting the dreamer's symptoms of posttraumatic stress syndrome. When such traumatic dreams recur, one should seek help from a Jungiam analyst or an insight-oriented psychotherapist, one who is trained to work with unconscious material and who honors the spiritual realm. At each recurrence, the dream should be reported, just as experienced, until one can notice a change in the dream. Then, the dream will contain something that did not happen. Jungian analyst Harry Wilmer calls this altered dream a "healing nightmare," signaling that the psyche has started to use normal processes of the unconscious to bind the wound.

For more than a year after my son died, I was awakened by similar frightening nightmares where he was in great danger, vulnerable because of his mental illness. I would vigilantly search for any red flags that might indicate his wanting to run away, jump off a bridge, or put himself in some precarious situation. In each dream, I would see such a red flag but remain powerless to protect him. Then I had the following dream:

> There is a big bright red flag. I worry that it predicts danger for my child, but just then the flag turns into a symphony. I see orchestra musicians performing, and the sound is as full as if I were sitting in the midst of them. The music fills me with joy.

The dream's beautiful music affirms the psyche's healing powers—gifts inherent in each of us.

Mothers often report finding great comfort when their deceased child appears in dreams, for they become convinced the beloved child is in a safe place, free from pain and harm. The child may bring words of reassurance that signal the time for tears to cease. The grandmother of thirteenth-century Dominican Thomas Cantimpratanus refused to be comforted when she lost her eldest son, until she had a dream of him lagging sorrowfully behind a group of joyful boys. When she asked the cause of his sorrow, he opened his cloak to reveal a heavy water pot and cried:

> Behold dear mother, the tears which thou hast vainly shed for me, through the weight whereof I must needs linger behind the rest. Thou therefore shalt turn thy tears to God, and pour forth thy pious and devout heart in the presence of the sacrifice of Christ's body, with alms to the poor. Then only shall I be freed from the burden wherewith I am now grieved.[3]

If you are really in touch with your intuitive side, you may be able to feel whether the figure of the dead child is being used as a symbol for some psychological reality or whether you are receiving an actual visit from the deceased. Many moms affirm that deceased children really appear in their dreams. Mary had the following dream which assured her that her daughter was safe in heaven.

> I am standing by a tree in a beautiful park filled with flowers, and I hear enchanted music playing. I am trying to fly, but I move to a treetop. Then I am able to fly. I call to Kim when I see her. She is dressed in flowing white gauze. She is directing a group of children dressed in white and seated on a pavilion. She looks up and sees me standing by a tree. She cries, "Mom" and runs into my arms. I am kissing her face and holding her. I can feel her hug; I can even smell her. When I woke up, there was such a feeling of joy.

Even if you are not blessed with a dreaming of your deceased child, recording dreams can still help you learn much about yourself. Working with dreams on your own, however, may be precarious. Generally, I recommend a dream group or seeking a licensed psychotherapist or Jungian analyst, someone skilled in helping people understand dreams. By devoting enough time to dream work, you will begin to see your path, and perhaps you can find your myth.

Writing Your Life Story

Besides journaling your feelings and recording dreams, you can also help healing by writing autobiography. Though you feel your life to be shattered, organizing events into a coherent history will broaden perspective. Writing your biography enables you to note and give value to all life's events, allowing you to see how you are more than *mater dolorosa*, a sorrowing mother, totally possessed by an archetype like Mary's grieving.

Good writing activates all four personality functions: thinking, feeling, sensing, and intuition. Using the thinking function, you can gather factual information derived from sensing and make order from seemingly unrelated events. For example, you may discover repeated behavior patterns and motifs, then determine their source. By interviewing her mother and two aunts, Victoria found a family connection that helped solve her current dilemma. A single woman, her baby had died three days before its delivery. After this tragedy, she looked to find solace in working, but though she had completed a year of law school, she didn't want to enter the legal world.

> I hated law school and I dreaded practicing law even more. I wanted to do something more creative, more true to myself. Unable to decide which path to follow and desperate to make a decision, I enrolled in a spiritual biography seminar at my church. During this course I also talked to some strong and successful women in my family. What I found out surprised me. My mother admitted having once longed to become an actress but settling for chemist—something safe, practical, and self-reliant. Aunt Maggie had given up her desire to dance, and Aunt Susie still wished she had studied painting. The mother of these three was an established poet who had taught her girls to be self-sufficient and practical because, she said, "men are always unreliable." After talking with my relatives, I decided not to take the safe-but-sorry route, and I enrolled in culinary school.

Victoria used her thinking function to gather information and reflect on her situation. When weighing what to do, her feeling function came into play, helping her decide what was valuable to her true self. Activating the feeling function enables making value judgments and helps you develop a unique philosophy based on personal experience.

Using your sensate function can enrich your autobiography with childhood memories that have become part of your inner landscape. In his World War I diaries, English poet Siegfried Sassoon first recalls such a scene and then is jolted back to the reality of war and the death of his brother. Nevertheless, his recollections momentarily freed him and doubtless can free him again.

> The roofs and stacks of the farm among its trees below the hill, the farmhouse chimney with its wisp of smoke, a bird winging out across the valley-orchards, and the sound of a train going steadily on, miles away—all are as I would have them, as I would keep them remembered. I am back in childhood; home with my kind of dreams; soon I shall hear my brother's voice along the garden, where moths will be fluttering like flowers that are free from their hot parades in sunshine, free to go where they will among the dimness of

quiet alleys. O brother, tell me what you have seen to-day, what have you done?

He will not answer, for he is dead. And I am far from the garden, far from the summer that is past. I am alone in this bitter winter of unending war.[4]

Your sensate function also helps describe people, though character study involves thinking and feeling as well. Doris Lessing uses all three functions in this portrait of her father, enabling her to to experience him in a complex way that transcends his present appearance.

The boy who was beaten at school, who went too much to church, who carried the fear of poverty all his life, but who nevertheless was filled with the memories of country pleasures; the young bank clerk who worked such long hours for so little money, but who danced, sang, played, flirted … this naturally vigorous, sensuous being was killed in 1914, 1915, 1916. I think the best of my father died in that war, that his spirit was crippled by it. The people I've met, particularly the women who knew him young, speak of his high spirits, his energy, his enjoyment of life. Also his kindness, his compassion and—a word that keeps reoccurring—his wisdom. "Even when he was just a boy he understood things that you'd think even an old man wouldn't find it easy to condemn." I do not think these people would have easily recognized the ill, irritable, abstracted, hypochondriac man I knew.[5]

Lessing's understanding about why her father changed also relies on her intuitive function which arises when we engage the inner voice of our heartfelt wisdom. You start your story with memories which generate feelings. Then your thinking and intuitive functions help you select the most important events, eventually allowing you to create a structure. Because such a process takes time, you may falter in the beginning, feeling overwhelmed at its magnitude. In that case, I find no better way to keep encouraging yourself than attending to Ann Lamott's family story in *Bird by Bird.*

Thirty years ago my older brother, who was ten years old at the time, was trying to get a report on birds written that he'd had three months to write. It was due the next day. We were out at our family cabin in Bolinas, and he was at the kitchen table close to tears, surrounded by binder paper and pencils and unopened books on birds, immobilized by the hugeness of the task ahead. Then my father sat down beside him, put his arm around my brother's shoulder, and said, "Bird by bird, buddy. Just take it bird by bird."[6]

Ira Progoff suggests one way an autobiographer can move from bird to bird: listing chronologically the stepping-stones of your life, create a "table of contents." You focus on the most important events, enabling you to begin writing a chronological life story. Another way to create such an outline, leading to a different structure for your eventual autobiography, is to catalogue events that influenced different levels of your psyche: your outer life, your psychological life, and your inner most true self. Whatever your approach, the outline you start will not be the final one: you will add, subtract, and move items as your writing proceeds.

Writing Your
Psycho-spiritual Autobiography

The Face You Show the World

Jung called the face one shows the world "Persona," after the ancient Greek actor's mask which signals his role within a play. We use this part of our personality in our social interactions, and it changes to meet various situations—the business woman doesn't display her loving face when driving a hard bargain. In a general way, however, we maintain a single set of attitudes in usual acts of daily living. Most people have such a set of attitudes—a Persona—one that includes seeming competent, strong, and intelligent, in most roles we play (child, parent, mother, bridge player, motorist, motorist stopped by police officer, doctor's patient, and so forth). When we feel crushed by loss, however, we may forget this important aspect of Persona, of ourselves.

Exploring our entire Persona by creating a detailed written picture of yourself leading your daily past and present life can be exhilarating. At the very least, it will shift your perception away from your present sense of having lost everything. Taking account of all aspects of your social identity alleviates feelings of powerlessness caused by grief. You will recall, for example, how others have loved and appreciated you and your accomplishments. Perhaps you excelled in sports, have a good sense of humor, made friends easily, finished college, or landed a good job. Besides being a mother, what other roles have you played? Identify important milestones in your public life. What people have helped you most along the way? Whom have you helped? How do you present yourself to others in typical situations? By answering such questions you gradually build a picture of your entire persona, your being in the world. We may think of our shadow, what we hide from everyone, our conscious self included, as standing opposite to this entire Persona.

Your Psychological Self

Go deeper into your identity, by examining how your family of origin helped form your unique psychology. This exercise will help you identify the myths you are living. In a family, there are always myths that direct how we relate to each other:

As a child, Jill, the adult peacemaker in her family, didn't demand as much attention as her "baby" sister or her mischievous older brother. As Jill grew older, her mother often confided marital problems and how she was "beside herself," because her son was always in trouble at school. Because her parents were fighting and her mother was depressed, Jill decided to go to community college and help out at home. After completing her two-year program, she still felt needed at home and guilty about moving out. Though often "frustrated," she seldom expressed anger and nothing seemed to bother her. Later marrying a medical student, she worked while he finished school and and continued staying close to her parents. After waiting six years, she and her husband had two children, but while fishing with his dad, her seven-year-old fell off the dock and drowned. Her husband buried himself in his work, while Jill tried to be good and strong, holding her remaining family together and taking care of their needs. Two years later, Jill ended up in a psychiatric hospital with a "nervous breakdown." In psychotherapy, she learned how her original family role had required her disregarding her own needs. The family myth had been that Jill was the strong dependable one on whom everyone should rely.

In addition to her family myth, each individual has a personal one. If you were blessed with a warm and well-balanced family, you can draw upon support you received when a child. If you come from a troubled family, however, now is a good time to find out how you played your part in *keeping the family together.* For it to continue functioning, you may have assumed such positive roles as caretaker and pleaser or negative ones like scapegoat, rebel, and victim.

After losing a child, Lorelei and Allison had almost opposite experiences. The oldest of thirteen children in a strict Catholic family, helping mother care for brothers and sisters made Lorelei feel deprived of her own childhood. In order to leave home, she married at eighteen, and four years later her third child Mark, born with a defective heart, required hospitalization throughout his short life. Worn out from staying at the hospital day and night with a sick baby, Lorelei would limp home to two toddlers and her husband who "loved the kids more than I did." After her baby died, in place of grief work, she left her husband and kids. "I needed a break from parenting," she said. " I wanted to have the youth I never had."

A year later, realizing she couldn't run away from her problems, Lorelei returned home.

> I was very depressed but medication helped, and when my husband and I went to counseling, I started to understand how much my past affected me. I'm ashamed for having left my kids, I really do love them, and I want to make it up to them. I think I had post partem depression after Mark was born. Death is hard, even when you aren't sure you want the baby, and I have a lot of guilt and sadness over all that happened.

Allison, who also grew up in a large Catholic family, lost her third child to SIDS, but she had happy memories of her childhood and a loving, supportive family.

> I don't know what I would have done without my sisters. We've always been a close family, and they were with me throughout the horrible ordeal. By researching articles about SIDS, my mom made sure I would never feel blamed, and my Dad, too, especially during the investigation, he was right

there. In our family we believe that, for some unfathomable reason, God wanted David in heaven, and believing that makes us closer.

Not all of us are as fortunate as Allison. Though we may have families who love us, we may grow unable to relate to them the way we did as children. Sometimes we need distance—psychological, geographical—from family in order to redefine ourselves, developing new ways to protect ourselves and others. Thomas Moore calls us to continually *reimagine* our family in order to preserve the family soul.

> The fundamental problem with the family is one of imagination. We need an appreciation of the family shadow—the tensions, differences, antagonisms, and clashes—that play a constitutive role in the family soul. It's often a struggle for family members to forge a new imagination of what they are, especially as various members go through their individual rites of passage and life transitions. But if they have the courage to reimagine themselves continually as a family, while remaining loyal to their traditions, they will be caring for the family soul.[7]

Annie has read Moore's book and is applying his concept of reimagining to her family of origin.

> For a long time I felt unloved by my sister. I realized after Donald died that I had intruded too much in her life. She never encouraged her kids to be close to me as they were with her husband's family. Now I am childless, so that really hurts. But I am trying to reimagine our relationship, more from her point of view. I see that her life is full and perhaps she doesn't understand how it feels to lose a child.

For a mother whose child has died, neither her nuclear family nor her family of origin will ever be the same. As we have seen, other family members often do not accept the changes, making efforts to keep you and relationships as they were or simply denying alterations. But because so much personal and archetypal energy is contained in family life, we do well to explore its past so we may better understand both it and ourselves. By recording the losses in your family, for example, including the death of a pet, a family move, or other seemingly small events, you can examine your family's reaction to loss as well as your own behaviors. As you examine the coping mechanisms you and your family used, you discover old patterns conditioning how you currently handle your greatest loss.

Families commonly use secrecy as a coping mechanism, either to protect an individual or because of shame. In writing your psychological biography, deliberately recall some parts of your story—both trivial and important—that you've never told to anyone. In my psychotherapy practice, I see healing begin when a patient can break silence and reveal her deepest secret. Putting untold parts of your story on paper is an act of healing in and of itself.

Your Spiritual Life

Inside you lies knowledge of what is true and unique to yourself, that which embodies all your potential and can guide you to wholeness and immortality. This force, whether called "Higher Power," "Soul," or "God Within," (Jung's Self as opposed to the ego) also includes the entire personality, all that is innate and all that transcends. As you write about your spiritual life, try to connect with your inner power, your strongest resource for mourning.

As a child you may have been confident about God and His creation, but as an adult, following a spiritual path requires questioning. Our received religion is a system of doctrine and stories, much of which can be interpreted on different levels. Write about what you used to believe, what you still believe, and what you hope to believe. Write about your participation in religious rituals. Then turn to spirituality itself, your direct experience of the sacred. What were the moments? What kind of spiritual experiences have you had whether inside or outside of church? In the following chapters, we will learn how to truly value those moments when we touch the sacred.

In writing your biography on every level, you will begin to identify archetypal motifs that lend universality to your experience. How each individual moves through birth, childhood, motherhood, and death varies, but some elements are shared throughout time. Often we find a myth or fairy tale profoundly moving because the patterns of our own life are reflected in it. These narratives can lead us through the developmental stages of our life and give new meaning to a world that may seem senseless. Myths attempt to answer that for which there is no answer. They contain motifs about creation, death and rebirth, mourning, following the way, loyalty and devotion. They can confirm or help correct how we are living. We can reinterpret these tales to meet our contemporary situations, or move the story forward, imagining a different ending. We can find new myths to live by that give significance to our existence.

NOTES:

1. Ann Finkbeiner, *After the Death of a Child*, Baltimore, 1996, p. 256.
2. Ibid., p. 263.
3. G. Coulton, ed., *Life in the Middle Ages*, London, 1967, pp. 118–119.
4. From *Siegfried Sassoon Diaries, 1915–1918*, edited by Rupert Hart Davis and quoted in a remarkable collection of poetry, fiction , and essays, *A Broken Heart Still Beats: After Your Child Dies*, by Anne McCracken & Mary Semel, Center City, MN, 1998.
5. Doris Lessing, *A Small Personal Voice*, New York, 1974, p. 86.
6. Ann Lamott, *Bird by Bird*, New York, 1994, pp. 18–19.
7. Thomas Moore, *Soul Mates*, New York, 1994, p. 75.

Chapter Twelve

FINDING A MYTH TO LIVE BY

*We look back and analyze the events of our lives, but there
is another way of seeing, a backward-and-forward-at-once
vision that is not rationally understandable.
Only God can understand it.*

— RUMI

My Discovery of the Myth I Was Living

Because all the stories we tell ourselves about who we are arise
from the collective unconscious and contain archetypal characters and
plots, at any given time, whether consciously or not, each of us is living a myth. A long process of discovering the myth I was living, began
several weeks after Duncan's funeral, when my sister suddenly spoke to
me about our half-brother Billy, a family taboo matter hitherto: "Don't
you know Duncan looked just like Billy?"

Like a gestalt, sudden images of Billy emerged in my memory, and
I felt profundity in her statement. Billy and Duncan must have had the
same bad gene! I recalled myself as a young girl, visiting my brother in
a mental hospital, and how I had imagined his cold and lonely death
at Christmas, when he hanged himself in the bathroom. In only a
moment, much of my life passed through my mind. I knew I had to
sort through so many memories; I returned to my journal that very
night. Previously focussing little on my own life, I had written there
only prayers, poems, letters to Duncan, and recurrent nightmares of

Duncan's needing help and my being unable to save him. But now I wanted to understand the impact my brother's suicide had on *my* life so I started digging.

I wrote how, when Billy died, my father said, "It was all for the best. Billy had quit school, stolen money, and left his wife." In my father's eyes, Billy hadn't been worth much. My adolescent awareness of Daddy's feelings had led me to work hard proving to him that I was different. I would be a success, not only winning Daddy's love and esteem but redeeming the disgrace to my father's life which Billy had brought down upon it. Accordingly, I had thrown myself into a lifelong pattern of workaholism, studying hard, and marrying well. I had also joined my father in a complicity of silent denial about his son and the three grandchildren he led all of us in abandoning.

As I wrote on that night, I understood for the first time that beneath my youthful compliance, I had nursed unconscious resentments at my father's turning his back on one of our family; he might turn his back on me, too, were I to stray from his wishes. I pieced more of the puzzle together. "As I got older, my resentment had flared in heated arguments between him and me about civil rights, Vietnam, and later Duncan's long hair." I also recognized that as an adult I was "always fighting for the underdog," just as I had wanted to fight when a child for my brother.

"Finally," I wrote, "it wasn't long after Daddy's death that David, my half-brother's son had telephoned. Recently learning the truth about Billy's being his natural father, he wanted to meet me, his aunt. David told me how he had searched for his father and found his remains *in an unmarked grave.* The news had enraged me, and pumped me further full of unconscious shadow energy to fight against the stigma of mental illness."

That night's self-analysis was very useful, but as I have said, more years working with a Jungian analyst needed to pass before I could begin effectively questioning the healthfulness of my roles as therapist and mental health advocate. That helped prepare the way for greater liberation, triggered by happenstance one night when I saw a production of Sophocles' *Antigone* and clearly recognized the mythic story I had been living.

Dwelling on the Significance of "Antigone"

After becoming engaged to Haemon, son of Thebes' King Creon, Oedipus' daughter Antigone suffers new family conflict arising from the assault on the city of "Seven Against Thebes." Creon has prohibited the burial of one attacker, her brother Polynices. In the opening scene, Ismane learns of sister Antigone's plan to defy the King's decree.[1]

ANTIGONE: Listen Ismane:
Creon buried our brother Eteolces
With military honors, gave him a soldier's funeral,
And it was right that he should; but Polynices,
Who fought as bravely and died as miserably,
They say that Creon has sworn
No one shall bury him, no one mourn for him,
But his body must lie in the fields, a sweet treasure
For carrion birds to find as they search for food.
That is what they say, and our good Creon is coming here
To announce it publicly; and the penalty —
Stoning to death in the public square.
There it is
And now you can prove what you are:
A true sister, or a traitor to your family.

ISMANE: Antigone, you are mad! What could I possibly do?

ANTIGONE: You must decide whether you will help me or not.

ISMANE: I do not understand you. Help you in what?

ANTIGONE: Ismane, I am going to bury him. Will you come?

ISMANE: Bury him! You have just said the new law forbids it.

ANTIGONE: He is my brother. And he is your brother, too.

As I watched this exchange, a sense of the archetypal injustice which had punished my half-brother filled me to bursting. I felt one with Antigone, *affirmed* in her brave willingness to do the right thing. Her archetypal courage and defiance *gripped* me, for I no longer felt alone in the fight I had been waging but could rejoice in her—in the whole community of women who redress family wrongs at all cost.

Later that night, I looked up the play's text, reviewing details of Antigone's determination and of her sister's grave warning about its consequences.

ISMANE: Think how ... terrible ...
Our own death would be if we should go against Creon
And do what he has forbidden!
The law is strong, we must give in to the law
In this thing, and in worse, I beg the Dead
To forgive me, but I am helpless: I must yield
To those in authority. And I think it is dangerous business
To always be meddling.

ANTIGONE: If that is what you think
I should not want you, even if you asked to come.
But I will bury him; and if I must die,
I say that this crime is holy: I shall lie down
With him in death, and I shall be as dear
To him as he to me
You may do as you like,
Since apparently the laws of god mean nothing to you.

ISMANE: They mean a great deal to me; but I have no strength
To break laws that were made for the public good....
I am so afraid for you!
So fiery! You should be cold with fear.

Replaying scenes in my mind, I was automatically reminded of my own provocative, quick-tempered nature. I wrote at length about many occasions when I had jumped into situations without thinking of consequences. My parents and sister saw me as a "trouble maker" or at best as one "who was always in trouble." Watching me, I came to see, my sister learned the truth in what Ismane says: it is "dangerous business to always be meddling."

In the second scene, a sentry witnesses Antigone giving her brother last rites and brings the edict-breaking woman to her king. Enraged by her defiance, Creon declares that she is "both headstrong and deaf to reason! She has never learned to yield." Antigone's fate seems clear and she embraces it ever more tightly, even mocking Ismane, who now wants to stand by her.

ISMANE: Do you refuse me, Antigone? I want to die with you:
I too have a duty that I must discharge to the dead ...
What do I care for life when you are dead?

ANTIGONE: Ask Creon. You're always hanging on his opinions.

Even when Antigone softens toward Ismane, she maintains her iron
resolve to do family justice.

ISMANE: You are laughing at me. Why, Antigone?

ANTIGONE: It's a joyless laughter, Ismane.

ISMANE: But can I do nothing?

ANTIGONE: Yes. Save yourself. I shall not envy you.
There are those who will praise you; I shall have honor, too.

Because Haemon threatens suicide if Antigone is slain by stoning in
the public square, Creon tries a legalistic wiggle, changing details of the
execution but not its hard outcome.

CREON: I will carry her far away
Out there in the wilderness, and lock her
Living in a vault of stone. She shall have food,
As the custom is, to absolve the State of her death,
And there let her pray to the gods of Hell:
They are her only gods.

At this point, Antigone momentarily pities herself, likening her fate to
Niobe's, the eternally mourning mother.

ANTIGONE: How often I have heard the story of Niobe,
Tantalus' wretched daughter, how the stone
Clung fast about her, ivy-close: and they say
The rain falls endlessly
And sifting soft snow; her tears are never done.
I feel the loneliness of her death in mine.

But the chorus reminds Antigone that the case is different, for she is
choosing her fate. So Antigone is led into the tomb.

Before she learns that Teiresis has persuaded Creon to yield, she
takes her own life. Haemon comes too late to save his bride and kills
himself in despair.

After seeing and rereading and dwelling on Antigone's story, so much became clear. Unconscious desires to free my brother and son from the stigma of mental illness had fed my angry busyness and single-minded concentration on improving mental health care. But in the process, I was now making myself into a tragic heroine both to escape pain at my son's loss and my father's refusal to face the truth, and also to affirm some wished-for justice and family solidarity that life had not in fact allowed me. I realized that if I continued living her myth, like Antigone, I would end up dead, dragging my devoted husband after me. Turning again to my journal, I began to list my own story's rough parallels to Antigone's, a woman who cared for her father Oedipus until his death, and then, returning to Thebes, fought King Creon for her brother's sake until she perished.

Parallels

1. I knew my father had blinded himself, unable to face many truths about his life.

2. Though knowing his flaws, I stood by him until his death, even bringing him into my home to pass his final weeks.

3. For my father, I sacrificed myself in my first marriage, choosing a man he could brag about rather than one I could love.

4. For the most part, my mother was absent, unable to teach me more feminine ways of living.

5. I felt my sister had betrayed me.

6. I had always caused trouble in my family.

7. I was hotheaded, strong-willed and passionately principled to a fault.

8. I tended to challenge popular political views and wanted to buck the system.

9. Deep down, I didn't care if I lived or died.

By further journaling, sifting memories and feelings over a period of months, I slowly learned how to lessen the intensity of my outrage and how to protect myself. I started looking at my own inner life rather than working so vehemently to change other people's attitudes. In brief, I stopped fighting and found new ways to honor my brother and my son through prayer and life-giving ritual, not in bitter acts of defiance like Antigone's.

However, I never trivialized some real truths in her stand. Throughout the play, Antigone defends her actions as based in personal feminine principles of kinship, love, and loyalty. She argues that she "and Polynices are from the same womb." In stating this position, Antigone reopens the debate between Apollo and the Furies in Aeschylus' *Eumenides*, but in contrast to the Orestes trial, Antigone affirms that the woman's womb is the decisive blood tie rather than the father's seed. Creon has no use for such thinking and bases his decisions solely on the authority of the state. Any hope the audience may have for a new order—one synthesizing two views of justice, masculine with feminine, society with family, and reason with passion—unhappily dissolves when Creon's son Haimon dies alongside his fiancé.

Though seeing Antigone's flaws, I also knew that I had the courage to go into darkness, places that Ismane would not tread. Deep inside I had once embraced archetypal suicidal desires, feeling it better to kill myself than disgrace my father. Though I now wanted to live, death is no stranger to me, and I am stronger for it. I remembered the ancient Greeks' belief that the moment of perfection can only be reached at death. Perhaps that perfection can give us a wiser perspective of what is important in life, in Antigone's words, "It is the dead, not the living who make the strongest demands." Rather than drowning in our own misery over the loss of a loved one, we should require ourselves to ask questions about how we conduct our lives and prepare for our own death: "What do the dead want? How does my dead child want me to live?"

Finding a New Myth to Live By

If we are drawn to a particular movie, story, myth, or fairy tale, we may be able to recognize the myth we are living. After carefully examining how our personal ways of being connect to the motif, we may choose to rewrite part of our life script. As we grow further, we may also discover other myths and stories that speak to us more deeply.

In *Antigone,* both the dramatic action and mythic allusions declare that after death there is no hope for rebirth. Antigone is indeed more like Niobe, petrified in stone and forever weeping for her lost children. Encased in a cave-tomb, she will never have the experience of motherhood, but only cold and desolate death. By contrast, myths like the Demeter and Persephone story instill hope for reunion and rebirth.

In preparation for a trip to Greece, I allowed myself to be drawn to the ancient mystery religions and more particularly to the Eleusinian Mysteries honoring Demeter and Persephone. I became ever more clear that their tradition and central myth have much to offer bereaved mothers.[2]

The Eleusinian Mysteries

As has been already mentioned, secret cults in the Greco-Roman world offered individuals direct spiritual experiences not provided by official established religious worship. Though originating in ancient tribal ceremonies, initiation later became a matter of personal choice. Thousands of Greeks and others who could speak Greek chose initiation at Eleusis, a place near Athens, in the Sanctuary of Demeter. After fasting nine days, initiates put on dark clothing and made sacrifices, cleansing themselves. Then as many as thirty thousand men and women began the twelve mile procession along the Sacred Road from Athens to Eleusis. There, they reenacted the myth, sitting by the town well, grieving just as Demeter had grieved when disguised as an old woman. Next they entered the temple, where the high priest commanded that a great fire be ignited, a funeral pyre. The Hierophant beat a huge gong, similar to one the Greek theater employed to imitate thunder. Then came a cry, "Persephone has given birth to a holy boy. A birth has arisen from the fires of death!"

The secret revealed was so well-guarded that we have no precise information about it today. We do know, however, that it involved a vision of Persephone and a birth through fire. The beatified initiates experienced a life-changing epiphany and now expected to enjoy a special status in the afterworld. Whatever the exact details, their initiation was based on the myth of Demeter and Persephone, a story of archetypal mourning, reunion and rebirth.

The Demeter / Persephone Myth

In the full blossom of youth, the story begins, Persephone wanders away from her friends and mother to gather flowers in a meadow at Nysa, a beautiful place but dangerous because of its entrance to the underworld. When Persephone reaches down to pick a narcissus, the earth opens, and the God Hades drags her into his dark kingdom.

When she hears Persephone's desperate cry for help, a sharp pain grips Demeter's heart. The mother knows instinctively that something dreadful has happened to her daughter. Tearing off her headband and letting her hair fall, she clothes herself in dark mourning.

She wanders for nine days, never tasting food or drink nor bathing her skin. On the tenth day, she meets Hecate, goddess of home and hearth, who also heard Persephone's screams but couldn't see what happened. With bitter determination, Demeter persists in her search. Finally, at the assembly of Gods, Helios, the sun god, informs her almighty Zeus himself allowed the girl's abduction. Although Helios pities Demeter's loss, he chides her, "Stop your wailing; you mustn't give yourself to grief so great and fruitless."

Hearing those words, Demeter feels more savage anguish sweep her soul. Stricken, she withdraws from other gods and wanders the earth until she enters the town of Eleusis and disguises herself as a nurse. Looking like an old woman deep in grief, she weeps beneath the olive tree by the town well. Noticing her modesty and graceful air but not recognizing a goddess, the king of Eleusis' four daughters bring her home to be nurse to Queen Metaneira's baby, Demophoon. She cares for the child, and also places him in the blazing fire each night, hoping to immortalize him. Failing to understand the meaning of this ceremony, his mother interrupts it, and he dies. Furious, Demeter reprimands Metaneira.

> Humans are too foolish to know ahead of time the measure of good and evil which is yet to come. You too were greatly blinded by your foolishness. Now it is not possible for him to escape the fate of death.[3]

Then revealing herself as a beautiful goddess, Demeter demands that a temple be built at Eleusis. Brooding alone and still angry, she refuses the company of other gods and brings a dreadful drought on the earth, ready to destroy all humans with famine. Fearing catastrophe, Zeus finally sends his messenger Hermes to Hades, demanding Persephone, who meanwhile has become Queen of the Underworld.

Hades tells Persephone she may leave, but reminds her that when she is with him, she will be greatly honored among gods and all mortals will perform sacred rites and sacrifices in her name. Because she misses her mother, Persephone decides to go, but before departing, tastes a honey-sweet pomegranate seed. For the indiscretion of having tasted the fruit of the underworld, she will be compelled to return to Hades for part of each year.

Demeter accepts this compromise, causing the earth to become fertile again with seeds and flowers. Mother and daughter joyfully embrace, joining the other gods in Olympus. To the people of Eleusis, Demeter communicates sacred rites embodying the great mystery of life and death, but they are not allowed to reveal the secret.

Archetypal Reactions

The myth offers much to assist a mourning mother, firstly by showing how not even a goddess escapes the trials of child death. Demeter's unrestrained grief enacts our own devastation at losing a child. Giving herself completely to grief, she searches for Persephone as if she has lost part of herself. Nothing else exists but fear, shock, sorrow, and rage.

By continuing her angry protests despite chastisement from other Gods, by separating herself from them and challenging the will of Almighty Zeus, and by weeping at the well and becoming a nurse, Demeter enacts archetypal, normal, and natural responses of a mother whose child has recently died. Like Isis, who also nurses a baby boy, and nightly places him in the fire, Demeter dramatizes women's common attempts to find relief by giving to another. Such caring partly satisfies one's own desire for protection and repair, while little endangering a mother's mourning process, for she does not tie her dreams for the future to the particular child she helps. Nevertheless during the sensitive period following her loss, her ardent sympathy, tenderness or wish to prevent others' suffering must not become excessive. The myth also makes this point, for though Demeter wants to make the baby boy immortal, she is ultimately forced to surrender this hope.

Both the continuing anger, the drought where nothing grows, and the threat of famine all symbolize Demeter's despair. Even Zeus is moved to intervene, but because Persephone has tasted the fruit of the underworld, things can never be the same. Demeter must finally agree to a new kind of relationship with her daughter. As she puts it: "Mere mortals can never understand the entire scheme of things. A mystery in life is that what looks so evil may in time be good." Their mutual suffering must become transformative, reuniting them, not just as mother and daughter, but on a higher plain, where the two become one.

The Mother / Daughter Bond

The ancient Greeks envisioned the Underworld as a place where souls dwelled in another form. Differing from such mainstream Greek notions as Homer's, whose afterlife is shadowy and sad, the Eleusinian Mysteries call the Underworld "the place of happy arrival." Though missing her mother, dead Persephone has apparent satisfaction living as the Queen of Hades.

In his particular retelling of the Demeter myth, the poet Ovid even criticizes her excess grief, having the nymph Arethusa declare: "Demeter, this is too much. I saw your daughter. She is sad, but she is queen." Moreover, Persephone has eaten the pomegranate of her own free will. One popular version of the myth even has her plucking fruit from trees in Hades' garden.

Persephone dwells in Hades only in each winter, afterward returning with spring to the sun-filled land of the living. On the other hand, some Greek lore holds that Persephone remains in the Underworld. Always with Hades, she is in both places at once.

Initiates of the Eleusinian Mysteries also affirmed the spiritual unity of maiden and woman, accepting a unity-in-duality even when it is beyond the reach of rational mind. In this view, mother and daughter are a single entity: the soul. In nature's facts, daughter becomes mother, mother surrenders to death and then becomes a daughter: such cyclical transformations being part of the Great Round of all human existence, including our own.

Further uniting duality, Persephone is both Queen of the Underworld and Goddess of Spring. Even her name also carries this unifying meaning, *pertho*, to destroy, and *phonos*, death. Wearing a veil symbolizing her mystery, this beautiful maiden comes to the Underworld to destroy death. Accordingly, though often feared, Persephone is always praised.

To sum up, while Demeter's and Persephone's relationship has been forever changed, the mother understands the new reality of her daughter's being in both realms at once. Such realization can come to any mother wishing to maintain a deep relationship with her deceased child.

Breaking the Earthly Bond

Until she finished high school, Kim's and her mother Mary's shared life seemed as lovely as the flowering meadow from which Persephone was stolen. Preparing for college, Kim looked upon the task of separating from her mother "with both fear and excitement." Once away from home, she gradually grew into a successful young woman, easily passing her engineering license exam. Her early death, however, broke her mother's heart. Mary tried to articulate the unique close relationship they had enjoyed.

> I have three boys I love dearly, but they never want to involve themselves in the kind of deep conversations I shared with Kim. The boys always seemed to have a different philosophy from us girls. They are tough goal-oriented guys who knew you had to work hard. Kim and I shared more compassion for the world. And, too, we had a mutual admiration for each other.

When Kim gave her senior speech at the Academy of the Sacred Heart High School, she evoked the pathos of leaving.

> Stages of life come and go, each leaving a mark on our character, but no mark is as sweet as that left by youth.

Only seventeen, she had an unusual appreciation of time's changes and precious remembrances.

It seems only yesterday that my mother was singing me this children's song, always hesitant at the thought of the last sentence:

"Where are you going my little one? Where are you going, pigtails and all? Turn around and you're two, turn around and you're four, turn around and you're a young girl going out on your own."

Though only an adolescent, Kim understood how separation and loss inevitably accompany the gifts of motherhood: a healthy daughter completes her education, she continues to separate, beginning a career, then marrying and nurturing a family of her own. But separation brings both mother and daughter rewards. When reenacting the myth of Demeter and Persephone, the Greeks manifested their mature understanding of separation and union. In their mystery rites death's wrenching break also amplifies and dramatizes the mother-daughter bond. Death, the great Separator, tears at mother and daughter's soul-bond, but it never breaks and may even become stronger in another realm.

NOTES:

1. Sophocles, "Antigone," in *Greek Plays in Modern Translation*, Dudley Fitts, ed., New York, 1964, pp. 459–499.

2. The reader will notice many similarities to the Isis-Osiris myth in Chapter Two. Joseph Campbell held all such stories were "the monomyth" of ancient agricultural civilizations throughout the world. Demeter-Persephone offers particular utility to a nourishing mother, for many reasons, some of which I explicate below. In addition, I find especially moving its pervasive femininity: one combining passion, strength and hope with beauty and floral sweetness. Many women will resonate with these qualities and find consolation in the myth's other archetypally feminine qualities. We may think of the monomyth as offering us hundreds of variations, each of which can speak to us in somewhat different ways, even as they create their single chorus of hope.

3. Apostolos N. Athanassakis, trans., *The Homeric Hymns*, Baltimore, 1976, pp. 8–9.

Chapter Thirteen

CREATIVITY:
BRINGING INTO BEING

He who hopes to grow in spirit
will have to transcend obedience and respect.
He will hold to some laws
but he will mostly violate
both law and custom, and go beyond
the established, inadequate norm.

— C. P. CAVAFY

ALL OF US have the ability to perform creative acts, *to bring something new into being.* When we make something new and become completely absorbed in the process—whether writing, painting, cooking, or gardening—we may lose all sense of time and be free of distraction. So engrossed, we reach a higher, more integrated state of consciousness, one which seems to have a general healing effect on the psyche.

Creativity as Repair

Not surprisingly, engaging in creative processes can also help repair a grieving mother's wounded psyche. In the following examples we see creative healing at work in three artists: a world renouned sculptor, a local portrait painter, and myself, a beginning student.

Sculptor Kaethe Kollwitz, whose eighteen-year-old son Peter enlisted in the German army at the outbreak of World War I, was already suffering deep depression and unable to work when he was killed. But by imagining Peter with his artistic talent, standing beside her giving encouragement, she mobilized her own creativity. Painting and sculpting again, she believed she could live the life denied her son. She began a memorial that took eighteen years to complete. In the middle of the project, she decided to dedicate the memorial to all grieving parents. Her two stone sculptures, "Morning Father" and "Morning Mother" stand at the soldiers' cemetery near Roggevelde, Belgium. Kaethe created other works with maternal themes, including a deeply moving Pieta and arresting woodcuts depicting outrage at the futility of killing. In such works as "Mary and Elizabeth," showing Elizabeth pregnant with John the Baptist and Mary pregnant with Jesus, Kollowitz exemplifies how identifying with a dead child's creative potential can bring forth new life.

Although our local artist Theresa had been working steadily as a portrait painter, following her son's suicide, she stopped doing portraits and instead chose religious themes, a move that gave her much comfort.

> Painting and sculpting don't just occupy my time. They are a means of creating new life. My friend also lost her son to a drug overdose. She asked me to paint my own version of the Pieta "because Mary saw her son die and maybe she could find some kind of connection there." I studied a lot of Pietas and then I painted one. My work has deepened, more depth than I ever thought I had.

Though I had never touched a paint brush before, after Duncan died I felt like making art, so I sought out an art teacher who encouraged students to paint whatever came up from the unconscious rather than asking them to depict any preconceived idea. We painted without our teacher's instruction or criticism, letting our work pile up in her students' studio. Every few months we reviewed our own paintings with her, not from any aim of judging competitive accomplishment, but simply to notice what was there in color, line, and movement. The first time I reviewed my work this way, I was surprised to discover several images of Madonna and Child—the nurturing mother beside or holding the baby—faintly visible in every painting.

The compensatory nature of the unconscious revealed itself in these obsessional representations. The image had come unsought and unremarked, yet serving to correct my conscious attitude. Consciously, I had identified myself too exclusively with the *Mater Dolorosa,* the grieving mother motif. The Madonna and Child image had risen from my unconscious, connecting me with the Great Mother Goddess within. Over time, I came to understand that new images of a noble and nurturing mother helped to heal my negative self-concept as a woman incapable of aiding her child. The Divine Child in paintings spoke of new life within me, movement toward growth and wholeness occurring outside conscious awareness.

Healing Arts: Bricolage and Gardening

More informal means exist for creating healing art. One is *bricolage. Bricolage* is a French word commonly meaning home repair, home maintenance, or more dynamically, tinkering. A *bricoleur,* like any household Ms. Fix-It, is constantly inventing solutions to little problems, which she executes more or less well depending on her supply of tools (from small to large), construction materials (wood, concrete, bricks, etc.) fasteners (brads, long and short nails, screws, plastic ties, etc.), finishing materials (primer, colored paints, shellacs, etc.), brushes, sandpapers and so forth ad infinitum.

A household *bricoleur* proceeds by constantly matching her collection of dozens of different kinds of things to the task, sometimes using a great many of them in such a simple job as installing a light fixture in a ceiling and afterward refinishing the surface. The process inevitably yields new solutions to problems and even new creations, as *bricoleur* carries on a multiplex dialogue with tools, materials, and goal, and her enabling or limiting environment.

Such people are inveterate collectors of little bits of things: a piece of 00 type sandpaper, a one-inch paintbrush, and a stray piece of two-inch wood. The spirit of the bricoleur is that of the Hunter/Collector/Piecer-Together/Inventor/Discoverer.

Anthropologist Claude Levi-Strauss also applied the word *bricolage* to an elaborate way of knowing discovered among primitive tribes. Not subordinating one datum to another, they make new connections. An active balance of sensing, thinking, intuition, and feeling characterizes their work.

Psychologists have also used the general bricolage approach to make creative art and release new potentialities in the creator. For example, Dr. Jose Cedillos begins groups by giving each person a 4'x4' piece of cardboard and a big trash bag. They have one hour to pick up trash. Then they take their materials, once valueless, and make them into something of value.

This folk art is available to everyone, including mourning mothers. Here's how. Collect some of the deceased child's personal objects. Rather than preserving them intact, as a way of clinging to the past, use them to create something new, without knowing what it will be as you start. For instance, one mother cut up an old T-shirt, spray painted her child's shoe, and with other such materials made an unexpected set of forms. Working with such personal remains, you are collecting colors, textures, and even smells all mixed with your memories surrounding the deceased's precious objects. Though retaining the powers deriving from its original materials, the image that emerges is also a newly created motif; you have reached down to tap archetypal forms and energies not rational or preconceived. These motifs may continue to inform a mother, holding numinous mysteries not fully understood. More encompassing than collage (pasting together materials not normally associated with one another), such bricolage with charged materials not only creates something new and unique, it causes changes in one's inner world. Images, ideas, objects, signs, and symbols have become raw materials for creating, thinking, and doing. Bricolage art is like improvisation in theater, and while we may hope for more seriously useful results, they come out of creative play. The playful attitude behind bricolage is itself useful to the mourning mother.

Creative play like this helped Sandy complete her doctoral program in spite of her husband's unexpected death. Though advised to discontinue her studies for a time, she pursued the theme of "Creative Process and Women's Art" by shifting her thesis focus to "Working through Grief by Making Art." Her contact with Dr. Jose Cedillos led to her utilizing bricolage.

> More than we know happens to the human spirit after a loved one dies. If we could connect to what we are truly experiencing, we would realize our deep understanding of the natural reciprocity of all life. Making bricolage provided me with this

connection. As I taped, then sprayed, then stripped the surface, layer after layer, I began to understand how the physical (mortal) world comes together, falls apart, then comes together again. That the messages gleaned through these experiences translate, in my art, to a personal system of knowing.[1]

The most lasting and poignant project in Sandy's grieving process, however, came from her connection with the earth. By focusing on the relationship, or metaphor, of flowers to life's human cycle, she realized how to immortalize death and celebrate life at the same time. With help from a landscape designer, she put together a garden design with 10 of her husband's favorite perennial flowers. In a summer ceremony, friends and family members planted a garden, then spread the deceased's ashes throughout.

By midsummer, the flowers were in full bloom. The Russian sage planted at either end and in the middle of the garden were five feet tall. Their purple hue provided a backdrop for the yellow coreopsis and magenta miniature geraniums. The delphiums stood tall next to each other while white and lavender cone-flowers sat between them reaching for the sun.[2]

Planting and cultivating a garden is another way to enlist the psyche's curative powers. Working with our hands and feet in the soil literally grounds us, helping us feel earth's archetypal support. We activate our imagination, by planning a design, choosing colors, and deciding where to place seedlings. In time, the fully-blooming plants delight us with their colors, textures, and scents, bringing with them the archetypal energies of Beauty.

Claude Monet used gardening to recover from a debilitating depression. Realizing its great contribution to his healing, he painted garden scenes to lift the souls of Frenchmen and women suffering World War One's psychological aftereffects. Because the restorative benefits of gardening are well-recognized, horticultural therapists regularly work in hospitals and prisons teaching people how to help heal themselves.

Keeping Connection Through Creating Images

There are infinite ways to seek the consolations of creative activity. Although we are often unaware of it, our knowledge and love of family and friends is based on images: my grandmother knitting by the fire or uncle showing off his new car to the neighbors. Archetypal psychologist James Hillman maintains that by actively creating such images we maintain and renew our sustaining intimate connections.

> If the character of a person is a complexity of images, then to know you I must imagine you, absorb your images. To stay connected with you, I must stay imaginatively interested, not in the process of our relationship or in my feelings for you, but in my imaginings of you. The connection through imagination yields an extraordinary closeness.[3]

We learn to know a person intimately when we recall her many images stored in our memory. Like Isis collecting pieces of Osiris, we continue knowing our absent but surviving children by imagining how they are maturing, how they react in certain situations, what personality traits they are acquiring. Similarly, if we continue to imagine our deceased child, we maintain a connection with her throughout life. For some grievers, like Jungian analyst Harry Wilmer, this connection occurs naturally, a gift of grace, enabling them to feel their child's presence. In *Quest for Silence* he presents a series of dreams showing his journey in grief following his son Hank's death. Four months after the tragic automobile accident, Dr. Wilmer wrote in his diary:

> In this dark time of grief, Hank's image seems everywhere, clear, strong, with a warm smile of recognition. I marvel at what I see and remember. There is a radiance, and my soul's eye accommodates to the darkness that struck with his sudden violent death. Hank's presence, even now, comforts and holds my sadness and tears. In death the invisible filial bond is as strong as in life. If this is a gleam of heaven, then we are with Hank.[4]

Most mothers report that this lifelong bond is a "natural" part of their inner life, and Theresa even believes she is closer to her child in death.

> Actually, my husband was the one who had close times when our son was alive. They played golf, went to ball games, did lots of things together. But now I have a spiritual relationship with Will, while my husband only cries.

Almost eight years after her son's death, Matilda keeps him ever present.

There is never a day that goes by when I don't think of him. Some thoughts are joyful, some sad.

Such examples further bring home the powerful truth of sustained life we discovered in the Demeter-Persephone story.

Creating a New Home for Your Child

As mothers begin imagining a child's future life, starting with conception, so they can willingly continue creating her life after death. We can start by imagining a place for our deceased child to live, for example, safely placing her in a heavenly home. Such inner acts can help a mourning mother more fully answer her most urgent question: *Where is my child now?* While response to the question may involve many psychological levels—including religious beliefs, subjective experience, or spontaneous connection with symbols, she can also actively seek to find a home where she meets her child.

The precise location takes infinite forms. Some women go to the cemetery with fresh flowers, others see their child in all of nature, still others find another person or even an animal that symbolically holds the child's spirit. Other common solutions imagine a child's continually developing in heaven, looking down from heaven at her family, seeing her lovingly surrounded by deceased grandparents, or simply feeling the child living by one's side.

For Matilda, a flower has become a symbol and therefore a locus or home for Reed's presence. Soon after her son died, she volunteered to chaperone a group of students traveling to Assisi. But she found being around his friends more difficult than anticipated. One night, laying her head against her hotel room's window sill, she sobbed herself to sleep. Awakening the next morning, her eyes opened on a field filled with tall sunflowers. She took active notice of the event, choosing to see it as significant response to her yearning. Since then, she has noticed that sunflowers repeatedly enter her life, and they do whenever she is certain Reed's spirit is nearby. Such was the time when years later Reed's unknowing schoolmate sent her a single beautiful sunflower with his thank you note. Later on in a moment of synchronicity, she discovered a newspaper photo of herself at age nine, holding the blue ribbon she had won for submitting the Garden Club's most beautiful sunflower.

In Alice Sebold's imaginative novel, *The Lovely Bones*, fourteen-year-old Susie Salmon looks down from heaven, her strange new home. Though its playground is much like hers on earth, in heaven, she gets whatever she wants just by thinking it. Counselors introduce her to new friends and otherwise help her adjust. She is also able to flow down to earth and brush against her loved ones, who then sense her presence. Susie's main concerns are those left behind—her parents' strained marriage, her sister's being overly protected as a replacement child, her little brother's inability to understand death, and her father's efforts to ensnare her murderer. She tries to help them as they stumble and grow through their grief. When her mother and father finally reunite, her father at last is able to talk about Susie's presence.

"Don't tell me you don't see her," he says.

Her mother admits she sees Susie everywhere. Then Father asks, "So if I tell you Susie was in the room ten minutes ago, what would you say?"

"I'd say you were insane and you were probably right," Mother answers.

From then on, Susie's parents share the moments when they feel her presence. Talking about her becomes a normal part of their life, as does their belief that the dead truly talk to us: "In the air between the living, spirits bob and weave and laugh with us. They are the oxygen we breathe."

Imagining our children residing happily in the afterlife and occasionally visiting us brings great comfort. Psychotherapist Sukie Miller laments that Westerners' concept of heaven grows foggier and clergy describe it in less detail.

> Today I encourage my clients to steep themselves in imaging the afterworld, to ask their minister or rabbi or priest for explicit descriptions of life after death, to picture a life as full and rich as they can for their children now. For this is the way people in other places find solace when their children pass out of their world—not by freezing them in a familiar time and place but by imaging them in a well-defined world after.[5]

Not surprisingly, many mothers grow fascinated with the idea of reincarnation and actively pursue the belief that we return to earth many times as another being. They take encouragement from widespread reports of people sensing that a friend or family member is familiar from another life or of many individuals' common speaking of certain contemporaries as "old souls," wise from living many lives. If we choose to imagine our child has been reincarnated, we have hope for her living a full future life. Some mothers even report meeting a child much like their deceased one, and believing she is reborn in that child's body.

How Does My Child Want Me to Live?

Jung employed a special way to explore the psyche he called "active imagination," a process of dreaming with open eyes. To engage your imagination with this technique, you must first concentrate on a specific point, picture, mood or event and then allow whatever series of images spontaneously develops. Gradually these images become dynamic, creating a new psychological situation within you. Many who have never heard of active imagination spontaneously carry on imaginary dialogues with their deceased children, but even they, wishing to go deeper, may benefit by reading about Jung's method.[6]

Whenever conducting dialogues with our dead child, however, we should be wary of becoming too self-absorbed. We can learn more if we try and see life from our child's perspective, asking her useful questions: "How would you want me to live my life? What unfinished business do we have? What can I do for you now? What is left incomplete that I may be able to fulfill?" As has been suggested, in doing so, we evoke the archetypal wisdom of the dead, and our child may become our psychopomp, a guide leading us toward the life beyond.[7]

Before her son died, Rheba had been dominated by her workaholic husband who involved the entire family in his business. She went to her Venetian photographs, "Women of Hope" and 'Women of Despair" when she wanted to seek counsel with her son Carter. In time, he pointed her in new directions.

> Yeah, I had all that rage going on, but now Carter gives me a new focus for that energy and makes me feel how fine life is and how I'm not going to waste it by just being mad all the time. He has insisted I put away "Woman of Despair."

"It's enough, Mom," he says, "feed on 'Woman of Hope.'" Carter gives me a lot of courage, and he died for our sins, sort of. Sins of the parents. To show how you have to get with life and make it worthwhile. Even if it is just enjoying yourself and having a good time. I think part of my rage was the inferiority I felt about being a woman and not powerful. And now I think you can be empowered by just loving life and trying to live it.

Through her imaginative interchange and shifting emphasis from her loss to Carter's viewpoint, Rheba finds meaning in Carter's death. Wanting to experience some of her son's unlived life, she has become passionately alive.

In considering that were it not for her son's fatal accident, Andrew would be full of imagination and creativity, Kate also learned to incorporate some of her son's unlived parts. In one of her many letters to him, she praises his imagination.

Dear Andrew,

Dad read *Embraced by the Light,* and one passage made him cry. The author talks about part of our purpose being to use our imagination to the fullest. Andrew, you did that so well. I love your school paper where you say, "I have a great imagination and sometimes I let it go wild!" Andrew, that is what makes your leaving so hard. Your life was filled with happiness and promise. How could it have been cut short?

When she later came upon a video Andrew had made of his family, Kate was suddenly moved to take snapshots of every imaginable household activity. With her renewed energy, she began living out her son's creative wildness. Her pictures eventually led to her becoming the photographer at her children's school, and after composing more letters to him, her creative writing expanded into poetry and creative meditations for her church.

Ginger remembers how much Peter's volunteer work meant to him. Though he was successful, as AIDS incapacitated him, he became unable to maintain his interior design business. Ginger continued her work as a nurse, and Peter moved home with her. No matter how bad he felt, however, each day he made himself go to the AIDS Task Force, delivering meals to bedridden patients.

Throughout the long ordeal caring for her son, Ginger never knew another parent whose child had AIDS, but after Peter died, she decided to carry on her son's work by preparing and delivering meals. Because she has made many friends through the task force, today she no longer suffers her old isolation. Remembering their deceased child's needs helps Ginger and all the rest of these women be more meaningfully alive. In essence, they live as their child would have wanted.[5]

Creative Moves Toward Transcendence

In teaching his grandson, a Cherokee Indian grandfather describes the internal battle of good and evil, familiar to most of us.

"There are two wolves fighting inside me, one is evil, full of anger, greed, arrogance, self-pity, and resentment. The other is filled with joy, peace, love, humility, and kindness."

"Which one is going to win?" the boy asks.

The grandfather replies, "The one I feed."

As we have seen, solitude is an important and recurrent phase of mourning. Looked at another way, creative living, by whatever means, requires time and space to be alone and feed the soul. Ann Morrow Lindbergh, who lost her child and much later her husband, writes eloquently about the value of aloneness and the art of solitude.

I am again faced with woman's recurring lesson. Woman must come of age by herself. She must find her true center alone.[8]

And Jung stresses that if we hope to evoke divine power and use it in our lives, we must find a place to be alone.

The patient must be alone if he is to find out what it is that supports him when he can no longer support himself. Only this experience can give him an indestructible foundation.[9]

For those of us with active children, like Jill, creating sacred time and space to be alone is a challenge. She solved the problem by hiding away in her large walk-in closet. With no children at home, Kay, on the other hand, has designed an elaborate meditation area in a separate room, complete with beautiful candles and religious objects on an altar. Rheba, as we have seen, sits by her pictures "Hope" and "Despair, but

Terri, another grieving mother, retreats to a wrought-iron love seat at the foot of her garden fountain. All these people can be said to be "praying." During our alone time we offer our personal prayers, which may or may not correspond with traditional religion. Prayer serves both the nonbeliever and the believer alike, for the act of praying more often changes us than it changes outside circumstances. Prayer may mean no more than sitting for fifteen or twenty minutes a day, providing a basic mental hygiene to a mind filled with chatter. Even the very devout are sometimes unsure about what constitutes prayer, as Peter, a contemporary novice monk, makes clear.

> I don't know what prayer is. On an existential level, I am quite incapable of saying, after a time of prayer, whether or not I have really prayed. I just can't determine the dividing line between prayer and what is simply a rambling mind, or dreaming, or an emptiness which is only a completely natural rest or peace.

No matter how performed or to whom addressed, prayer is always a creative act. Whether we pray to God, Jesus, or the Blessed Virgin, Buddha or Allah, Father/Mother God, the Great Goddess, the Tao or the Universe, receiving answers requires our imagination. Solutions depend on one's own strength, whether that divine strength is found by connecting to the Greater Power within or to our God without.

Although prayer in all religions contains certain patterns—petitions, confessions, intercession, praise, and thanksgiving—the supreme form is considered to be adoration in holy silence toward the immeasurable mystery of God. Mystical union, the experience of ecstasy, described by the German Dominican Meister Eckhart, brings complete identification with the divine.

> The eye in which I see God is the same eye in which God sees me. My eye and God's eye are one eye and one seeing, one knowing and one loving.

Meditation is a form of prayer which can be based on a set of cognitive religious beliefs or can simply use some other system to move one's consciousness to a different level of reality. Contemplative religions often combine repetitive prayers with the use of prayer wheels or beads to reach a meditative state. Some use a Sanskrit *Mantra*, a word or phrase repeated in the mind that helps us quiet thoughts and find a deeper level of consciousness. Sometimes focus is placed on breathing or imaging a sacred symbol like a mandala. In his "creative theology," Dominican scholar Matthew Fox recommends extroverted meditation: walking, swimming, or playing the drum with a consciousness of immersing oneself in the rhythms of life.

At the Center for Creation Spirituality and Culture in Oakland, California, Fox teaches theology with painting, music, dance, poetry, and other activities, encouraging students to listen to the cosmos within and around them and give birth to a creative theology. He defines spirituality as a way of life, dictating our response to everything with a sense of awe and wonder, and mysticism as a form of religious practice centering on firsthand experience of the divine. His numerous books—*Creation Spirituality, Original Blessing, The Coming of the Cosmic Christ*—speak of an authentic spirituality derived from community celebration, social justice, compassion, ecological awareness, and valuing our own moments of ecstasy.

Living Creatively By Honoring Subjective Experience

Today there is widespread yearning for psychic wholeness and spirituality that is not necessarily based on institutionalized religion, yet many mothers are finding these deepening experiences within their church or synagogue. What all long for is connecting to a Holy Presence so as to feel its power in our lives.

In a series of lectures delivered at Edinburgh University at the turn of the last century, William James explored the "varieties of religious experience." He described our normal rational consciousness as but one special type surrounded by other entirely different latent forms of consciousness. James found a certain mystical state was similarly described by people in all times and places, though it was ultimately ineffable and must be directly and individually experienced. Sometimes called "cosmic consciousness," it involves being enveloped by an overwhelming Presence, which we may call "God" or "The Absolute." Through long and disciplined spiritual practice, the devoted of all creeds and religions can touch God in this way, but others, even atheists, have received the gift spontaneously. Uniformly, they know it is one of the most important moments in their lives. They come away with gratitude and humility, returning to life as an ordinary human being, but not needing to have faith because they "know."

I think of my own mystical experience as a gift from God in a moment of severe trauma. I had never engaged in meditation or any spiritual discipline before this life-changing event. In subtle ways, the experience has become my ultimate authority, breaking down my total reliance on rationalistic consciousness.

Early Sunday evening we were all at home when we heard rushing footsteps and Duncan's girlfriend Lori crying, "He's shot himself!" I rushed upstairs to his bedroom, then climbed the ladder to his loft. My son was dead. I called for Lori, who sat next to me in her pretty white dress, now full of blood. I held my dead son in my arms and screamed.

It was then, while holding Duncan, that an incredible sensation came over me. I began to feel embraced by an ever-loving presence, and my capacity for love also became so sweet. I was held in love. At the same time the air became quite different, as if it were filled with tiny sparks no bigger than pinheads. I soon lost my sense of embodiment and felt at one with the special atmosphere around me. It occurred to me that I understood everything there was to know. I had no questions to ask. This sense of knowing has stayed with me throughout my ten-year quest for healing. It is as if I know everything of importance when it comes to a higher realm, and yet what I know can not be stated. In addition, it is with a sense of utter humility that I have this knowing. I am overwhelmed by the awesomeness of God. I know all and I know nothing.

I am not certain how long that night I remained in this blissful state, dimly aware that my husband handled the terrible practical matters surrounding suicide. I clearly recall, however, that I returned to a state of hysterical grief. Angry and unforgiving when I had to be finger-printed (a requirement for investigating violent deaths), I raged against the police, the mental health systems, and God. I was determined that they were not going to put my son in a body bag. But because I knew he was dead, what else could I do?

As I've already made clear, the mystical experience had no sudden power to make my behavior saintly, but it did start my ten-year quest to find some meaning in my son's suffering and my own loss. During

the early months of alternately raw and deadening grief, I was sustained
by a memory lying just on the edge of consciousness, a tender knowing
that my son was safe and embraced by love. Two years later an intern
I was supervising introduced me to Siddah Yoga, a meditative practice
that led me to India. I knew the goal of yoga was union with God, and
I wanted to develop the kind of awareness I had been given on the night
of Duncan's death. At Gurumayi's ashram near Bombay, I learned spiritual practices that enable me to feel connected, not only to Duncan, but
to the entire universe. When I read my journal entries today, the weeks
at the ashram seem remote yet greatly comforting.

> I arrived at Gurudev Siddaha Peeth just as the dawn lightens
> the sky. The entrance to the ashram is filled with statues and
> turrets. I pass the Indian guards, enter the courtyard, and fol-
> low the walkway past shrines and temples surrounded by beau-
> tiful tropical gardens. I have been traveling for forty hours so I
> welcome the continuous energy supplied by the chanting. "See
> God in everyone and in yourself."

> The next day, I begin chanting myself: "Om Naamah Shivaya,"
> "I worship God within me."

> This mantra proves the meditation treasure that connects
> with the God in me. It is me becoming the chant. After enough
> repeating, I find the mantra leaves me. I am then lost in the
> space. I rest in this space and I am open to the universe within
> me. High on a mountain at 4:30 in the morning, I sit in lotus
> position under the protection of a large white tent. My body
> is clammy from the heat and the monsoons. After two hours,
> enmeshed in its sweetness, I hope the chanting will have no end.
> Periods of unbelievable bliss leave me with tears of gratitude.

> I am the sun rising over the mountain at daybreak. I am the
> elephant rain pouring ponderously. I am as strong and as still
> as the mountain. I am the mountain. I am the Self of Duncan
> and the same Self is me; I am the Self and not the mind. I am
> overwhelmed with love for the whole world. My son calls to me
> in a clear and certain voice, "Mom, I'm home," he says.

Though in India I felt connected to God and to Duncan, no experience ever approached immediately after his death. Years later a German
Jungian analyst explained to me the precise grace I had received that

night, when knowing Duncan was embraced in love and free from pain. "You were experiencing in those moments just what Duncan was experiencing," he said. I immediately knew the interpretation was right for me. With this new understanding, I had what Jung called an "Ah Ha!" moment. Why wouldn't a mother and child, so connected in the womb, be connected that night in death in a *participation mystique* of joyful bliss?

William James coined the term "Nothing but" to denote the common practice of explaining and thereby negating mysterious or even mystical events, reducing them to ordinary phenomena. We devalue higher experiences by equating them with inferior ones: "Oh, this is nothing but a dream, or it's nothing but a coincidence." Even when we personally take our unusual subjective experiences seriously, we are reluctant to admit so doing to others. Though it is not necessary to share these sacred times, we must privately honor our special ways of knowing.

Sally had several times made contact with her deceased son Chip. These experiences "uplifted, reassured, and healed" her. Nevertheless, as time went by, her rational side relentlessly began to diminish the events. Then she had a dream: her deceased child was sitting in a room with the police, his principal, and his doctor. All rational authorities confirmed her son's ongoing existence. Thus she awoke from the dream elated.

> I am in his school, and I have lost Chip. I am frantically searching for him. I am looking for the principal's office.
>
> "Where is the principal's office? Chip is only three. I can't find my son."
>
> So I run to the principal's office and they are all there—the police, the doctor, the principal, and Chip—all in one room.
>
> "Oh, my God, I've found you."
>
> I was so happy. After two years, I had found him.

Integrating the sacred into our being is a lifelong process with tasks similar to the mourning process. We must never use sacred experience to replace the hard work of personal growth: for example, seeking spiritual highs to bypass emotional problems or interpersonal problems.

We need to always keep our inner self dialoguing with our ego, lest we over identify with the archetypes, as if we were they, rather than a single person participating in psychological realities all people share. In the following inner dialogue, for example, Kay, a devout Buddhist, checks carefully before affirming her experience to be genuine.

> I meditate with my eyes closed, but this morning my right eye kept wanting to open slightly, and after several futile attempts to keep it closed, I finally let it be as it wished. A light was coming up from the floor, and as its rays got closer to me, they broadened and were directed to my chest, or center, or heart. It continued to pour into me, neither waxing nor waning the entire thirty minute meditation, which seemed like five minutes. When my timer went off, I thought: "I will never be the same again." I finished by bowing over and touching my head to the floor and the light struck me directly in the middle of my forehead. By the time my dedication was over, in which I offer my practice to the liberation from suffering of all human beings, the light was gone. I assume all the light was inside me but I have to be careful not to make spiritual experiences out of illusions. I can, of course, say the light came from the window, in front of which I meditate. But how do I explain my right eye (which has never done this before) or the exact location of the light, or the timing of the light, just during my meditation?
>
> One of my meditation practices is to breathe in suffering and breathe out love, compassion, healing. At first I resisted this, thinking that I was the one who needed the love and who needed to breathe out all the suffering. But I encountered the heart as a transformer.
>
> Now I see that breathing in love would actually be a sign that I couldn't love myself from the inside; and that breathing out suffering would not help the world to heal.

NOTES:

1. Sandy Mayo, "Creating a New Surface: Growing Through Grief,"
    Network: A Publication of The Union Institute, vol. 17, Cincinnati, 2001,
    pp. 24–27.
2. Ibid., p. 28.
3. James Hillman, *The Force of Character,* New York, 1999, p. 185.
4. Harry Wilmer, *Quest for Silence,* Einsiedeln, Switzerland, 2000, p. 142.
5. Sukie Miller, *Finding Hope When A Child Dies,* New York, 1999, p. 88.
6. See Robert A. Johnson, *Inner Work: Using Dreams and Creative Imagination for
    Personal Growth and Integration,* San Francisco, 1989, and Joan Chodorow,
    Jung on Active Imagination, Princeton, NJ, 1997.
7. Greg Mogenson, *Greeting The Angels: An Imaginal View of the Mourning Process,*
    New York, 1959, pp. 101–126.
8. Ann Morrow Lindbergh, *Gift from the Sea,* New York, 1955, p. 134.
9. C. G. Jung, *Psychology and Alchemy,* vol. 12, *Collected Works,* par. 32.

Chapter Fourteen

CONNECTING OUR INNER
AND OUTER WORLDS

*There is a time for mourning, a time for dancing
(Ecclesiastes 3:4). But mourning and dancing are never fully
separated. Their times do not necessarily follow each other. In
fact, there time may become one time. Mourning may turn into
dancing and dancing into mourning without showing a clear
point where one ends and the other starts.*

— HENRI J. M. NOUWEN

IN ORDER TO live authentically, we must close the gap between our
inner and outer worlds as much as possible. What we first experience "outside" must be taken seriously "within oneself." Conversely,
what is initially experienced within oneself must eventually be lived
in our outer lives as well. D. W. Winnicott observed children linking
their two worlds with what he called a "transitional object," a favorite
blanket or teddy bear which they have heavily invested with subjective emotions. He called this connecting of inner and outer "creative
apperception," which he says, "more than anything else makes life
worth living." The following discussions of synchronicity, pilgrimage, ritual, advocacy, sharing, and forgiveness—topics we have already
touched on from other points of view—suggest how these may all aid
in mourning, but they can also serve more generally to bring congru-
ence to our subjective and objective existence.

Synchronicity

Modern atomic physics reveals us all connected in a cosmic web where human observer and the observed interact, time and space are a continuum, and a particle of matter may also be a wave of energy. Such interconnectedness corresponds well with some Eastern religions' views, and with the mystics' experience everywhere, but because Western theology has been dominated by spirit-matter duality, our minds have difficulty understanding profound interconnection. By letting ourselves experience synchronicities, however, we may become more open to our dynamic interrelationship with the universe.

Jung described *synchronicity* as "an acasual connecting principle that manifests itself through meaningful coincidences which cannot be explained rationally." A powerful example is Cookie's dream about her daughter's drowning in the Bayou shortly before the girl's actual death. Some synchronistic moments can be associated with traumatic events, but others reveal comforting knowledge important for our spiritual growth.

Shortly before her mother's falling ill, Theresa dreamed she felt her dead son Neil embrace her and rest his head on her own. Feeling his strong arms around her, she awakened with an enduring new strength, which later helped her through the crisis of having to put her mother in a nursing home. When signing the admission papers, though the actual season of the year was early Spring, she saw a calendar opened to December 9, the date of Neil's birthday. She imagined the synchronicity to be a sign of Neil's sustaining presence, supplying her with the courage she needed.

Using their imagination, mothers can amplify possible connections, giving special moments precious meaning. Kate describes such an incident after the death of her son Andrew.

> The day after he died, the sunset was the most magnificent I've ever seen—the most brilliant pinks and reds. Many friends connected it to Andrew, and one little girl said, "Andrew was painting the sky."
>
> The next week, a neighbor met a fishing buddy who happened to mention he had witnessed the most gorgeous sunset he'd ever seen in thirty years of outdoor fishing. He even took a picture of it. The buddy knew nothing about Andrew,

but our neighbor was shaken when he learned that the picture was taken on October 14, the day after Andrew died. He gave us the photograph because the camera had an automatic date function. October 14 is printed right on it!

Playing with the possibilities is certainly a fuller way of living than passing off such events as mere coincidences. Taking non-logical synchronicities seriously helps us make our inner and outer lives compatible, enriching the well-balanced person whose ego does not easily divorce everyday reality or become flooded by infantile superstition. It is a matter of mobilizing psychic poise when interpreting what happens to us, for a healthy person may well label many concurrent events as "false synchronicities."

Funerals and Mourning Rituals

The work of grieving usually starts when you plan your child's funeral, celebrating her life and marking her death with ritual. Imagining and designing funeral rites, you begin to give words and actions to your deepest inner sorrow, joining your two worlds. In the best circumstances, the priest or rabbi doesn't just offer you standard funeral procedures but also acts as consultant, encouraging all family members to suggest their own ways for making the service most personal and meaningful.

Concentrating on memories of the child provides endless means for celebrating her life. You can place photographs or pieces of her art work at the site or have a musician play her favorite pieces inside the sanctuary. As friends enter it, you may wish to give them a beloved flower along with the program. Having previously asked them to write their thoughts on memory cards, you gather these in a specially designed box.

Mentioning your child's name in the service's opening remarks will ensure her presence throughout. Then participants should learn how the child died and how profoundly she is missed. Inviting close friends or family to speak assures that the child's life will be celebrated. Some of us strongly bound to a particular faith may be adequately consoled by traditionally sanctioned rituals. Others should choose to adhere to personally meaningful readings or otherwise express how they feel.

Even if the family holds no religious belief, a ceremony should always take place because dying is a rite of passage that demands ritual for the sake of those who mourn.

Remember that participants will depart unchanged and ill-satisfied from an impersonal service or when a clergyman glosses over conflicted feelings about death with easy dogma about "eternal peace." A meaningful service will express how we feel, provide a time to say good-bye, and comfort people, enabling them to leave with a sense of hope.[1]

While most of us do not question the need to plan a funeral for our dead child, we should also understand the importance of additional ritual throughout mourning and perhaps all our life. The human need for ritual is linked to what Mircea Eliade calls the "Celestial Archetype." For archaic peoples, neither objects nor human acts had an intrinsic value; they became significant only when imbued with transcendence. Daily taking of nourishment, for example, meant more than merely satisfying a physiological need: always accompanied by prayers, it renewed the need for communion with God. To participate in transcendent reality, people performed rituals learned from ancestors and originally, they believed, from God. In many places, even today these same traditional ceremonies provide a natural way, for moving into the spirit world. For example, ritual acts before and after eating, like the Christian saying "Grace," or specific Jewish Barruchas—prayers blessing God for bread, wine, and water or meat—still live among many modern people as ways to sanctify everyday events.

In our more secular society, however, many people only enact customary rituals on special holidays, but these traditions may have become too painful for the family of a deceased child. In such cases, it may be better to find a new place for a Thanksgiving gathering, for example, or to change ways we celebrate Christmas or Hanukkah. Some mothers may want to ensure the deceased child is clearly present to consciousness on these special days by planning a ritual in the child's memory. One family noticed that their aunts, uncles, and grandparents seldom mentioned Chip's name after his death. The next Christmas Mom, Dad, and two surviving siblings all wore t-shirts with big red letters exhorting, "ASK ME ABOUT CHIP!"

Creating such new rituals can help us move through mourning's most painful days, particularly the death anniversary and birthday of

our dead child. Birthdays of deceased children have been commemo-
rated with cakes and candles, special family dinners, gifts to needy
children, collages and mementos, cards and letters sent to heaven, and
a broad range of other acts. Because mothers imagine their little ones
growing up in an afterlife, the idea of a birthday celebration often
seems right. Then too, many mothers expect their child will be remembered by others if she is honored on her own special day.

Do not be surprised, however, if friends or extended family don't
appreciate the day's importance. One mom baked a cake for her dead
son each year, but her family thought preparing food for a dead person
was ghoulish. Another mother planned a birthday dinner, but after
the second year, she realized her extended family didn't honor the date.
They preferred watching an important football game. Another mother
had gathered her friends to share the burden of the first anniversary,
but after they arrived, no one mentioned her son's name or acknowledged his death. Though difficult to do, observing friends' and family's disengagement and accepting it is better than remaining hurt and
embittered about their lacking understanding.

Even if you are alone in your deep feelings, it is helpful to know
that the anticipation of the dreadful anniversary of a child's death is
oftentimes worse than the actual day. In addition, taking time to plan
a meaningful ritual, thereby knowing what you will do then, gives you
some control in a world that may have come to seem chaotically unpredictable. Further, by committing yourself to ritual every year, you
establish a predictable, structured activity. As with birthdays, put into
the ritual what you believe and value. You may go to a sacred place
or enhance an ordinary space with candles and music or share special
food, showing gratitude for life. Our prayers and meditations should
center around our child but also be a commitment to living our own
life as truthfully as we can.

During the first year, some mothers also perform a daily ritual.
For eleven months after her son's death, Rebecca embraced traditional
Jewish custom, reciting the Kaddish prayer, hymns sanctifying the
Name of God. But the Kaddish also pleas for the speedy realization
of the messianic age. Because the resurrection of the dead is associated with the coming of the Messiah, gradually Kaddish became the
ritual prayer of mourners. Part of any service where the congregation

numbers ten or more, Kaddish calls the dead to remembrance, creating a bridge to their mysterious realm and encouraging them to live in our hearts. For Rebecca, the discipline of attending synagogue also imposed a helpful routine.

> I was waking up early because I was depressed, so going to the synagogue gave me something to do every morning. I had a routine and I was drawn into a community rather than being so isolated in my grief. I didn't believe, like some Jewish mystics, that my son was suffering and I had to pray for his redemption. But I turned to Kaddish because reciting it put me in touch with my boy.

Years later, Dianne, whose son died on a Friday, June 13, still follows a ritual begun in her first year of mourning. Knowing the superstition surrounding that date, she has always had a sense of dis-ease when it turns up on the calendar. But June 13 is also the feast of St. Anthony, and Dianne has become deeply connected to him. Traditionally, St. Anthony is the patron saint who helps us find things that are lost, and in many ways he has helped Dianne connect to her lost son. On her way to or from work, she stops for prayer at St. Anthony of Padua Church. Someday she hopes to make a pilgrimage to Padua, where St. Anthony is as revered as he was in the thirteenth century when the entire city flocked to hear him preach, welcoming him as another St. Francis. Dianne greatly respects St. Anthony's having left a prominent monastery to take vows of poverty and service, becoming a Franciscan friar. When enacting her prayerful ritual, she likes to imagine her son protected by St. Anthony's love and wisdom.

Rhonda gave her life new dimension by beginning repeated activity that eventually became a ritual. Hindu philosophy helps us understand her progress. According to the Hindu Deity Lord Krishna, one's highest good is performing one's *dharma*, or duty. When we do so without personal motives, we reach heights beyond worldly things, becoming content and even-minded. Accordingly, we should be willing to fulfill whatever duties the outer world requires, but the highest *dharma* is recognizing and following the truth in our own heart.

After her son Stan completed suicide, Rhonda was filled with guilt feelings about not having fulfilled her motherly duties, though as an immature divorced mother, she had had little support rearing her troubled and difficult child. Making matters worse, on the night Stan took his life, Rhonda was in an operating room suffering a stroke. Struggling with both her child's death and her illness, and unable to work, she was forced to go on disability.

Understandably, she felt worthless and useless, until learning that Carolyn, a high school friend with multiple sclerosis, needed a ride to a water-therapy class three times a week. Rhonda began driving her friend Carolyn to therapy and also participated herself in the water exercises. These acts became a ritual for Rhonda, because they gave much deeper meanings than just providing transportation. Getting the wheel chair in the car, helping Carolyn dress in her wet suit, and assisting her to the swimming pool required slowing down, patience, and full attention. During these times Rhonda stepped outside her own troubled life and into a routine where she felt usefully needed, calm and centered. As she became more involved with Carolyn's life, Rhonda grew, recognizing her own empathic caregiving qualities and following the wisdom of her heart.

Not only did she discover a capacity for compassion, Rhonda also worked through her feelings of having neglected her child. Carolyn, who had previously striven for independence, also became changed by their ritual, understanding that her willingness to receive helped someone else. Both women felt renewed by the repetitive, structured time they spent together.

Making A Sacred Journey

Older cultures, which draw no lines between sacred and profane, offer their people experiences of The Archetype of the Way—our felt need to progress with and toward divinity—in repeated everyday actions. In addition, they provide special culturally constructed journeys to Mecca, Canterbury, Lourdes, the Ganges—where individuals find companion seekers. In contemporary Western society, however, we are more likely to feel no ready-made Way for us exists, frequently feeling we have lost our way. Not surprisingly, The Way Archetype may then manifest itself in our longing to make a sacred journey.

Even when we know that truth lies somewhere buried within ourselves, we may feel a need to leave our familiar surroundings in order to find answers. By designing a pilgrimage, we prepare to embrace The Archetype of the Way, leaving everyday worries and crossing into a separate psychic space where we can better connect inner and outer worlds. We have great choice of destinations: as far away as the Holy Land of Israel or the sacred mountains of Tibet, or as near at hand as the old family home, a gravesite, or a local shrine.

A pilgrim differs from a tourist by intention and attention. Her destination is a sacred center, a higher plain of consciousness, and she hopes to be transformed by the experience. Desiring to contact the sacred, a pilgrim continues journaling, praying and meditating as she travels, and lets imagination complement her seeing.

In his excellent guide to making travel sacred, Phil Cousineau outlines some preparations for the journey: seek a blessing before leaving, take books that express the soul of your destination, always have your journal, be prepared to perform a sacred ritual, and imagine all you can about your destination. While journeying, recall the words of the thirteenth century Sufi poet Rumi, "As you start on The Way, The Way appears." Imagine all the seekers who have traveled this road before you. Soak in the beauty of your destination. Also, pay attention to the sacred Source of your own being. Choose a piece of the sacred place—without and within—to remind you of your journey, and end your pilgrimage with rituals of gratitude.[2]

My own first experience of pilgrimage was vicarious, when we moved to Spain to take a break, three years after Duncan's suicide. As it happened, our rented house belonged to a grieving mother whose sixteen-year-old son had died in an automobile accident two years before. Whenever Elena had business with us, she would break down in tears: being back in the house where her son had grown up was too much for her. She sought refuge from her grief in activity—learning to play golf, taking Flamenco dance lessons, and the like. But when she could no longer run from her sadness, she convinced her husband Carlos to accompany her on the Camino de Santiago de Compostella.

Several routes actually constitute the "Road to Santiago," traveled since 1100 by pilgrims seeking the sacred tomb of St. James. From every direction, kings and bishops, merchants and troubadours, the penitent and the sick, sinners and saints wended their way to Galicia in Northwestern Spain. Villages and towns grew up along the routes, and hospitals, hostels, churches, bridges and wide roads were built to accommodate the masses. Today's Spanish government has restored ancient landmarks and created a network of wayside *refugios* for the pilgrims, who include thousands of foreigners, most of them entering Spain by crossing the Pyrenees at Roncesvalles and winding their way through lush fields and quaint towns, making the steep climb to the hostel at O Cebriaro and then walking on to Cruz de Hierra, where they unburden themselves of the stones they have carried as penance. At Santiago de Compostela, the weary travelers first come to a massive courtyard and then they enter the cathedral, where they place their right hand in the hand print worn into St. James' marble statue by millions before them. They then attend the pilgrims' mass under the great *botufumeiro*, once used to fumigate them and now swinging down to fill the cathedral with incense.

Elena and Carlos overcame significant obstacles during their thirty-two-day walk—blisters on their feet and muscle pains in their legs, losing sight of the yellow government markers, getting lost at nightfall far from a *refugio*, and fearing wild dogs. Nevertheless, they returned home grateful for space to grieve and also for the pilgrimage's restoring their marriage and their faith. They reported that "the camino contains the energy of all the millions who have walked it." Elena, particularly, felt the presence of those who died along the way. For her, daily keeping the dead pilgrims in her memory made certain her own deceased son would never be forgotten. In short, the spiritual exercise of walking the camino helped them find a healing source within themselves.

For those unable to make such journeys, during the Crusades, the Pope constructed labyrinths to symbolize pilgrimages. The labyrinth in Chartres cathedral was also walked by many whose bad health interrupted their progress to Santiago. Such labyrinths combine circles and spirals into a purposeful path. Walking the labyrinth symbolizes our typically passing through many ordeals to reach the center.

Today a labyrinth revival enables seekers to experience a sacred journey in many places. New labyrinths can be found in numerous churches and parks, and traveling labyrinths circulate among cities. Cindy walked the Washington, D.C., labyrinth when it came to New Orleans.

As I entered it, I started letting go of outside worries and concentrating on the path. I began to feel less anxious as I moved toward the center. It is an incredible experience! I can't really express it. After standing in the center a minute, I had to turn around and find my way back. Reworking the path, I felt empowered and very, very thankful. The feelings are impossible to describe. You have to walk it yourself.

For Kay, however, walking the labyrinth was insufficient. To propel her from her son Scot's death, she felt need of "cataclysmic change for a cataclysmic tragedy." While practicing Himalayan Buddhism at her American Dharma Center, she noticed a poster advertising a pilgrimage to sacred sites in Nepal, followed by trekking in the Solu Kdhumbu to visit several monasteries. At the time her physical condition was as poor as her emotional one, because fibromyalgia and neck disk degeneration had created bone spurs and muscle spasms, requiring physical therapy three times a week. When younger, however, she had been a runner and a hiker, so despite warnings from friends—dangers from Nepalese TB, her susceptibility to bronchitis, and tourists being kidnapped by Maoists—she borrowed money for a ticket to Katmandu. At fifty-eight and worn out with grief, Kay either wanted to really live again or die; she didn't know which.

On the day of departure, five travelers met at the airport, including twenty-year-old Charles, who had been hired to run the video. His parents were very worried about their son. Kay's thoughts:

> I vowed secretly to offer my life for his, even if it were not necessary, just so his mother would not have to go through what I was and so I would not have to go through it any longer, at least not in this human form.

After acclimatizing themselves in a small village near Katmandu, the group flew to Lukla to begin their pilgrimage. They climbed five hours a day, ascended trails whose switchbacks alternated with boulders too large to step over, slept on hard wooden platforms beside porters, and suffered dry December's lung-clogging dust.

The *mani* or prayer walls (stones into which the mantra for compassion is carved) helped transform trek into pilgrimage. Just when Kay believed she could go no farther, she would come upon a new *mani* and her attention would go to the prayer that ends all suffering: "*Om Mani*

Padme Hum," All hail the Jewel in the Lotus, a traditional evocation of the Divine Self, both within and outside each person. She also realized that her attending to her body chased away obsessive thoughts of Scot's fatal accident and severed leg. She knew she had to climb higher, for she was not yet at their destruction. Finally the trekkers reached 14,000 feet, and Kay saw the Rimpoche, a spiritually advanced monk, standing on the other side of a deep gorge.

> ... the only way to reach Rimpoche, rest, and food was to slip and brake our way to the bottom, cross it, and then claw our way up the other side, one small, careful half-step at a time. At the bottom of the gorge, it seemed to me that great boulders could come flying down at any moment, crushing me with a roar. It was my first sense of being in *bardo,* a sort of afterlife before-life psychic place, similar to the feeling with which I started the trip. The riverbed seemed so much like the bottom of something, perhaps I was already dead. No. I could live or I could die. If I wanted to find out, I had to climb to where my Lama stood in his orange down jacket, tattered prayer flags flapping all about him.

Only Charles, Kay, and the porters and guides made the last ascent to Tengpoche Monastery, where they entered a beautiful lodge whose guests were reading and playing cards. Stunned by the contrast to their journey, they wondered how they had gotten to such lovely, safe, and comfortable surroundings. To shatter the illusion of having entered some unearthly realm, they slapped each other's hands and pulled the porters and guides into a dance. It was one of the greatest moments in Kay's life. In Charles, she knew she had acquired what Buddha calls a *putta orasa,* "a son of the breast." Writing in her journal on the last day descent, she reflected on her life and her son Scot.

> I have survived a violent childhood and made amends to my father and myself for holding my resentments too long. I have married and buried a husband; I have borne three children, after which I put myself through college and landed the only teaching job for which I ever applied. I have recovered from alcohol and drug addiction. I have buried a son and not grown bitter. But I no longer suffer under the illusion that I have done this on my own. It looks like, in fact, I am going to live again with the joy we all deserve. My pain is neither larger

nor smaller than anyone else's. It simply or complexly, is. I am Charles, my lama Pema, my porter Dawa, the stone I slipped on, the white water that rushes down, the dust in my lungs, and the rhythm of my breath. Every mother's son dies, sometimes before the mother. My son was someone else's son before he was mine, and he is most likely someone else's son now. When I think about it, I feel jealous, but I thank him for choosing me to give him exactly what he needed in this life. His sudden disappearance is not complete: He is a string of Harley-Davidson Mardi Gras beads flying around the world on the neck of a beautiful woman; he is Charles who makes me laugh; Dawa who gallops me down the mountain; the broken watch on his broken wrist; and the young guard of the sacred temple in rainbow socks. We are only a couple hours from Lukla, and we are going to walk it, on this, the last day of what most people believe is the year 2000.

As I have hinted, one need not travel to unusual or faraway places in order to be a pilgrim. The essentials are longing for a deeper experience and an active imagination. Peggy Lou's and Lacy's outwardly ordinary trip became a pilgrimage because of their intentions.

Shortly after her husband's death, Peggy Lou moved to New Orleans to live with her son and daughter. Tragically, several months later, her son Ed died of a drug overdose. The circumstances of his death made Peggy keep much of her suffering private, to the point that many people back home had not learned of Ed's death. Her son was cremated, but the ashes were not interred in a cemetery.

After a year passed, Peggy Lou and her daughter Lacy decided to take a trip to Maryland. Ever since her father died, Lacy had hoped to visit distant relatives and find out more about his family. Peggy Lou wanted to scatter Ed's ashes in places where he had been happy. Planning their trip with great care, the two women researched Carl's genealogy and wrote to cousins they hadn't seen in years, some they had never met. They chose small quiet hotels or bed and breakfast establishments that would be conducive to the meditative state they hoped to achieve. Their activities all revolved around their quest to find roots and honor their dead.

After losing both father and brother, Lacy wanted to know all she could about family. During their three-day drive to Maryland, mother and daughter shared intimate stories and laughed a lot, and cried. Lacy said, "It was the closest we had ever been." In Baltimore they visited her father's grave and searched out the tombstones of lost relatives. Then they drove to the Eastern Shore, where they knocked at an old farmhouse and declared to the owner, "My father was born in this house." They received permission only to walk around the grounds, but Lacy felt satisfaction, "a little more rooted."

In Glen Burnie they visited Lacy's great aunt, whose family photo Lacy copied at the drugstore. Then they drove to Annapolis to see the place where Lacy and Ed had grown up. They scattered some of Ed's ashes on the Severn River, where he liked to sail, and some more on his high school football field. Then they stopped to pray in the town's lovely old Episcopal church, Lacy saying afterward that "some memories were too overwhelming to hold in our hearts."

When the two returned home, they immediately made a photo album of pictures copied and others taken during the trip. They placed photos of Dad and Ed on the dining table and shared food and a bottle of wine to mark the end of their journey. "Feeling changed in some important way," they gave thanks for all their experiences on the sacred journey.

Protest and Advocacy

When we reflect upon what we value, we may begin championing a cause that can change our outer world. Mothers frequently express hope that their child did not die in vain. Driven by such feelings, some form organizations bearing on social issues connected to child death. Here is another way to bridge our inner feelings and our actions.

Founded in 1980, Mothers Against Drunk Driving, began as one mother's reaction to the tragic death of her thirteen-year-old girl, killed by a repeat offender drunk driver. In 1994, another woman founded Mothers Against Violence in America, to create safe neighborhoods and promote gun control. As we have seen, Parents of Murdered Children helps guide surviving victims through complicated court procedures.

Fueled by mothers' outrage, all these advocacy groups have grown profusely over the past twenty years.

In every language and time bereft mothers have organized, moaning and wailing and speaking their demands to be heard. Perhaps the groups most widely known across the world today are the *Abuelas de Plaza de Mayo and Madres de Plaza de Mayo* (grandmothers and mothers of May Square in Buenos Aires). They aim to locate children who "disappeared" after 1976, when a military dictatorship seized the Argentine government and systematically caused 30,000 people to vanish from society. In the United States, Women in Black—a group of outraged mourning mothers—marches in protest against inhumane deaths, carrying photos of the martyred. Recently, the day after a jury exonerated police officers who shot an unarmed black man, Amadou Diallo, forty-one times, this group put on their black veils and haunted New York streets with their quiet vigils.

> When your loved one's heart stops, so does the clock. Let the politicians move on to other business. Mothers know that the strong-backed refusal to get over it is their final weapon. They rightfully have no faces because they are living ghosts. They are the nagging regrets that fuel insomnia, the ache that will not cease. They are everyone's unfinished business.[3]

Two years after the 1964 death of Andrew Goodman, a twenty-year-old white activist murdered by the Ku Klux Klan in Philadelphia, Mississippi, Carolyn and Bobby Goodman formed the Andrew Goodman Foundation to aid other young activists. The foundation provides advice and raises money for a variety of projects such as multicultural curriculums and environmental programs. Continuing this work after her husband's death, Carolyn, at age fifty-four, earned a doctorate in clinical psychology at Columbia University, later creating a therapy program for disturbed mothers and their young children. Interviewed, she explained her motivation.

> I have always felt that if the bastards who murdered my son had experienced a more humane life, they would have become more decent people. So I felt if I could help these abused and abandoned mothers grow in self esteem, if I could impart the idea that they were basically good people even though they'd

had bad experiences in their youth, they would be able to relate to their children in a more positive way.[4]

You can probably find similar examples of mothers making meaning out of terrible social and personal loss. In my town, I found Dana Na-Champassak inspiring many others to take community action. One morning in front of their home, as Dana buckled her eleven-month-old son Etienne and two-year-old daughter into their car seats, a gang member shooting randomly killed her boy. Transforming sorrow and anger into action, Dana became a visible advocate for creating peace and lessening poverty in our city. She started a campaign urging every citizen to give two hours of volunteer work to the community. During the long trial of the murderer, she worked as a volunteer herself, tutoring disadvantaged youth. Though strongly wanting the murderer incarcerated, she used her passionate energy in serving peace rather than obsessing about the trial's inevitable ups and downs.

Kevin's mother, on the other hand, worries that her son's murderer will never get to trial. Because of all the problems she had with the judicial system, she is comforted and thankful that Kevin's friends responded to his cause by establishing a foundation in his name. The focus, Unity in Community, helps fund crime prevention and youth outreach programs. Each year a benefit, popular with Kevin's contemporaries, is held at the House of Blues. His friends believe the foundation is very important, not only for its focus in the community but also because it keeps Kevin's name, lessening the chances that his case will fall through the cracks.

Sharing and Connecting

When friends share our burden by responding to our children's cause, we find comfort, but their kindness and concern does not necessarily help us share our problems and worries. We feel intimacy only when we have the sense of *being in touch with our truth in the presence of another person.* More often, however, we are acting from persona, the part of ourselves we show the outside world. Mothers in mourning frequently declare they can "put on a good front," or "keep their problems to themselves." Although we may give away too much of ourselves when trying to share our inner world, we desperately need intimate experiences, ones validating our deepest feelings and convictions.

At a Coventry, England hospital in 1969, two grieving couples whose boys had died at the same time first met as strangers but soon found they were able to support each other. Their meetings led to founding The Compassionate Friends, probably the most comprehensive self-help group available today to parents whose children have died. Monthly meetings in cities throughout the United States offer friendship and understanding to bereaved families. In our local Compassionate Friends, newly bereft parents share stories about their child's life and death, receiving comfort from those further along in their grieving. Here the broken-hearted can take off their masks and share parts of their inner life.

On the other hand, some mothers who do not like participating in groups can find a single confidante—a psychotherapist, clergyman, family member, or close friend. One of the most frequently voiced complaints among women whose children have died is feeling alienated in the presence of others. Here the connection between inner and outer is severed, but worse, the mother is disconnected from her own true nature and is responding from a false self, a position she has chosen to protect herself or perhaps to please others. If she is unable to speak her truth, no one's support or validation will seem real to her.

More about Forgiving

As you begin living in ways that reflect your inner world, you must decide how important forgiveness is to helping you feel whole. In his book *Forgive for Good*, Dr. Frederic M. Luskin champions both the physical as well as the emotional benefits of forgiveness. Though understanding the journey to forgiveness may be long, he uses rail travel metaphor to suggest how to forgive along the way. People board the train, but it makes various stops before they reach a destination of final forgiveness and can get off.

The following story of forgiving parents raises the question: What price are we willing to pay to remain imprisoned in our needs for revenge? I believe Judy and Denis Shepard's forgiveness came from innate compassion, but by agreeing to lessening the murderer's sentence, they were also able to escape from being engulfed by a court system's impeding their grief work.

Their twenty-year-old son was beaten, burned, and strung to a prairie fence, where he hung in freezing temperatures for eighteen hours before he died, killed because he was gay. Afterward, tear tracks showed in crusted blood on his cheeks. The Shepards told the court they would accept a punishment of life in prison without parole. In their act of mercy, they showed compassion and their desire to take a stand against violence, but they were also pragmatically mindful about their own future, knowing that when a murderer accepts a sentence with no parole, he forfeits any right to appeal the verdict. Thereby, the Shepards spared themselves years of watching a case slowly go through the criminal justice system.

"Sixty Minutes" featured another story of extraordinary capacity for forgiveness. Amy Biehl, a Fulbright scholar from Southern California, who had gone to fight against apartheid, was stabbed to death by a South African mob of angry black militants—she was killed by the very people whose cause she had embraced. Her parents, Linda and Peter Biehl, deciding to try and understand their daughter's commitment, visited the squatter camps of Guguletu, where Amy's killers had grown up. On returning home, they established the Amy Biehl Foundation, funding welding classes and school tutorials. By participating in Archbishop Tutu's Truth and Reconciliation Commission, the Biehls enabled their daughter's killers to be pardoned and released from prison after serving only four years. Nobel laureate Archbishop Tutu complimented them by saying, "You have *Obuntu*, the essence of humanity."

To many, the Beihls' compassionate response to murder seemed incredible, even shocking. "That's not me, I'm no Mother Teresa," one angry women said. Yet, if our goal is to have our daily actions reflect our true selves, we must work to rid ourselves of all that interferes with living freely. Each of us will have a different answer. The inspiring story of Parker Sternburgh tells of a woman who, after her three-year-old son's death, found joy through absolution.

Parker and Charles Sternburgh had moved to New Orleans to work at Ochsner Hospital, he as a vascular surgeon and she a hospital administrator. Parker enrolled her daughter in school and placed an ad for a nanny for Jared, diligently checking the background of each applicant. Finally she settled on a forty-three-year-old woman, Terri Lynn Revere, who seemed a perfect fit.

Terri took neighborhood walks with Jared and especially enjoyed driving him around town, but no one knew that Terri had an overwhelming gambling addiction, becoming hypnotized by video poker machines she found in shops, restaurants, and public malls. One day she entered a restaurant having several such machines, leaving Jared sitting peacefully in his car seat. When she emerged four hours later, she discovered him unconscious. Rushed to Oschner Hospital, he was diagnosed with severe heat stroke and dehydration. By the time his parents arrived, their baby's temperature was 107. He died the next morning, one month short of his third birthday.

Terri's forty-year sentence brought Parker no closure, but she continued working hard to recover. Although an active Episcopalian, she was not wed to any single religious system or cosmology so she explored both Eastern and Western views on forgiveness, transcendence, and love. She made a pilgrimage to Turkey, visiting the place where Mary reputedly spent time mourning after Jesus' death. Parker further studied religious teachings, took counsel with her priest, and mustered all the activities she could discover to heal herself.

> I went to the National Cathedral and arranged flowers for a week and did the training on the labyrinth, lots of meditation, a lot of therapy, especially shadow work: accepting hidden parts of myself and turning them into strengths.

Nonetheless, only after years of soul-searching could she begin preparing to confront and forgive Terri. Louisiana law provides for meetings between victims' families and convicted murderers, but no one had ever done it. To accustom herself to prisons, Parker visited a distant one where she met Charles Gervais, a man serving a life sentence but artistically gifted, whose paintings hung in the Vatican. Parker accepted his offer to paint a portrait of Jared.

> Because he's trying to help me with my pain by painting a portrait of this child that I loved so much. And so, if we can help each other that way, if we can connect and create some light, then only good can come of this.

She had schooled herself to expect no remorse from Terri, who had already passed long dreary years in prison. Parker planned only to forgive, but when they met, Terri broke down, tears flooding her face, and confessed her fault and remorse. When she left the prison, Parker felt only happiness for both Terri and herself.

> I wanted to do this because my son was just this joyful kid. What better can I do with the rest of my life than just love people, trying to have the joy he had. Right after he died, I knew that I'd get back to myself somehow. I had to, because joy is so innate to my soul. I wanted to take the gift Jared's life had been to me and use it responsibly. Not returning to the joy, to this joyous mystery of life, would dishonor his memory.[5]

Though her path can inspire, no one can follow it exactly. Rather, we must each find our own unique way to wholeness.

NOTES:

1. Sarah York, *Remembering Well: Rituals for Celebrating Life and Mourning Death,* San Francisco, 2000.
2. Phil Cousieau, *The Art of Pilgrimage,* Berkley, California, 1998.
3. Debra Dickerson, "The Silence and the Fury," *Mother Jones,* San Francisco, September-October, 2000, pp. 60–65.
4. Patricia Burnstein, "Mother Courage," *Modern Maturity,* March-April 2000, pp. 23–24.
5. Richard Harth, "Forgive and Remember," *Southern Woman,* Winter 2003, pp. 22–23.

Chapter Fifteen

LIVING SYMBOLICALLY: TRANSFORMATIVE ASPECTS OF THE BLACK MADONNA AND THE PIETA

Mary,
ground of all being,
Greetings!
Greetings to you, lovely and loving Mother!
You birthed to earth your son,
You birthed the son of God from heaven
by breathing the spirit of God.
— Hildegard of Bingen

Becoming an Actor in the Divine Drama

We have seen how archetypal motifs arise from human depths in religion, myth, and dreams, and how they unconsciously influence all of us. When individuals can become *conscious* of the dominant themes and ideas in their lives, however, they open themselves to many benefits. Self-understanding and voluntary control increase, and their psychological isolation gives way to feeling part of the human family. Moreover, they actively gain wisdom from those who have lived before and can imagine life in the world beyond. They can now use archetypal images to create meaning, purposefully, leading what Jung calls "The Symbolic Life."

Symbols are commonplace (e.g., the flag, the cross), but always refer both to themselves and larger realities not fully knowable. When certain symbols seize our beings, however, they become vital bridges between these manifest and hidden realities. Such symbols can come to impart a kind of divine energy to us, restoring our health and wholeness.

Jung found that people become neurotic when their lives are too rational: They lack a dimension that allows them a role as one actor in a divine drama. He once met a tourist who restlessly traveled around the world, always returning home with the same painful feeling of meaninglessness. He thought that had she been able to imagine, to genuinely discover and enter into the realities of symbolic living, she might have found something to live for.

> But if she could say, "I am the daughter of the Moon. Every night I must help the Moon, my mother, over the horizon"—ah, that is something else! Then she lives, then her whole life makes sense, and makes sense in all continuity, and for the whole of humanity. That gives peace, when people feel that they are living the symbolic life, that they are actors in the divine drama. That gives the only meaning to human life; everything else is banal and you can dismiss it. A career, producing children, are all *maya* compared with one thing, that your life has meaning.[1]

My own symbolic journey, which I sketch in this final chapter, illustrates the personally transforming nature of symbolic images. I hope that you may share my fascination with these particular archetypal motifs, but more importantly, that you will find your own way to stand in relationship to life's mysteries. By bringing our personal experiences and mythologies to a sacred image, we give it power. Over time, however, particular symbols will lose their forces, and others will arise. Clinging to a symbol too long, or as James Hollis says, interpreting it literally and demanding its worship, is "the oldest of sins, idolatry."[2]

Seeking the Symbolic

Three years after my son's death, we sold our family home in July and moved to Spain. My friends asked, "Why Spain?" We had no answer except that we had never been there. We felt a need to heal that only a radical break with our past might satisfy, so drawing on our savings, ignorant of the language, we simply settled ourselves down in San Lorenzo de Escorial.

During Philip's reign, when she enjoyed supreme Western power and felt herself the universal champion of Catholicism, Spain felt certain God smiled on her conquering the new world and Christianizing its heathen. By the time we arrived, centuries later, the influence of the institutionalized church had weakened, but Marionite sightings, festivals, and rituals borne of the people's longing imagination still remained ubiquitous.

In our first weeks, I had no contact with the vital remnants of these sacred traditions. Despite my mystical experience just after my boy's death and other work journaling and interpreting dreams, I was still very confused by his loss, longing for meaning, and, somewhat desperate, unable to imagine a future for myself. Routinely, we began to take long walks, following the highroad which afforded a view of the monastery below. But climbing the Machotas Chicas hills with our two Springer spaniels leading, we walked only in search of mushrooms, or collecting thyme, rosemary, and laurel. Each afternoon we joined the village people in their afternoon *passe* along paths winding through the Finca de la Herreria. Gradually we made friends with those who bowed themselves to pat our dogs. Often we stopped at the Hermita de La Virgin de Gracia, sitting in its cloister and chapel. Gradually, moments of thankfulness and joy came upon me, and these happy times grew longer.

As months passed, I entered into the El Escorial religious festivals, thereby realizing how lightly I had been wearing my own religion. My Presbyterian upbringing, stripped of images of saints or Mary and mainly devoid of ritual, had left me clothed only in scripture. In India I had felt moved by the young, beautiful, feminine deity, Gurumayi. Here, at Escorial and the Hermita I started to understand Mary's love and compassion, and her willingness to submit to the heavenly messages she received. In order to heal, I needed to *experience* figures of divinity, and I longed for a feminine face of God.

In early October we began rising at daylight to join the solemn crowds of believers in the Romeria, the annual pilgrimage honoring

Mary. Carrying lighted candles and singing Ave Maria, we followed the Virgin's ancient statue through the narrow streets to her Hermita. The following Spring, we witnessed even more impressive processions during *Semana Santa,* when each evening at dusk *confradidas,* religious fraternities as old as the Middle Ages, swayed slowly to beating drums, following behind wooden images of Christ's Passion. In this sacred theater, Mary, the mourning mother, *Mater Dolorosa,* was always central. Troops of women, wearing their best black dresses and high heeled black shoes, their heads covered in black mantillas, accompanied the Virgin Mother through the streets.

These and other symbolic images increasingly moved me, subtle changes not yet brought to full awareness. In Avila, city of that fulfilled mystic St. Teresa, a Latin inscription above the doorway of the Palacio de los D'Avilia repeatedly seemed to speak to me, "Where one door shuts, another opens."

The Black Madonna of Einsiedeln

I was beginning to understand that God had some other plan for my life. But what was it?

On my own I had been reading Jungian psychology, attempting to broaden my psychological background to include spiritual material. Inspired himself, my husband decided he should drive me to Zurich so I could consult a Jungian analyst. Inside Dr. Baker's safe office, I wept and wept, surprising myself. "How many tears are still to be shed?" I thought. "What more must I do to dissolve this grief?"

After our initial consultation, Dr. Baker suggested that we drive on to Einsiedeln and that I visit its sculpted Black Madonna. I had come upon several Black Madonnas in Spain, but somehow one didn't seem to belong in the snow-covered mountains of Switzerland. Dr. Baker assured me that this image of spirituality's darker side had been worshiped at Einsiedeln for over a thousand years.

We passed through the heavy monastery doors and immediately faced a small dark chapel. I gazed, kneeled in front of her, and at once, a voice inside me cried out, "*This,* my child's death can happen. I know *the worst* has already happened!" In the face of such knowledge, I was filled with shame and awe. I prayed to the Black Madonna, reputed miracle worker, Queen of Heaven, Descendant of the prehistoric Great Mother, of Isis and Demeter:[3] "Heal the wound from the sword that has pierced my heart."

Idolatry or True Self?

Praying before a sacred statue need not be idolatry, it can rather be a means to connect with one's own true self. The symbol will contain divine energy only to the extent an individual can project important significations onto it. Sue Monk Kidd's novel *The Secret of Bees* contains an excellent example.

Fourteen-year-old Lilly Owens has spent much of her life longing for the mother who died amid mysterious circumstances ten years before. With her black caretaker, the girl flees an abusive father to search out some friend or relative. She carries her remaining $38 and her mother's picture of a black Virgin Mary with the words "Tiburon, South Carolina" written on it. Through a series of synchronistic events, they are taken in by three black beekeeping sisters who worship the Black Madonna. At first skeptical of their rituals and prayers to a black icon, Lilly later realizes that the divine feminine is something inside herself. Her teacher August drives home the point.

> Our Lady is not some magical being out there somewhere, like a fairy godmother. She's not the statue in the parlor. She's something inside you.

When Lilly begins her new life, she continues to pray before the Black Madonna, feeling Her power within herself.

> Each day I visit black Mary, who looks at me with her wise face, older than old and ugly in a beautiful way ... I feel her in unexpected moments, her Assumption into heaven happening in places inside me. She will suddenly rise, and when she does, she goes further and further inside me. August says she gets into the holes life has gouged out of us.

In Einsiedeln, I was graced to see Mary's blackened face with my inner eye, at last accepting her as Virgin, at once true to her destiny's terrible pain yet also participant in a *hierosgamos*, a sacred marriage, symbolized by the Holy Dove's inspiriting her flesh with her divine child. It became clear to me that the archetypal motif of virgin birth which appears in many goddess stories had been too literally interpreted regarding Mary, making her inaccessible to us rather than inspiring and fortifying. Broadly speaking, I felt that we need to reimagine Mary's characteristics for she is our only contemporary Western Goddess.

Like me, I began to think other women throughout the world were seeking images of the dark-skinned Madonna, longing for a feminine face of God. After rejecting the passive submissiveness projected on her lighter sister, the dark Mary had enabled some to return to Catholicism. In her face others had found multitudes of many cultures reflected, particularly the poor and oppressed. My visiting the Virgin of Guadeloupe in Mexico and the Black Madonnas in Spain had made me feel connections across time and space, but the Black Madonna of Einsiedeln spoke to me more personally, reaching the shadowy part of my inner world.

Filled and troubled by the goddess, I left Einsiedeln with my husband and drove to the Hotel Sonne by the Zurichsee in Kusnacht. The lake's rough, cold water and the gray sky echoed my mood. But that night I had a dream.

> I am standing near a little hermita surrounded by freshly fallen snow. My two Springer spaniels are with me. I look down at the dogs, and I'm amazed that they have turned black.

My Jungian studies had by this time much advanced, and I knew that in almost every tradition, the dark deathly side of the Great Mother is linked to the dog motif. Cerberus, for example, the triple-headed dog guards Hades' underworld deep inside Mother Earth. I was struck by the dream's miraculous change in my dogs' color. It seemed that the beloved Springers, symbolizing my instinctive nature, were calling me to go deeper into the unconscious, metaphorically to enter the underworld. Apparently I again needed to confront hidden realities and discover what blackness required of me. But the dream had been promoted by my prayer to the Black Madonna, and it showed me standing near the Virgin's hermita. I grew confident that by trusting her guidance, I would be led toward wisdom.

Discovering the Pieta

From my experiences of Jungian psychology, I already knew that successive dreams can indicate our path toward personal growth, the "individuation" process bringing us to terms with both our own nature and external events. People are often called to their process of individuating after a painful wound, one leading them to give meaning to their suffering. The unique process has been described as resembling a wandering spiral, organized by a center that is our own true Self. Each person is wired to follow a given path, and our greatest achievement is to fulfill our destiny.

Accordingly, I spent increased time gazing on Europe's beautiful paintings of Madonna and Child and visiting shrines dedicated to the Black Madonna. The culminating symbol of my mourning, however, proved to be the *Pieta*, the image of a mother holding her dead child on her lap. *Pieta*, the Italian word meaning "pity," "compassion," and "sorrow," also derives from the Latin *pietas*, signifying "loyalty to the highest degree ... a profound love that neither life nor death can destroy."

As I studied ornate paintings and carvings in Spain's cathedrals, I found myself lingering at two types of art: works depicting The Virgin holding her infant and others representing God's Mother holding the dead Christ in her lap. In the Vatican, fascination with Michaelangelo's Pieta prompted me to purchase a marble replica.

In the intervening ten years, Michaelangelo's statue has inspired me to an ever deepening realization of beauty and faith. He has captured our loss and sadness, but by contemplating it, our sorrows can be assuaged by love.

Both men and women have been drawn to the statue's mysterious powers. Robert Hupka, for example, made thousands of photographs from different angles, testifying to its infinite meanings and transformative powers.

> There is so much in the Pieta that if you lived a thousand years and wrote a thousand books you can never express it. In other words, there is a divine quality in it. It must have been inspired, because how could a boy, twenty-four years old, create a work like that? You can't imagine how. It was a special grace from God....

What makes the Blessed Virgin remarkable is that his whole love for her is in that face ... You couldn't describe her in words better than that face does. In fact, you can't describe her in words, that is, that ineffable expression.

This is his tremendousness, excelling even the Sistine Chapel. The Sistine Chapel reveals artistic grandeur. The Pieta portrays simple faith. There is sanctity in that statue.[4]

I wanted to learn how the art form evolved. The sculptural image began in Germany in the fourteenth century, then moved into France and Italy, reaching its highest spiritual and artistic fullness in Michaelangelo. After starting my analytic training in Zurich, I frequently took advantage of Sunday free museum admission, riding the tram to Kunshaus to gaze at a German version. There, Virgin and dead Christ await us at the top of a stairway. Though no photograph or other information is available at the desk, art historians date the statue from 1300. It is thus the earliest surviving representation.

Carved of wood, then vividly painted to enhance its impact, Mary's face is both rapturous and pensive, as if she has transcended all suffering. Her eyes, almost closed, seem to look both outward at her dead child and to attend inward in a contemplative spirit. Gaunt and doll-like, bearing his wounds and crown of thorns, Christ rests like a small broken child in his mother's lap. A chest upon which the two sit is partly covered by Mary's blue robes. Objectifying mysterious archaic and archetypal principles, this complex image, topped by Mary's peaceful face, seems to hold the answer to all I wish to know.

Pietas like this earliest one, first appeared in German convents as parts of sculptural groups called called *die Marienklage* or *das Vesperbild.* Connected with Good Friday Vespers, the images were placed close to the worshipper, kindling her meditative spirit to identify with Mary and Christ's suffering, but culminating in the joy of redemption.

Medieval artists depicted Mary's grief in scenes showing the Seven Sorrows of Our Lady. Later painters and sculptors eschewed her lesser sorrows in favor of the most poignant moment, when late Good Friday afternoon, her friends having left, she holds her dead son in private, solitary despair. The moment is not found in any Gospel passage, nor the apocryphal gospels, but to human experience alone. Freed from any specific reference to the Bible, the theme has been repeatedly interpreted with emotional intensity by artists of every age.

It existed as an archetype of human consciousness long before Christ, when 5,000 years ago Sumerian goddess Innana held her dead son-lover Dumuzi. Marina Warner compares an ancient Mesopotamian poem about Inanna's weeping with Romanos Melodos' sixth century Christian hymn.

Inanna's lament

Into his face she stares, seeing
what she has lost … his mother
who lost him to death's kingdom
O, the agony she bears
shuddering in the wilderness
she is the mother suffering so much.

Mary's lament

I am overwhelmed, O my son
I am overwhelmed by love
And I cannot endure
That I should be in the chamber
And you on the wood of the cross
I in the house
And you in the tomb.[5]

The weeping Mary we know follows a historic succession of great goddesses mourning their child's death: Inanna and Damuzi, Isis and Osiris, Aphrodite and Adonis, Cybele and Attis. As we have seen, these myths of sons who died and rose again from the dead represent the decay and revival of life, their weeping mothers foreshadowing the Christian Mater Dolorosa.

Archetypal Attitudes in the Pieta

Though mourning underlies all Pietas, individual artists chose to ignite a varying range of strong emotions and tender feelings in their images. Those hardest to look at portray Mary feeling fear and terror, her expression and her dead son's broken body almost grotesque.[5]

When the bubonic plague ravaged Europe, causing pessimism in all levels of society, fear and terror were further fueled by both physicians' and clergy's attributing the epidemic to God's punishing the world's sinners. Flagellants roamed from town to town, scourging themselves in public penance and, particularly in Germany, carrying wooden, polychrome statues depicting Christ's and Mary's anguish. People had always seen the Virgin as having participated in agonies like their own, but when the Black Death struck, ending life swiftly and taking a child in a single day, Pietas reflected this unique shock and terror in Mary's anxious face. Today these images may be understood as showing a mother's dark lonely despair evinced by sudden news of her child's death before hope can intervene.

People who are moved by images of the sorrowing *Mater Dolorosa* believe Mary participated in a human's experience of grief; she knew how it felt. Tears falling down Mary's face in thousands of Pietas portray sorrow. A counterpoint in poetry is the scriptural *Statbat Mater*, later set to liturgical music by Palastrina, Haydn, and Rossini. Here the unknown Franciscan poet presents himself as an eyewitness at the crucifixion and ponders, "Who would not weep to see the mother of Christ in such torment?"[6]

To combat the despair they projected onto her, medieval worshippers prayed to the Virgin for protection from the plague and all life's sorrows. In Pietas reflecting her role as Protectress, Mary sometimes doesn't stare at the dead Christ but looks outward with a straightforward strong expression closer to the poise of the Great Mother.[7]

Supporting modern research showing mothers feel increased compassion following child death, many other Pietas depict the Virgin as full of love and compassion. In these images, the Virgin Mother intervenes with God asking mercy for his people. Because she has suffered so much, worshippers have often believed she performs miracles. Sometimes she is even depicted smiling, suffused with the joy of redemption, or when not even looking at her dead child, she may instead present his body to the world as God's sacrificed son. In complete contrast, others image her as protectively holding the son to her breast, with all her strength, never wanting to let him go.

As I studied the attitude portrayed in each Pieta, I recognized different parts of myself that needed attention. I found it difficult to acknowledge some of what I saw, but other characteristics gave me strength. For months, motifs present in or aroused by the Pieta continued to haunt me.

I would remember how proud I was to be Duncan's mother, before he became ill. People were always complimenting us on Duncan's "charismatic nature," "his talents," and "his love of life." There were times, despite myself, when I wanted to "show him off." I found the Biblical Mary that exhibits such pride in her son. After the Annunciation, she boasts joyfully:

> From this time forth, all generations shall call me blessed, for
> He who is mighty has done great things for me. (Luke 1:48)

But when Jesus is presented at the temple, the devout and upright Symeon warns her about the role her son will play and her own sorrowful destiny:

> This child is destined to be a sign that will be opposed so that
> the inner thoughts may be revealed – and a sword will pierce
> your own soul, too. (Luke 2:34–35)

The figure of Mary resonates with many mothers' different experiences. Perhaps that explains why so many stories having no Biblical reference developed around her. My musings about Mary and the Pieta seem to me to be only a personal strain of motifs arising for hundreds of years. The sword symbol in Symeon's prophecy is a good example. Through the imagination, dreams, and visions of believers, one sword piercing Mary's heart grew to seven, representing seven sorrows in her incarnation as Our Lady of Sorrows. Believers would meditate on these sufferings for hours, imagining and participating in her grief. Meditating on the first sorrow, fourteenth century mystic Bridget of Sweden learned in a vision that "of all mothers Mary was the most afflicted by reason of her foreknowledge of Christ's most bitter Passion."[8]

We can certainly assume that Mary's own suffering was heightened by her anticipating his painful fate. Other mothers often report knowing in advance something terrible would happen. Obviously, mothers' constant worries about a child's fatal illness, drug addiction, or military misadventures excite a uniquely feminine suffering. Because Symeon's sword was part of Mary's consciousness, theologians still argue about Mary's acquiescing to the crucifixion. Like many other mothers, I, too, have searched for ways I may have contributed to my child's illness and suicide.

What does the sacrifice of the son-lover show us about feminine consciousness? Esther Harding's interpretation can help women who have grown stronger from experiencing the loss.

> A woman who has not yet sacrificed the son, that is, sacrificed the instinctual maternal within herself, may have no actual children, but will none the less carry the maternal attitude into her relationships. She is under an inner compulsion to mother all for whom she cares. She cannot bear to see anyone unhappy or in difficulties. Motherliness dominates in her. She never realizes that her inability to accept the hardness for her friends reflects her own ability to accept hardness of life itself.[9]

We must recognize how much we needed our child to be the object of all our maternal instincts. Our instinct is as strong as the sexual, and it carries the same potential to abuse power. Maternity can both fulfill and limit our humanity, so losing the object of our maternal fixation can be the terrible price we pay for a more fully developed existence. Naturally, we would have given almost everything to have our child live, but his death, if we hear this archetypal message, can open new doors which might otherwise have remained closed. There need be no guilt in such a realization, because, in fact, we are innocent of his death. But we may be guilty if we do not use well what can be considered a sacrifice for our benefit. Getting in touch with our instinctive nature, we begin to combine our passion with our suffering, opening the door to "co-passion," becoming increasingly compassionate.

Aspects of Transformation in the Pieta

Archetypal expressions of Mary as a loving mother nurturing baby Jesus contribute to those Pieta images which imply transformation. In some depictions, for example, Christ's body appears scarcely larger than an infant's. These versions express the mystic's belief that the Virgin is reexperiencing motherhood, as St. Bernardino of Sienna explains:

She believed that the days of Bethlehem had returned, she imagined that he was sleeping, and she cradled him to her breast. She imagined the winding sheet in which he was wrapped to be his swaddling clothes.

The divine mother holds her dead child in the same *participation mystique* which formed a dual union with the live infant. Her holding and cradling is Eros-filled, and she is overmore the container of all the child needs. Consciously, even now at his death, she wishes to protect, though intuitively, she also feels his peace. Such Pietas' archetypally positive Great Mother portray a transpersonal role for her, both unconscious and instinctive.

Participation mystique belongs to the same family of experiences as the mystical, for in both we reach a psychological state of original unity, where ego and unconscious intermingle. In the highest numinous experiences the world's contradictions become suspended or reconciled. It is possible that the paradoxically positive mystical state some mothers experience at the death of their child arises more readily because her previous unions in the mother-infant bond prepared the way. On the other hand, the shock of a child's death and the outpouring of grief lowers the inhibitory quality of our ordinary level of consciousness, enabling numinous contents to emerge from the unconscious. Mary's rapturous expression in many Pietas can also be understood as portraying the moment when a mother experiences a "nothingness," a state beyond consciousness.

Just as symbiotic bonding is appropriate to one maternal developmental stage, so is the movement toward "disinterest" a right goal at a later one. Indeed, a mother's move toward separation begins when the infant is a mere eighteen months old, during the period that Piaget called *rapprochement*, and continues through the adolescent years and after. It must be a mother's goal whether the child lives or dies. All separation entails real loss, for women are fed by relationships; yet only with detachment can one really love.

In Meister Eckhart's talk of instruction, "About Disinterest," the fourteenth-century mystic elevates disinterest above love, humility, and even mercy. Disinterest brings God *in*, which, according to Eckhart, is better than one's moving *toward* God.

Disinterest comes so close to zero that nothing but God is rarefied enough to get into it, to enter the disinterested heart.

To use better known words, the kingdom of heaven comes to the poor in spirit, for she can not want to fulfill the will of God. Instead, empty of her own will and the will of God, she has room for God to come in.

We have now arrived at a final paradox the symbolic Pieta offers the mourning mother: her need for detachment and what Eckhart terms "disinterest." In some sculptures, this stage of growth has been foreshadowed by Mary's expression. There her face shows a restraint and self-forgetfulness, born of disinterested impulses rising from her heart. This facial expression firmly suggests that, in the end, a bereaved mother must remove the dead child from her lap. She has passed through a period of mourning, and she has touched God experientially and not through faith alone. But in order to recreate, she must separate, removing the beloved dead from her tight embrace. Only then will she bring new life both for herself and her child's soul. In "Maria Leben," Rainer Maria Rilke's lines embody the essence of this mother's condition. "Now you lie across my lap, and I can't birth you anymore." The body must go into the ground.

This hard truth of necessary burial helps to ground both child and self. Her feminine psyche requires that the body be moved from her lap and buried, just as before, the body has been removed from the cross, giving it the comforting embrace of the Great Mother. The bereft woman, yielding her power as mother of life by placing her child in the moist earth, creates space for transforming her and the beloved's Soul. The fertile moist soil now safely incorporates the body, enabling its Soul to transcend. As nature's womb from which all life proceeds and the grave into which it returns, Earth becomes the source of blossoming.

I have had many dreams about the death of my child. Late in our years in Spain, one particularly pointed me toward new possibilities.

Along the wooden dock, opposite the lake, where a ship is anchored, there is a beautiful wall made of fresh fertile soil. Ivy vines cover it in all directions. I begin pulling the ivy aside, for I know that there are important documents buried in the moist dirt. I dig inside the dirt until I find a very important document, the Magna Carta.[10] It is written on a beautiful tapestry, and the cloth is very thick, almost like quilting, and the needlework is beautiful. I wipe the dirt from the Magna Carta. I am going to take this document into the world, where it will serve me well. I begin carrying it away from the dock and into the crowded street.

At the same time that I examine the Magna Carta, I become aware of another very important document inside the dirt wall. Hidden beneath the ivy is the Corpus Christi (the body of Christ). Though a document, it also looks like a body ready for burial. I am certain that it is quite safe here, buried in the moist fertile earth. Somehow I am certain that this document should remain safely buried in the wall. It belongs there, whereas the Magna Carta must be shown to the people.

So my ship of my being lies anchored, and I am also grounded in the soul of life's greatest sorrow. I have sacrificed my son, but like the Corpus Christi, his body lies safely in moist earth. It is time to move on in life, to bring the Magna Carta to the people. (The original 13th-century document limited the power of the King, giving property rights to citizens.) In its own symbolism—tapestry, needlework, quilting—my "Magna Carta" points to an intuitive way of knowing that must not be overpowered by more masculine (kingly) thinking. I need to disseminate a personal message from the depths of feminine wisdom.

Though I didn't know it at the time, this book which I hope will bring comfort and freedom to other grieving mothers, is no doubt part of the personal Magna Carta with which I have been entrusted. Even though the dream may seem exaggerated to some, such archetypal "big dreams" have a profound and lasting effect on all of us who experience them. Certainly, it helped give me the courage to find and articulate a message useful to others.

In later years my relationship to the *Pieta* changed as I discovered new ways this artistic motif spoke my truth and helped me live. When we returned to New Orleans from Europe, we bought a house a few blocks from The Mater Dolorosa Church, more than a coincidence, a synchronicity. Every morning for about a year I'd walk to see the church's Pieta. Then gradually, I began to disengage from the symbol. My nighttime dreams about Duncan changed: no longer a troubled young man, Duncan has grown wise and helpful and no more dreams of "red flags" warn me of danger. The following dream told me my storm had ended.

There is a hurricane coming to New Orleans. We prepare by boarding up windows. We protect our plants in the garden.

I am surprised the storm is very short and that the plants are unharmed by the forces of wind. I am fascinated by verdant, green, new growth on the plants. I hear a voice in the background: "And all is well, and all is well, and all will be very well."

My son's girlfriend Lori appears and suggests that I put on pink eyelash mascara, but then she agrees that it doesn't look good on me.

During the long stormy period of my life, I was in danger shutting out everything but anger, bitterness, self-pity, and meaninglessness. Like the boarded up windows in the dream, intense grief would block my vision. By doing purposeful grief work, however, I protected enough of my psyche to allow for new growth. Though my only child's illness and death consumed me for most of fifteen years, like the storm, that time seems short compared to the entire scheme of things. I hear the well-known assuring message from Julienne of Norwich's vision, "And all will be well, and all will be well, and all will be very, very well." I have also been to the underworld, and the dark experience has made me wiser. Youthful pink mascara is no longer fitting.

In Part Two of this book, I have given aids I believe will help women mourn their children's death. In the last section, I have also shared some experiences in hopes that they can stimulate your imagination to lead to your own symbolic healing. Because I have found my path and am moving on, I no longer feel so deep a connection to the grieving mother, the Mater Dolorosa, but I will always honor her archetypal image for offering me new life.

Pieta

Holding him there
Blood-stained child in the bosom of my body
All suffering ceased
All questions answered
Only the rapture and the bliss
I dissolve into the divine power
All in one, I am nothing
But the knowing and the loving.

Is this what you feel my child?
At peace at last, no more to endure
No more fear, no tortured thought
No urgent need to answer to the call
No worried wanting to please, and no pretending?

Oh, the awesomeness of all; thank God it's finished.

Remembering this
I stand at the Pieta
Spellbound
How long will I be there
Living what a word cannot express
Only wonder.

How was I singled out?
How much was I forewarned?
To birth this child so perfect in my eyes
To marvel at the miracle of life
It was too much-too joyful to behold
Such fullness cannot last
A child can't suckle long at mother's breast
But who would guess that it would end like this?

So many sorrows compressed into one this Pieta
The agony, the world turned upside down
No natural order here, all time has stopped
The earth shakes from foundations of belief destroyed.

How strange then is this face of Mary filled with peace
Compassion born from suffering
Detachment born from understanding
I'm energized—something inside has changed
There's something settled, some new way of being

My womb is full now as I give birth to myself.

WITH GRATITUDE, CM

NOTES:

1. C. G. Jung, *The Symbolic Life*, vol. 18, *Collected Works*, par. 630.
2. James Hollis, *Tracking the Gods*, Toronto, 1995, p. 9.
3. China Galland, *Longing for Darkness*, New York, 1990, pp. 135–169.
4. Robert Hupka, "A Contemplation," *Pieta*, Angers, France, 1975.
5. Marina Warner, *Alone of All Her Sex*, New York, 1976, pp. 206–208.
6. In Cosome Tura's painting "Pieta," Mary kisses the wounds of Christ's gaunt and grotesque body. Adoration of Christ's wounds was customary in fourteenth century devotional art. (Venice, Museo Correr)
7. Emile Male, *Religious Art in France*, Princeton, 1986.
8. Ibid., p. 216.
9. M. Esther Harding, *The Way of All Women*, Boston, 1990, pp. 157–192.
10. The Magna Carta is a thirteenth-century British document that limits the power of the King and gives property rights to the people.

Appendices

I

In Historical Perspective

Many social observers have said that we live in a society which normally hides death, routinely delegating social and personal rituals to funeral directors, and rewarding the robust griever who "can get on with her life." Unfortunately, such common praise for seemingly strong, highly functioning, bereaved mothers shows that most friends, relatives, and even helping professionals have inaccurate ideas of mothers' actual experiences losing children.

We grieving mothers can be comforted, however, by examining records. There we discover that women in western cultures have always felt unbearable loss when a child dies. Examining their experiences can help us feel less alone, even leading to our seeing ourselves as part of a timeless sisterhood of sufferers. Becoming aware of the normality of other bereaved mothers' pain can also help us grow in compassion.

Today's historical researchers have also discovered that most mothers never cease mourning the deaths of their children. Using such primary sources as old letters, diaries, and coroners' reports, they agree that women have always felt the strongest bonds with their children. These may seem obvious ideas to any bereaved mother who knows the wrenching loss experienced when her child died, but historians previously believed that, until the eighteenth century, affective bonds between mother and offspring were weak. Studying medieval England, for example, they used to adduce such common practices as swaddling babies, using wet-nurses, and infanticides. Trying to explain the maternal coldness they thought to have existed, the older historians reasoned that because so many children died natural deaths their mothers found it excessively distressing to become emotionally attached to them. Earlier historians did trace a gradual increase in motherly concern from the eighteenth century on, but thanks to current historiography, we now know mothers' intimate reactions to the death of their children were perennial.[1]

This constancy of response can be found even during the middle ages when infant mortality rates were of such great magnitude that we find it hard to imagine how mothers coped. Then, only fifty percent of children reached age five, and disease, accidents, and malnutrition killed many youngsters up to ten years. When the Black Death ravaged Europe from 1348 until the end of the fifteenth century, destroying one third of the population, over one half its victims were children. As for accidental deaths, a study of coroners' inquests in medieval England shows cradle fires to have been the leading cause among infants. Commonly swaddled or tied to their cradles, they could not crawl about, so busy mothers sometimes left them unattended. Yet inquest records also show mothers not liking to leave their babies alone, nor did other villagers approve the practice. Arranging child care was often difficult, however, and the baby-sitters might not be much older than their charges. Among toddlers, accidental deaths were most often caused by their being burnt in hearth fire, drowned in nearby lakes, streams, or wells, or being attacked by wandering animals. Here is one particularly moving example of accidental infant death.

> On Friday last (Aug. 9, 1298) John Trivaler and Alie his wife were in a shop where they abode in the parish of St. Mary late at night, ready to go to bed, and the said Alice fixed a lighted candle on the wall by the straw before it was discovered and immediately the fire spread throughout the shop, so that the said John and Alice scarce escaped without, forgetting that they were leaving the child behind them. And immediately when the said Alice remembered her son was in the fire within, she leapt back into the shop to seek him, and immediately when she entered she was overcome by the greatness of the fire and choked.[2]

According to religious documents of the middle ages, the responses of mothers to losing their children trace a spectrum of pain.

> A weeping and wailing mother, tearing her hair or beating her breast and head; a mother fleeing to the forest after the death of her infant and refusing to come home, a bereft mother refusing to hand over the corpse of her son for burial.[3]

Evidence from English History

In early modern England, women's beginning to write diaries has clarified our knowledge of mothers' reactions to their children's death. Two passages from 1660 give poignant descriptions. The first mother reveals strong positive feelings toward her infant, and though she makes an effort to restrain describing her grief, a reader nonetheless feels its depth. She prays to God both for her dead son and His forgiving unworthiness which, by implication, might possibly have helped cause the death or could now interfere with the child's happy life in eternity.

Mrs. Alice Thornton

My delivery of my son William, my sixth child, and of his death, April the 17th, 1660, at St. Nicholas:

It was the good pleasure of God to continue me in the land of the living, and to bring forth my sixth child at St. Nicholas. I was delivered of a very goodly son, having Mrs. Hickeriggill with me, after hard labour and hazardous, yet, through great mercy, I had my life spared, and was blessed with a happy child about 3 or 4 in the morning upon Tuesday the 17th of April 1660. Thus was I blessed with the life and comfort of my dear child's baptism, with its enjoyment of that holy seal of regeneration; and my pretty babe was in good health, sucking his poor mother, to whom my good God had given the blessing of the breast as well as the womb, of that child, to whom it was no little satisfaction, while I enjoyed his life; and the joy of it maked me recruit [recover] faster, for his sake, that I might do my duty to him as a mother. But it so pleased God to shorten this joy, lest I should be too much transported, that I was visited with another trial; for on the Friday sennight after, he began to be very angry and forward after his dressing in the morning, so that I perceived him not to be well; upon which I gave him Gascoyne powder and cordial.... And having had three hours sleep, his face when he awaked was full of red round spots like the smallpox, being of the compass of a halfpenny...these continuing in his face till night; and being in a slumber in my arms on my knee he would sweetly lift up his eyes to heaven and smile, as if the old saying was true in this sweet infant, that he saw angels in heaven.... He grew very sick all night, and about nine a clock on Saturday morning he sweetly departed this life, to the great discomfort of his weak mother, whose only comfort is that the Lord, I hope, has received him to that place of rest in heaven where little children behold the face of their heavenly Father, to his God and my God; whom I humbly crave to pardon all things in me which he sees amiss, and clean away my sins by the blood of my dearest Saviour and Redeemer.[4]

In another account, all a mother's dreams for her dear little girl are wiped out by smallpox. Though we see how this idealized child, almost perfect in her mother's eye, created feelings of great loss, her mother, like Alice Thornton, thanks God for joy felt during her daughter's short life.

The Countess of Bridgewater, Elizabeth Egerton, on the death of her daughter Kate 1660:

When I Lost My Dear Girl Kate

My sorrow is great, I confess, I am much grieved for the loss of my dear girl Katy, who was a fine a child as could be. She was but a year and ten months old when, by the fatal disease of the smallpox, it was God's pleasure to take her from me, who spoke anything one bid her...and was kind to all, even to strangers, and had no anger in her. All thought she loved them; her brothers and sister loved her with a fond love. She was so good she never slept nor played at sermon nor prayers. She had received the sacrament of baptism, which washed her from original sin, and she lived holily. She took delight in nothing but me, if she had seen me; if absent, ever had me in her words, desiring to come to me; never was there so fond a child of a mother. But now she is not in this world, which grieves my heart, even my soul, but I must submit, and give God my thanks, that he once was pleased to bestow so great a blessing as that sweet child upon me.[5]

Both Alice Thornton and Elizabeth Egerton struggle to calm their grief with holy thoughts based in the deep religious convictions of the time. Nonetheless, the mothers also clearly declare their abiding pain.

A comparison of reactions by Romantic poets who lost children, with those of their wives, helps us understand maternal mourning in their time. Samuel Taylor and Sara Coleridge, William and Mary Wordsworth, and P.B. and Mary Shelley all were couples who had children die. The men's grief could find expression in their verse and become further mitigated by their expansive public lives, including their travels. By contrast, women, whose primary work was caring for children, suffered an immediate loss in their social role as mothers and had only limited access to the outside world.

Sara Coleridge was even urged not to tell her husband their child was dying, lest it interfere with the man's studies. When the infant did die, people praised Sara "because she never forgot herself," that is, she never let known her feelings as a mother. On the other hand, Mary Wordsworth, deep in despair after their four-year-old Catherine and six-year-old Thomas died within a few months of each other, refused to eat and wept bitterly day and night.[6]

Shelley's own verse shows his wife reduced to deep despair when their son William died less than a year after their daughter Clara.

> My dearest Mary, wherefore hast thou gone
> And left me in this dreary world alone?
> Thy form is here indeed —a lovely one
> But thou art fled, gone down the dreary road
> That leads to Sorrow's most obscure abode:
> thou sittest on the hearth of pale despair,
> For thine own sake I cannot follow thee.
> Let none look at me![7]

Sitting on "the hearth of pale despair" describes a private place of sorrow cut off from activities outside the home. Mary Shelly's apparent silence probably represents other mothers' unexpressed grief. Much may have been unrecorded because women were supposed to remain submissive to men, to appear modest, and to exhibit steadfast faith in God. In keeping with these expectations, we find women writing what seem to be rote formulas for responding to a child's death.

> God has been most merciful to us in this affliction, and, if bereaved, we are still a happy household and full of thanksgiving.[8]

Women felt obliged to affirm the strength of their faith, but this kind of testimony did not necessarily diminish the reality of their grief. Nor did their husbands' dictates to act with stalwart duty probably decrease their true sadness. When his daughter Dora died at eight months, Charles Dickens wrote to his wife:

> I cannot close without putting the strongest entreaty and injunction upon you to come home with perfect composure... to do your duty to the rest, and to shew yourself worthy of the great trust you hold in them.[9]

Only later in 19th century England did mothers begin to feel less obligated to show their unquestioning faith in heaven. Instead of emphasizing a child's joyful life hereafter, some people paid tribute to its personal history. When Emma and Charles Darwin's daughter Annie died at age ten, they were thankful for her likeness preserved in a daguerreotype. His written memorial to her made no reference to an afterlife, but instead stressed her innocence and uncomplaining acceptance of illness.[10]

Though most women continued to believe that their deceased children dwelled in heaven, by the 20th century new mythologies arising from the works of Charles Darwin, Karl Marx, and Sigmund Freud ushered in a period where traditional Christian teaching grew less influential.

American History over the Centuries

The prevailing reactions of grieving women in the United States were comparable to those in England. From American colonial times on, although families did not then lavish affection on their children, historians believe that emotional and expressive ties have remained essentially invariant. Nevertheless, two groups of women, those heading west and those bound in slavery, faced hardships that worsened their sufferings when a child died.

The great Westward expansion brought imminent danger of Indian attack, as well as a felt isolation from neighbors and extended families. Mothers moving West with their husbands lost their close-knit Eastern colony support systems. Often women were left for long periods of time without the companionship of any white people while their husbands searched for gold in the mines, or were off hunting, or seeking work, or accompanying cattle drives.

Narcissa Prentiss Whitman of Amity, New York, "a blonde beauty of high spirit," was one of two women who first crossed the Rocky Mountains. In 1834 she married a man who shared the same fervent ambition to save the heathens. The two set out to convert the Indians, and their only child, Alice Clarissa, was born at the Oregon Missions. When the girl accidentally drowned, Narcissa kept the corpse at home for four days before the burial so that she could sew a shroud. The mother's devotion and her attempt at consoling herself clearly emerge from her own words.

> She did not begin to change in her appearance for the first three days. This proved to be a great comfort to me, for so long as she looked natural and was so sweet I could caress her.... The Lord has taken our own dear child away so that we may care for the poor outcasts of the country and suffering children.[11]

Another woman, Maggie Brown, who had hoped to live a stable middle-class life with her physician husband in Virginia, followed him West to the frontier where her sole relief from loneliness, her seven-year-old daughter Mattie, died. Maggie's social support became circumscribed by her husband's limited time and letters of condolence from distant family and friends. Even though Maggie's own mother had lost six children, her letters as well as those of other friends demonstrate understanding of Maggie's loss and isolation.[12]

We all know how the evils of slavery have burdened the black family in America; for mothers there were any number of special trials. Especially in times of economic stress, the threat of a child's being sold was always a possibility, nor did slave families have equal protection against accidents and disease. Fredrika Bremer reports the terrible losses endured by one poor slave woman with six children: three died and the other three were sold.

> When they took from me the last little girl, oh, I believed I never should have got over it. It almost broke my heart.[13]

Only the most inhuman slave owner could not be moved by such a statement. Reading between the lines, we can more fully understand the depth of these losses to a woman whose only life has been obedience, lacking all opportunity to be heard, make plans, or develop an experience of self.

For many African-Americans similar historical sufferings continue today. Malnutrition, poor maternal health and infectious disease claim children's lives, and anticipation of premature death persists among mothers whose sons are particularly vulnerable to drug overdoses and street gang bullets. Those who escape death are often likely to endure overcrowded prisons, a death in life.

In her book *Passing On*, Karla F. C. Holloway has gathered African-American mourning stories, including her own for the death of her mentally ill adopted son. When her son was imprisoned, she knew that he would be given the death penalty despite his mental illness. While he awaited sentencing, she schooled herself for witnessing his death by lethal injection. She also rehearsed how she could prepare her son for this moment by guiding him toward some contemplative peace. In the end, however, her son's actual death evaded such modest remedial measure. He escaped from the prison farm in Odom, North Carolina, a place from which no person had ever successfully fled. His actual dying under police continues to haunt her.

> I have considered the moment again and again—how he took off running through the midsummer growth of the expanse of cotton fields. Although the scratchy saplings may have tugged at his pants legs, as if pleading for him to stop, all he could feel, I suspect, was something like the rhythmic heartbeat of 'took off running.' I imagine how he might have been surprised by the threatening combination of fear and exhilaration that his running provoked. Fear, because somewhere, even in the midst of the confusion and delusions that were the hourly manifestations of his illness, there were spaces in his childhood of sanity that must have let him know, that may have even prompted him to run...He was closer to freedom than he had ever been in his short, unhappy life. Certainly freer than in the series of mental institutions, jails, and prisons of the last five years. And absolutely freed from the angst of the ninety-five year sentence for rape and attempted murder that he was serving, the likely convictions for murder that were pending, and the nearly certain consequence of a death penalty that lay ahead in the fall, when the fields would be ready for harvest.[14]

NOTES:

1. Linda Pollock, *Forgotten Children: Parent Child Relations from 1500–1900*, 1983, p.p. 124–141.

2. Barbara Hanawalt, *The Tie That Bound*, London, 1986, pp. 174–81.

3. Shahar Schulamith, *Childhood in the Middle Ages*, London, 1990, p. 153.

4. Ralph Houlbrooke, *English Family Life, 1576–1716*, 1986, p. 121–22.

5. Ibid., p.152.

6. Lawrence Lerner, *Angels and Absences: Child Deaths in the Nineteenth Century*, Nashville, 1985, pp. 71–72.

7. Ibid., p. 66.

8. Ibid., p. 17.

9. Ibid., p. 17.

10. Mary Abbott, *Family Ties: English Families 1540–1920*, 1993, p. 30.

11. Nancy Wilson Ross, *Westward the Woman*, New York, 1944, pp. 40–41.

12. Lillian Schlissel, *Far from Home: Families of the Western Journey*, New York, 1989, pp. 153–155.

13. Eurgene Genovese, "The Myth of the Black Family," *The Black Family*, Robert Staples, ed., 1978, p. 24.

14. Karla F. C. Holloway, *Passing On*, Durham, N.C., 2002, p. 10.

2
MOVIES ABOUT GRIEF AND RECONCILIATION

USED AS CATHARSIS, the following movies can help clarify emotions and give grievers permission to cry. Mothers may want to see a video repeatedly, providing themselves with a contained time to weep. Identifying with a particular character's pain and coping skills will help them understand their own grief reactions. By sharing the film with their spouse and, when appropriate, with surviving children, they may enable loved ones to open up and talk to one another. Because these films are powerful presentations of devastating loss, however, I suggest mothers rent videos to view at home, with discretion and uninterrupted.

ACCIDENTAL TOURIST *(1988) 120 minutes*

Bereavement Themes:
>   Family history influences reactions to sudden death of son
>   Destructive results of shame and blame
>   How child death may end an already fractured marriage
>   Clinical depression and delayed grieving in father
>   Relationships with pets as part of the grieving process

Characters: Macon (William Hurt), Sarah (Kathleen Turner), Muriel (Geena Davis)
>   Synopsis: Two years after the death of their son, Sarah tells her husband Macon that she wants a divorce. Glimpses into Macon's family-of-origin life give clues to Macon's compulsiveness and lend understanding to his clinical depression. Sarah remains stuck in her grief, but Macon's relationship with his deceased son's dog leads him to Muriel, a dog trainer who changes his life.

IN AMERICA *(2003) 103 minutes*

Bereavement Themes:
>   Family dynamics after a child's death

Man's inability to cry
Children caring for grieving parents
Woman's struggle with replacement child
Sudden shifts in mood as a natural part of grief
The healing power of imagination

Characters: Sarah (Samantha Morton), Johnny (Paddy Considine), daughters Christy and Aerial (Sarah and Emma Bolger), Mateo (Djimon Hounsou)

Synopsis: Reeling from family tragedy, Johnny, Sarah, and their two imaginative young daughters move from Ireland to a Manhattan building populated by junkies and beggars. Ten-year-old Christy records the family's daily life on her camcorder, offering stability and continuity to her grieving parents and comfort to her younger sister. All hold the dead child Frankie in their heart in a different way. Mateo, a passionate Black artist dying of AIDS introduces hope by using imagination and "magic." The film is dedicated to Director Jim Sheriden's young son, who died of a brain tumor. Sheriden and his screenwriter family have created a story of grief and reconciliation that can only come from those who have been there.

In the Bedroom (2001) 120 minutes

Bereavement themes:
    Murder of a dearly loved 21-year-old son
    Reactions of a small community to murder
    Parents' struggle with blame and outrage
    Taking law into one's own hands
    Consequences of revenge

Characters: Frank (Nick Stahl), Natalie (Marisa Tomei), Matt (Tom Wilkinson), Ruth (Sissy Spacek)

Synopsis: Home from college for the summer, Frank takes up with Natalie, a sexually alluring mother of two boys whose estranged husband is prone to violence. The tender love between Frank and his parents, even when strained by his relationship with Natalie, makes the film's subsequent anguish acute. After Frank is murdered, his devestated parents live weeks of blame before they act out the fantasies of revenge that haunt so many parents of murdered children.

MASK *(1985)*, *120 minutes*

Bereavement Themes:
  Helping a child deal with the fact she is different
  Letting a disabled child become an adult
  Understanding suicide
  Viewing rage over the loss of a child

Characters: Rusty (Cher), Gar (Sam Elliott), Rocky (Eric Stoltz), Evelyn (Estelle Getty), Abe (Richard Dysart), Diana (Laura Dern), Babe (Nicole Merceirio), Red (Harry Carey Jr.), Mr. Simms (Ben Piazza)

Synopsis: Rocky Denis is a young boy afflicted with a horribly disfiguring condition called craniodiaphyseal dysplasia. His mother Rusty loves him for who he is. Though life's problems make Rocky anxious, Rusty makes the difficult decision to let him spread his wings. Rocky decides he's had enough of life and gives up. Rusty's powerful rage over losing her child comes from long having held her frustrations and fears inside her. Releasing her anger begins her healing. Any mother who struggled to help her child accept the limitations of illness, and had the courage to allow the child to find her own way, will identify with Rusty.

ORDINARY PEOPLE *(1980)* *124 minutes*

Bereavement Themes:
  Accidental death of a son
  Unresolved sibling grief
  Attempted suicide
  Survival guilt
  Mother's favoritism towards deceased son
  Crumbling marriage after child death

Characters: Conrad (Timothy Hutton), Beth (Mary Tyler Moore), Calvin (Donald Sutherland), Psychiatrist (Judd Hirsch), Neannine (Elizabeth McGovern), Karen (Dinah Manoff)

Synopsis: Conrad has been hospitalized for a suicide attempt stemming from guilt about being unable to save his brother during a boating accident. His mother Beth is hostile because she favored her dead son. His father Calvin can't emotionally connect with either Beth or Conrad. In therapy, Conrad realizes he cannot save his parents' marriage, but he can move through grief towards wholeness.

STEEL MAGNOLIAS *(1989)* 120 *minutes*

Bereavement Themes
    Anticipatory grief allows time to put things in order
    Different grieving styles can strengthen rather than divide a family
    Dilemmas about withdrawing life support systems
    Parents' issues with the death of an adult child
    Importance of friends for support

Characters: Shelby (Julia Roberts), M'Lynn (Sally Fields), Truvy (Dolly Parton), Ouisa (Shirley MacLaine), Clarice (Olympia Dukakis), Annelle (Darryl Hannah)

Synopsis: Despite of her mother M'Lynn's fear that she will be courting grave danger because of her diabetic illness, Shelby decides to become pregnant. After the child's birth, Shelby experiences kidney failure and undergoes a transplant. Her mother is the donor. Within a year, Shelby's kidney fails, resulting in coma and, finally, death. McLynn is enraged first by her daughter's decision to have a child and then by her death. Her friends Truvy, Ouisa, Clarice, and Annelle support her throughout the ordeal.

Music for Mourning & Transformation

By evoking our deepest feelings, music can help us reduce anxiety and release unresolved grief, providing comfort and lifting our spirits to a transcendent realm. A few suggestions for listening follow:

Hildegard Von Bingen,
11,000 Virgins: Chants for the Feast of St. Ursula

> Twelfth-century poet-composer and mystic Abbess Hildegard claimed to have received these chants in a vision. Based on the legend of St. Ursula, they were sung by convent nuns during services of the Divine Office—Matins, Lauds, and Vespers.

Johannes Brahms,
Ein Deutsches Requiem, Op. 45

> Based on the following Biblical texts:

> > Ye now have sorrow; but I will see you again, and your heart shall rejoice, and your joy no man taketh from you. (John 16:22)

> > I will comfort you as one whom his mother comforteth. (Isaiah 66:13)

> > Behold me with your eyes: a little while I have had tribulation and labor, and have found great comfort. (Ecclesiastes 51: 35)

GABRIEL FAURÉ,
In Paradisum, REQUIEM, OP. 48

> May the Angels lead you into Paradise; at your coming may
> the martyrs receive you, and conduct you into the Holy City,
> Jerusalem. May the chorus of Angels receive you, and with
> Lazarus, once a pauper, eternally may you have rest.

PETER GABRIEL,
"I GRIEVE," *City of Angels* SOUNDTRACK

> It was only one hour ago
> It was all so different then
> nothing yet has really sunk in
> looks like it always did
> this flesh and bone
> it's just the way that we are tied in
> but there's no one home
> I grieve...
> for you
> you leave...
> me
> so hard to move on
> still loving what's gone
> said life carries on
> carries on and on and on ...

JAN GARBAREK & THE HILLIARD ENSEMBLE,
Officium

> This is my personal mourning soundtrack, played hundreds
> of times to comfort and ground me and given to a best friend
> when her own son died. The music combines jazz and polyph-
> ony; both traditions are neither wholly composed nor com-
> pletely improvised. A saxophonist and a vocal quartet present
> Renaissance music, particularly three versions of Christobal de
> Morales' *Parce mihi domine.*

Henryk Gorecki,
Symphony no. 3 Opus 36 (*Three Sorrowful Songs*)

I. Lamentation of a 15th-century Polish monastery

> My son, my chosen and beloved
> share your wounds with your mother
> and because, dear son, I have always carried you in my heart
> and always served you faithfully
> speak to your mother, to make her happy
> although you are already leaving us, my cherished hope

2. Prayer inscribed on wall 3 cell No. 3 in the basement of "Palace," the Gestapo headquarters in Zakopane; beneath is the signature of Helena Wanda Blazusiakowna, and the words, "18 years old, imprisoned since 26 September, 1944."

> No, Mother, do not weep
> Most chaste Queen of Heaven
> Support me always
> "Zdrowas Mario." (Ave Maria)

3. Polish folk song

> Were my bitter tears
> to create another River Oder
> they would not restore to life
> my son

> Oh, sing for him
> God's little song-brids
> since his mother
> cannot find him

> And you, God's little flowers
> may you blossom all around
> so that my son
> may die sleepily

MICHAEL JONAS, "ON EAGLES WINGS"

This beautiful uplifting melody was sung at my son's funeral,
accompanied by guitar.

> You who dwell in the shelter of the Lord,
> who abide in His shadow for life,
> say to the Lord: "My refuge, my rock in whom I trust!
> The snare of the fowler will never capture you,
> and famine will bring you no fear:
> under His wings your refuge, His faithfulness your shield.
> You need not fear the terror of the night
> nor the arrow that flies by day;
> though thousands fall about you, near you it shall not come.
> For to His angels He's given a command
> to guard you in all your ways
> upon their hands they will bear you up
> lest you dash your foot against a stone.
> Refrain: And He will raise you up on eagles wings,
> bear you on the breath of dawn,
> make you to shine like the sun,
> and hold you in the palm of His hand.

GUSTAV MAHLER, *Kindertotenlieder*

A cycle of five songs based on Fredrich Ruekert-Lieder poems
about the death of children in a storm. Through expressing
anger and remorse that the children were permitted to go outside, a father finally regains a sense of peace.

GUSTAV MAHLER, SYMPHONY NO. 5 IN C SHARP MINOR, PART FOUR: *Adagietto*

This movement, often performed as a single work, was broad-
cast at the time of John Kennedy's death.

Sacred Treasures: Choral Masterworks from Russia ("Hearts of Space" Soundtrack)

> Large mixed choirs sing a capella, a traditional form of worship in the Russian Orthodox Church. The music expresses shades of religious feeling characterized by extremes of mood, tempo, and volume.

Franz Schubert, *Wiegenlied*

This lullaby is addressed to a dead child.

> Sleep, dear, sweet boy
> Your mother's hand rocks you softly.
> This swaying cradle strap
> Brings you gentle peace and tender comfort.
>
> Sleep in the sweet grave
> Your mother's arms still protect you.
> All her wishes, all her possessions
> Ah hold lovingly, with loving warmth
>
> Sleep in her lap, soft as down;
> Bare notes of love still echo around you.
> A lily, a rose
> Shall be your reward after sleep.

And Other Suggestions...

Dvorak's "Goin Home" from *New World Symphony*

Max Bruch's "Kol Nidrei" (a Hebrew melody from Yom Kipur)

Maurice Ravel's "Pavane pour une Infante defunte" (Dance for a Dead Infant)

Tchaikovsky's "None But the Lonely Heart"

Andrew Lloyd Weber's "Pie Jesu"

4
REACHING OUT FOR HELP

Compassionate Friends
National Office
P.O. Box 3696
Oak Brook, IL 60522–36961
www.compassionatefriends.org
630-990-0010
877-969-0010 (toll-free)

Mothers Against Drunk Driving
MADD National Office
511 E. John Carpenter Freeway, Suite 700
Irving, TX 75062
www.madd.org
800-438-6233

American Association of Suicidology
4201 Connecticut Avenue
NW Suite 408
Washington, DC 20008
www.suicidology.org
202-237-2280

National Association of People with AIDS
1413 K W Street NW
Washington, DC 20045
www.napwa.org
202-898-0414

National SIDS/Infant Death Resource Center
2070 Chain Bridge Road, Suite 450
Vienna, VA 22182
www.sidscenter.org
866-866-7437 (toll-free)
703-821-8955

National Organization of Parents of Murdered Children
National POMC
100 East Eighth Street, Suite B-41
Cincinnati, OH
www.pomc.com
888–818-POMC (toll-free)
513–721–5683

SHARE Pregnancy & Infant Loss Support
National SHARE Office
St. Joseph Health Center
300 First Capitol Drive
St. Charles, MO 63301–2893
www.nationalshareoffice.com
800-821-6819
636-947-6164

SIDS Network
SIDS Network
P. O. Box 520
Ledyard, CT 06339
www.sids-network.org

TAPS, Tragedy Assistance Program for Survivors
800-959-TAPS
2001 S. Street NW, Suite 300
Washington, DC 20009
www.taps.org
202-588-8277

INDEX